Wilfred J. Ethier
University of Pennsylvania

MODERN
INTERNATIONAL
ECONOMICS
Third Edition

STUDY GUIDE

W·W·NORTON & COMPANY

NEW YORK LONDON

W. W. Norton & Company, Inc. 500 Fifth Avenue, New York, N.Y. 10110
W. W. Norton & Company, Ltd. 37 Great Russell Street, London WC1B 3NU

ISBN: 0-393-96312-8

1 2 3 4 5 6 7 8 9 0

CONTENTS

How to Use This Study Guide

The international economics course can seem a formidable one. The best way to approach it is with an aggressive, participatory attitude: read with pen and paper at hand, question everything, and work out answers as you go along. This Study Guide encourages such participation. You will find several distinct aids here. A list of *Key Ideas* opens each chapter, so that you know what to expect. Next come the various elements applying to individual sections. First, the central points of each section of the textbook are highlighted in a description of *Basic Ideas*. These are similar to the textbook's end-of-chapter summaries, but much more detailed.

Next, are the exercises themselves. There are four levels of exercises comprising hundreds of items—plenty of opportunity to practice. First come *Self-Tests*, for which the answers are provided at the end of the section, to give you a quick sense of whether you need more work on the material in a particular section. Next, you'll find *Solutions to Problems from the Text*, which provides answers for the problems in the textbook. Not *all* of the answers are given—a few are withheld for pedagogical purposes—nor is every answer meant to provide the last word on the question. You are not lectured on *how* to solve the problem, but the answers provided should give you a clear sense of whether you have understood how to work the problems. Finally, come *Additional Problems*, just like the problems from the textbook, except that answers are not provided. In a separate section at the end of each chapter, a set of *Review Questions* will help you to pull together the entire chapter's material.

Sample examinations—both midterms and finals for both one-term and two-term courses—can be found in *Appendix II*. The best way to use these is to treat them like exams: give yourself the allotted time and do the best you can without text or notes. Then return to the text and to your notes to evaluate your answers and grade yourself.

But above all: never stop questioning.

Part One

Why Nations Trade

CHAPTER 1

Comparative Advantage

KEY IDEAS of Chapter One

1. Countries conduct comparative-advantage trade to *exploit their differences*.

2. The international differences that might cause comparative-advantage trade include: *technology, resources, and preferences*.

3. The net effect of all these differences between countries is summarized in *international differences in relative autarky prices*.

4. The simple Ricardian model assumes only *one factor of production* and focuses on comparative-advantage trade due to differences in *technology*.

5. Countries export those goods that would be *relatively cheap in autarky* and import those that would be relatively dear.

6. Engaging in comparative-advantage trade can never make a country worse off than if it were not to trade at all.

1.   THE SIMPLE RICARDIAN MODEL

Basic Ideas

1.   The simple Ricardian model, which imagines that two countries can each produce two goods by means of a single productive factor, labor, is a useful way to understand the basic idea of comparative advantage.

2.   According to comparative advantage, if labor is immobile between countries, each country should export the good which requires relatively less labor in its production than does the other good, compared to the other country, regardless of whether that other country can produce the good with absolutely less labor.

3.   Definitions to know: **efficient pattern of production; opportunity cost; comparative advantage.**

Self-Test

1.   True or false: A country should never produce a good in which it has a comparative *dis*advantage.

2.   True or false: A country should never export a good in which it has a comparative *dis*advantage.

3.   Multiple choice: The U.S. will have a comparative advantage in nothing:
     3.1.   Indefinitely.
     3.2.   If all labor requirements are low enough.
     3.3.   If all labor requirements are high enough.
     3.4.   Never.
     3.5.   If labor becomes completely mobile internationally.

Solutions to Problems from the Text

1.1   *Suppose that in England 5 man-hours of labor are required to produce each cask of wine and 5 man-hours are required to produce each bolt of cloth, whereas in Portugal 1 man-hour of labor is required for a cask of wine and 4 man-hours for a bolt of cloth. (Except for the choice of numbers, this is the example used by Ricardo to discuss comparative advantage.)*

    a.   *Who has a comparative advantage in what and why? Make two equivalent statements.*

    b.   *Prove that your answer to a is correct by showing in detail that when both countries are producing both goods, the world can be made better off by allowing England and Portugal to reallocate labor and trade in accordance with the pattern of comparative advantage. Derive the analog of* **Table 1.2** *in the textbook.*

c.   *Now suppose that it becomes possible to move labor between the two countries. What should be done?*

a.   England has a comparative advantage over Portugal in cloth relative to wine. Portugal has a comparative advantage over England in wine relative to cloth.

b.   If England produces one less unit of wine and Portugal one fewer bolt of cloth:

	Additional Wine	Additional Cloth
in England	-1	0
in Portugal	<u>-1</u>	<u>-1</u>
in World	-1	0

c.   All labor should be done in Portugal.

1.2 *In the context of the above problem, suppose that there is also a third country, France, where 1 man-hour of labor can produce either 1 bolt of cloth or ½ cask of wine. What statements can you make about comparative advantage? Which patterns of production and international trade are efficient?*

France has a comparative advantage over England and Portugal in cloth relative to wine. Portugal has a comparative advantage over England and France in wine relative to cloth. France should export cloth and Portugal should export wine. England's trade pattern cannot be prescribed without knowledge of tastes.

Additional Problems

1.   Given the data of Problem 1.1 above, what is the opportunity cost of wine in terms of cloth: in England; in the world if both countries are producing both goods; in the world if labor can be moved from country to country?

2.   Suppose that in Canada timber and steel each require 10 units of labor for the production of one unit of output, whereas in the U.S. 6 labor units can produce a unit of steel. What must be true of the U.S. labor requirements for timber production if: the U.S. is to have a comparative advantage in steel; the U.S. is to have a comparative advantage in timber; Canada is to have a comparative advantage in steel; Canada is to have a comparative advantage in timber?

Answers to Self-Test

1.   False

> **2.**   True
>
> **3.**   3.4

2.   EFFICIENCY IN THE SIMPLE RICARDIAN WORLD

Basic Ideas

> **1.**   In the simple Ricardian model, the pattern of comparative advantage is revealed by a comparison of the slopes of two countries' production possibility frontiers.
>
> **2.**   An individual country will be on its production possibility frontier if its entire labor force is productively employed.
>
> **3.**   The world as a whole will be on its production possibility frontier if the entire labor force of each country is productively employed, and if the pattern of production is consistent with comparative advantage.
>
> **4.**   Definitions to know: **production possibility frontier; marginal rate of transformation; productive efficiency.**

Self-Test

> **1.**   Multiple choice: Which of the following could cause a country's production possibility frontier to shift?
> **1.1.**   A change in tastes
> **1.2.**   Growth of the labor force
> **1.3.**   A decrease in labor efficiency
> **1.4.**   A change in the pattern of production
> **1.5.**   The commencement of international trade
>
> **2.**   True or false: A country has a comparative advantage in a good if its production possibility frontier is further from the origin than that of the rest of the world.

Solutions to Problems from the Text

> **1.4**   *Consider, as in Problem 1.1, that in England 5 labor are required for each unit of wine and each unit of cloth, while in Portugal 1 labor produces 1 wine and 4 labor produce 1 cloth. Suppose also that each country has 100 man-hours of labor available.*
>
> > ***a.***   *Draw the production possibility frontiers for England, Portugal and the world. How do they change if England's labor force increases to 1,000?*

b.   *If everyone in the world always consumes exactly one cask of wine for each bolt of cloth, what should each country produce and what should the direction of trade be?*

c.   *Draw the world production possibility frontier if labor is* internationally *mobile.*

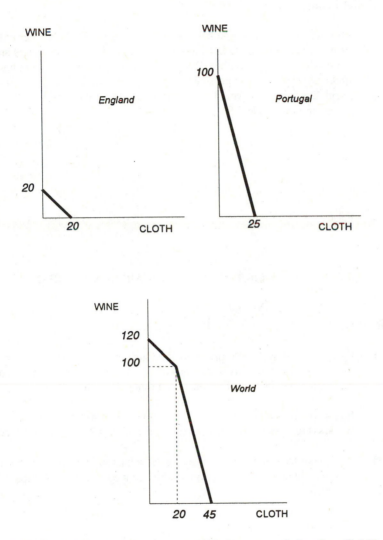

If England's labor force increases to 1000, that country's frontier will shift out by a factor of 10 (as will its part of the world frontier).

b.   England would produce 20 cloth and export 4 of them; Portugal would produce 16 cloth and 36 wine, exporting 16 of the latter.

c.   Just like Portugal's frontier, but twice as far from the origin.

1.5 *In the above problem, suppose that in France 1 labor can produce 1 cloth while 2 labor produce 1 wine, and France has 200 labor. Draw the world production possibility frontier. Who produces what at various points along it? Depict inefficient patterns of specialization.*

Additional Problem

Suppose that in Canada timber and steel each require 10 labor per unit of output, whereas in the U.S. 6 labor units can produce a unit of steel and 8 can produce a unit of timber. Canada has 1,000 labor and the U.S. has 9,600. Draw production possibility frontiers for Canada, the U.S. and the world. Describe what would happen if the world were to consume 400 timber and free trade were to take place.

Answers to Self-Test

1. 1.2 and 1.3

2. False

3. THE ECONOMICS OF THE SIMPLE RICARDIAN WORLD

Basic Ideas

1. In equilibrium wages and prices must be such that, in each country, the price of a good equals its cost of production if that good is produced, and is no greater than its cost of production if that good is not produced.

2. If two countries do not trade with each other, each will have a lower (autarky) relative price of the good in which it has a comparative advantage.

3. If two countries trade, their wage rate will adjust so that each can compete in the world market for the good in which that country has a comparative advantage.

Self-Test

1. True or false: A country with high wages cannot compete on world markets with countries where wages are low.

2. Give two reasons why a country might have low wages compared with its trading partners.

Solutions to Problems from the Text

1.6 *We have seen that the pattern of comparative advantage can be determined by comparing relative prices in the two countries when free trade is restricted. When the restriction is removed, trade proceeds according to comparative advantage, and prices in the two countries are driven toward common international prices. But if prices are the same everywhere, why should anyone bother to trade?*

Prices are the same everywhere *because* people trade.

1.7 *Suppose in the context of Table 1.1 on page 6 of the text that $w^F = 1$ and $w^G = 1$. Then both French prices are higher than both German prices, and, as we saw in section 3 of the text, international competition will cause the French wage to fall if the two countries trade. Does this not indicate that free trade will hurt the French worker?*

No, becaUse the purchasing power of French wages does not fall.

1.8 *In Problem 1.4(b), what will be traded and what will all prices be? Do both countries gain as a result of trade? By how much? If the world suddenly decides it will consume one cask of wine for every two bolts of cloth, how will your answers change?*

The world price will be $p = P_W/P_C = 1/4$ (Portugal's autarkic price). In Portugal, consumption consists of 20 units of each wine and cloth, the same as in autarky. England's consumption is 16 units of each, compared to 10 of each in autarky. England exports 4 cloth to Portugal in exchange for 16 wine, and England captures all of the gains from trade.

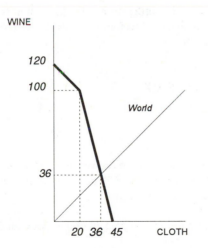

1.9   *The discussion in the text supposed that wages and prices in France and Germany adjusted themselves to each other entirely through inflation in Germany. Suppose instead that it happens entirely through French deflation, with German prices constant. Restate the argument in the text and write down the analog to Table 1.3. on page 16 of the text.*

	Machines	Wine	Wages
France	6	2	2
France (after 50% deflation)	3	1	1/2
France (after 66% deflation)	2	2/3	1/3
France (after 83% deflation)	1	1/3	1/6
Germany	1	1	1

Additional Problem

If France and Germany engage in free trade, what can you say about their relative wage levels, w^F/w^G? Is this ratio determined by absolute cost differences or, like the pattern and the terms of trade, by relative cost differences?

Answers to Self-Test

1.   False

2.   Because its labor is less efficient than the labor of its trading partners, and because world demand is low for the goods in which the country has a comparative advantage.

4.   THE GAINS FROM TRADE

Basic Ideas

1.   International trade leaves each country at least as well off as in autarky, in the sense that the country can still afford to buy the goods it would have chosen if it were not trading.

2.   The gains from trade are due to a difference between relative autarky prices and relative trading prices.

3.   Definition to know: **terms of trade.**

Self-Test

1.   Multiple choice: When we say that a country gains from international trade, we mean that
     1.1.   Trade makes everyone in the country better off.
     1.2.   The country as a whole consumes more of each good than it would without trade.
     1.3.   Free international trade is better for a country than restricted international trade.
     1.4.   All of the above.
     1.5.   None of the above.

2.   True or false: In the simple Ricardian model, trade between similar economies (in the sense of similar autarky price ratios) is unlikely to generate large gains for either country.

Solutions to Problems from the Text

1.11   *As in Problem 1.4, suppose that England has 100 labor and requires 5 to produce each unit of wine and of cloth, whereas Portugal has 100 labor units, with 1 required to produce each wine and 4 to produce each cloth unit. If the world relative price of wine in terms of cloth is 1, what will be the pattern of trade and production; what will be the prices in each country; and who will gain from trade?*

   If $p = 1$, the English autarkic price, Portugal must specialize in wine, Portugal exports wine to England for cloth, and all gains go to Portugal. If the English wage $= 1$, then $P_W = 5$ and $P_C = 5$ because England can compete in both markets. The Portuguese wage equals 5 because Portugal can compete in wine. Note that cloth costs 20 to make in Portugal, so that country cannot compete in that good.

1.15   *Suppose that when trade opens, for some reason, France is forced to continue producing at point A in Figure 1.3(a) on page 19 of the text, instead of specializing in wine. How is the argument in the text altered? Compare this situation with both autarky and the case where France specializes.*

   France would still be no worse off than in autarky, because she could still have A, and would now have alternative possibilities not available in autarky. But specialization would allow even better consumption possibilities:

1.16*   *From 1792 to 1900, the United States was legally on a* bimetallic standard: *the dollar was defined in terms of both gold and silver. As a result of the Coinage Act of 1792, the U.S. mint stood ready to convert gold or silver into coins, at the prices in the first line of the table below, for anyone presenting either metal. France was also on a bimetallic standard from 1803 to 1874, and the bottom line contains hypothetical French prices illustrative of the early part of this period.*

Mint Prices of One Ounce of Gold and Silver, Representative of 1804-1834

	Gold	Silver
U.S.	$11.60	$.77
France	0	Fr3.87

From the first line of the table, we see that the official U.S. relative price of an ounce of gold in terms of silver was $11.60/$.77 = 15 ounces. Similarly the French price of gold in terms of silver was Fr60/Fr3.87 = 15.5 ounces.

a.   *use the logical structure of the simple Ricardian model to deduce what happened after passage of the 1792 act. France was economically much larger than the United States in those years.*

b.   *The U.S. mint ratio was changed in 1834 and 1837 to about 16 silver ounces per gold ounce. The world price ratio by and large remained near 15.5 to 1. What do you think happened from 1834 to 1862 (the U.S. government abandoned metallic standards during the Civil War)?*

a. Gold and silver are analogous to the two traded goods of the simple Ricardian model, and the two national monetary units are analogous to labor. Since France was the 'large' country, the equilibrium international price could have been expected to be 15.5 ounces of silver per gold ounce. With the U.S. authorities maintaining a price of 15, the U.S. could have been expected to 'specialize' in, and export, gold. That is, any U.S. gold coins would have been melted down and exported to France where they could have been sold for more silver than they cost in the U.S. Thus the U.S. money supply could be expected to consist only of silver coins. This is in fact what happened.

b. In this case the above argument is reversed. In fact, the U.S. money supply quickly came to consist only of gold coins, so that the country in effect switched from a silver standard to a gold standard.

Additional Problems

1. List all the reasons that you can think of for why a nation might actually be worse off as a result of international trade. Reconcile them with the theory you have studied.

2. We have studied how international trade is beneficial for a country as a whole, but there are always people within a country who think that trade is harmful to them. Try to explain this.

Answers to Self-Test

1. 1.5

2. True

5. COMPARATIVE ADVANTAGE IN MORE GENERAL CIRCUMSTANCES

Basic Ideas

1. If we generalize the simple Ricardian model by abandoning the assumption that labor is the sole factor of production, the _MRT_ and the autarky price ratio in a country are no longer determined simply by technology. Instead they become variables whose equilibrium values also depend upon tastes.

2. If the pattern of comparative advantage is deduced by a comparison of autarky relative prices (= _MRT_s), nearly all of our earlier conclusions remain valid.

3. The exceptions: the pattern of comparative advantage depends upon tastes as well as technology; it is no longer necessarily the case that with free trade

at least one country must specialize completely in the production of a single good.

4.   Concept to know: **increasing opportunity cost**.

Self-Test

1.   Multiple choice: With free trade both countries will continue to produce both goods:
     1.1.   Under no circumstances.
     1.2.   Always.
     1.3.   Only if there are in fact no gains from trade.
     1.4.   Whenever there are increasing opportunity costs.
     1.5.   None of the above

2.   In the simple Ricardian model, a country neither gained nor lost from trade if the free-trade relative price equalled that country's autarky relative price. Is this still true with increasing opportunity costs?

3.   In the simple Ricardian model, a country neither gained nor lost from trade if it produced both goods. Is this still true with increasing opportunity costs?

Solutions to Problems from the Text

1.19   *Recall that in Section 1 of the textbook we considered the experiment of shifting labor from butane to apples in France and the reverse in Germany, recording the result in Table 1.2. Do the same now, in the context of increasing opportunity costs, and derive a table analogous to Table 1.2.*

	Additional Butane	Additional Apples
in France	-1	French *MRT*
in Germany	+ 1	- German *MRT*
in World	0	French *MRT* - German *MRT*

1.20*   *Suppose that France exports apples to Germany in exchange for butane under increasing opportunity costs. Neither country is specialized. Now suppose that the cost of transporting one unit of butane from Germany to France equals 50 percent of the (German) cost of producing the butane. The cost of transporting apples, however, is so low that it can be ignored. What must the free trade relationship be between the prices of each good in the two countries? Suppose that a "transportation revolution" is expected to reduce by one-half the cost of shipping a unit of butane within the next four years. Can you predict anything* *about the likely effects of this on international trade and upon the pattern of production in both countries?*

(Transportation Costs) Let P_A^G denote the price of an apple sold in Germany. Competition will ensure that French and German apples sell for the same price in the same market. If P_A^F denotes the price of apples sold in France, international competition and the absence of a transportation cost for apples will ensure that $P_A^G = P_A^F$, that is, all apples will sell for a single world price regardless of where the apples are produced or where they are sold. Denote this common price by P_W.

Similarly, within each market butane must sell for a single price regardless of where produced, but since there is a transportation cost in moving butane between markets, it need not sell for the same price in France as in Germany. As long as the price of butane in the two countries does not differ by more than this transportation cost, no one can make windfall profits simply by buying butane in the country with the lower price and then selling it in the country with the higher price. In this case we are told that the Germans export butane to France. Thus the price of butane in France must equal its price in Germany plus the transportation cost: $P_B^F = P_B^G(1 + 0.5)$.

Let p^F and p^G denote the relative price of butane in terms of apples in France and Germany respectively. Then $p^F = (1.5)p^G$ (Be sure that you can explain why!). That is, $p^F > p^G$. Then the principle of comparative advantage can be directly applied to conclude that the "transportation revolution" will cause Germany to shift production from apples towards butane, and to increase its exports of the latter, and will cause France to do the reverse.

Additional Problems

1. Suppose that two countries are identical in size and technology, and so have identical production possibility frontiers. Is there any reason for them to trade with each other? Explain.

2. How does your answer to the previous problem change if the two countries also have identical tastes?

Answers to Self-Test

1. 1.5

2. Yes

3. No

6.   TASTES AS A DETERMINANT OF COMPARATIVE ADVANTAGE

Basic Ideas

1.   Each consumer's *MRS* will equal the relative commodity price prevailing in an economy, regardless of whether different individuals have quite different tastes or not.

2.   Differences in *MRS*s across countries are a basis for mutually beneficial trade.

3.   The principle of comparative advantage continues to apply to this trade, as long as the pattern of comparative advantage is defined on the basis of differences in relative autarky prices across countries.

4.   Terms to understand: **production gain, consumption gain.**

7.* *EXPLORING FURTHER:* INDIFFERENCE CURVES

Basic Ideas

1.   An individual's tastes can be represented by a set of indifference curves, each connecting bundles of goods between which the individual is indifferent.

2.   Under some circumstances the collective preferences of an entire society can be represented by a set of community indifference curves.

3.   Such curves give a convenient geometric way to depict autarkic equilibrium and the gains from trade.

4.   Term to understand: **community indifference curve.**

Solutions to Problems from the Text

1.21   *Prove that, for a single individual, two distinct indifference curves can never intersect.*

Suppose that two indifference curves did in fact intersect, as at point *A* in the diagram below. Since *B* and *A* are on the same indifference curve, the individual is indifferent between them. She must likewise be indifferent between *C* and *A* since they are also on the same indifference curve. Thus she must be indifferent between *B* and *C*. However, this is not consistent with the two curves being distinct indifference curves.

1.22 *Draw community indifference curves in Figure 1.7 on page 28 of the textbook to show that international differences in tastes can serve as a basis for mutually beneficial trade.*

Additional Problems

1.23 Go through the discussion in Section 3 of the textbook of the gains from trade, using indifference curves.

1.24   Draw the community indifference curves that depict the tastes described in
Problem 1.4b: everyone always wants to consume equal numbers of bolts of
cloth and casks of wine.

8.   NORTH-SOUTH TRADE

Basic Ideas

1.   Trade between the DCs and the LDCs is in basic accord with intuitive
beliefs about the characteristics of those two groups of countries and the
principle of comparative advantage.

2.   There are, nevertheless, aspects of world trade which rest uneasily with
comparative advantage, even though they are not logically incompatible
with it.

3.   These include the fact that the largest part of world trade is the exchange of
manufactures between different DCs, and the large and growing share of
intraindustry trade.

4.   Terms to know: **intraindustry trade; interindustry trade; product differentiation; division of labor; NECs; NICs.**

Self-Test

1.   Multiple choice: The fastest growing part of world trade is:
1.1.   The export of manufactures from the DCs to the LDCs for primary
products.
1.2.   The exchange of manufactures among the DCs.
1.3.   The exchange of primary products among the LDCs.
1.4.   The export of manufactures from the LDCs.
1.5.   Intraindustry trade among the DCs.

2.   True or false: The principle of comparative advantage would seem to imply
that intraindustry trade is not very important from a welfare point of view.

Solution to Problem from the Text

1.25   *Since the Second World War, the DCs have substantially lowered trade barriers,
but the LDCs have not. Explain how Table 1.5 on page 36 of the textbook
seems to be consistent with comparative advantage. What would you expect to
be true of the relative gains from the various trade flows, as distinct from their
volumes?*

The principle of comparative advantage would lead us to expect proportionally more gains from trade between the DCs and LDCs, where comparative
cost differences are greater.

Additional Problem

What practical difference does it make whether or not the actual pattern of world trade is explained by comparative advantage?

Answers to Self-Test

1. 1.4

2. True

9.   REVIEW QUESTIONS

1. Explain the principle of comparative advantage.

2. What is *intraindustry* trade and how prevalent is it?

3. Describe the international trade of the United States.

4. Compare and contrast U.S.-Canadian trade with U.S.-Japanese trade.

5. What kinds of differences between countries can generate comparative-advantage trade?

Economies of Scale

KEY IDEAS of Chapter Two

1. Countries engage in scale-economies trade *to concentrate on fewer tasks and thereby do them better.*

2. Scale-economies trade *does not inherently assign countries to specific industries,* as comparative-advantage trade does.

3. Scale-economies trade *may possibly leave a country worse off than it would be in autarky.*

4. Economies of scale *internal* to the firm are inconsistent with a perfectly competitive equilibrium.

5. Economies of scale may be *national* in origin (productivity depends on national output) or *international* in origin (productivity depends on global output).

1. INCREASING RETURNS TO SCALE

Basic Ideas

1. Scale economies may be either internal to the individual firm or external to it.

2. Scale economies that are internal to the individual firm are not consistent with a perfectly competitive equilibrium.

3. Scale economies may be either national in origin or international in origin.

4. If scale economies are national in origin, the productivity of inputs depends upon the size of the national industry; if the scale economies are international in origin, productivity depends upon the size of the world industry.

Self-Test

1. Multiple choice: Which of the following is an example of increasing returns to scale?
    1.1. Labor becomes more productive as more capital is invested in an industry.
    1.2. A new invention makes labor more productive.
    1.3. Existing plants become more productive as new firms enter the industry.
    1.4. All of the above
    1.5. None of the above

2. Multiple choice: Which of the following is an example of external economies?
    2.1. Labor becomes more productive as more capital is invested in an industry.
    2.2. A new invention makes labor more productive.
    2.3. Existing plants become more productive as new firms enter the industry.
    2.4. All of the above
    2.5. None of the above

Solutions to Problems from the Text

2.1 *If France has 10 labor units, and if Table 2.1 on page 49 of the text describes the technology of both the apple and butane industries, draw France's production possibility frontier.*

2.2 *Suppose that Germany is identical to the France of Problem 2.1. Draw the world production possibility frontier.*

2.3   *How does your answer to **Problem 2.2** change if instead the scale economies are international?*

Additional Problems

1. What is the difference between increasing returns to scale and decreasing opportunity costs?

2. Give a practical example of increasing returns to scale that are internal to the firm, and a practical example of increasing returns to scale that are external to the firm.

Answers to Self-Test

1. 1.3

2. 1.3

2. SCALE ECONOMIES AS A BASIS FOR TRADE

Basic Ideas

1. Increasing returns to scale furnish a basis for trade that is independent of comparative advantage.

2. Comparative-advantage trade allows countries to *exploit their differences* for mutual benefit; it tends to assign specific countries specific tasks in the world economy. By contrast, scale-economies trade allows countries to

concentrate *on fewer tasks* and thereby do them better. Since this does not assign countries specific tasks, the pattern of trade tends to be indeterminate.

3.   If trade is due to international economies of scale, countries with similar patterns of resource allocation will engage largely in *intraindustry* trade while countries with divergent patterns of resource allocation will have largely *interindustry* trade.

Solution to Problem from the Text

2.4   *Industries are sometimes described as having* decreasing *returns to scale: increasing all inputs in proportion increases output in a smaller proportion. Try to deduce the consequences of such scale economies for international trade, when they are national and when they are international.*

If the decreasing returns are *internal* to the firm, individual firms will all remain at minimal size. Industry output will change by changes in the number of firms, each operating at this minimal size, so the industry as a whole will operate under constant returns to scale.

If the decreasing returns are *external* and *national*, the economy will behave just as it would with increasing opportunity costs but constant returns to scale. If the returns are *external* and *international*, this will be true of the world as a whole.

3.   NATIONAL EXTERNAL ECONOMIES OF SCALE

Basic Ideas

1.   If trade is due to national economies of scale, a single country could be worse off than in autarky.

2.   Trade due to national economies of scale *may* produce a situation where one country must gain relative to autarky and one must lose: trade jealousy.

3.   Neither of the two preceding basic ideas is a necessary consequence of trade based on national economies of scale, or even a likely one. But with comparative-advantage trade neither outcome is even a possibility.

Self-Test

1.   Multiple choice: The country of Malpensa possesses one productive resource, labor, and can produce good A under conditions of constant returns to scale and good B subject to national increasing returns to scale that are external to the firm. Free international trade *must* leave Malpensa worse off than in autarky if:

    1.1.   Malpensa exports *A*.
    1.2.   Malpensa produces only *B*.
    1.3.   Malpensa produces more *B* than in autarky, but some *A* also.
    1.4.   Malpensa produces some *B*, but less than in autarky.
    1.5.   Malpensa produces no *B* at all.

2.   Multiple choice: The country of Malpensa posseses one productive resource, labor, and can produce good *A* under conditions of constant returns
to scale, and good *B* subject to national increasing returns to scale that are
external to the firm. Free international trade *must* leave Malpensa better off
than in autarky if:
    2.1.   Malpensa exports *A*.
    2.2.   Malpensa produces only *B*.
    2.3.   Malpensa produces more *B* than in autarky, but some *A* also.
    2.4.   Malpensa produces some *B*, but less than in autarky.
    2.5.   Malpensa produces no *B* at all.

Solutions to Problems from the Text

2.5   *Suppose France has 10 labor units and that Table 2.3 describes its technology.
Each French resident always spends one-fifth of her income on apples and
four-fifths on butane. Describe autarky equilibrium: how much of each good is
produced and consumed and what is the price of butane in terms of apples?*

France consumes 2 apples and 5 units of butane, and the price of butane in
terms of apples is four-fifths.

2.6   *Suppose England has 6 workers and the following technology for producing
cloth and wine:*

To Produce This Much Cloth	Requires This Much Labor	Allowing This Much Wine
0	0	6
1	3	3
2	4	2
3	5	1
4	6	0

*Describe autarky equilibrium if all the English always consume equal quantities
of wine and cloth.*

The English consume 2 cloth and 2 wine, at a relative autarky price of cloth
in terms of wine of 2.

2.7   *Suppose Portugal has 8 workers and the following technology for producing
cloth and wine:*

To Produce This Much Cloth	Requires This Much Labor	Allowing This Much Wine
0	0	8
1	3	5
2	4	4
3	5	3
4	6	2
5	7	1
6	8	0

Describe autarky equilibrium if Portugal always consumes equal quantities of wine and cloth.

Portugal consumes 3 wine and 3 cloth, at an autarky relative price of cloth in terms of wine of five-thirds.

2.8 *Suppose that the England of Problem 2.6 and the Portugal of Problem 2.7 engage in free trade. Describe an equilibrium in which England completely specializes in the production of cloth. What is the free-trade relative price, and how does it compare with autarky prices in the two countries? Who gains and/or loses relative to autarky?*

England produces 4 cloth and 0 wine; Portugal produces 1 cloth and 5 wine. The international price of cloth in terms of wine is 7/5. Portugal exports 2.33 wine to England for 1.67 cloth. Portugal consumes two-and-two-thirds units of each good (compared to 3 of each in autarky), and England consumes two and one-third units of each good (compared to 2 of each in autarky). Thus England gains, Portugal loses, and the world as a whole neither gains nor loses as a result of free trade.

2.9* *Find another possible free-trade equilibrium in Problem 2.8 and describe it as completely as you can. Compare the various free-trade and autarky equilibria from the perspective of world welfare.*

Another international equilibrium features England specialized in wine production, producing 6, and Portugal in cloth, also producing 6. Portugal exports 3 cloth to England for 3 wine. Each country thus consumes 3 of each good, so that England gains from trade and Portugal is neither better off nor worse off. England, Portugal, and the world as a whole are each better off in this international equilibrium than in the one of Problem 2.8.

Answers to Self-Test

1.   1.4

2.   2.3

4.   INTERNATIONAL EXTERNAL ECONOMIES OF SCALE

Basic Ideas

1.   When external economies of scale are international in origin, concentration of the industry does not matter for the scale economies. Thus the industry's location will be determined by other considerations, such as comparative advantage.

2.   International economies of scale arise from the division of labor, which requires intraindustry exchange among firms in the industry. Thus if the industry operates in more than one country, those countries will engage in intraindustry trade.

3.   The division of labor is limited by the extent of the market because individual operations have to be conducted at some minimum scale of operations. Thus these individual operations are subject to national economies of scale.

Self-Test

1.   Multiple choice: The country of Malpensa posseses one productive resource, labor, and can produce good A under conditions of constant returns to scale and good B subject to international increasing returns to scale that are external to the firm. Free international trade *must* leave Malpensa worse off than in autarky if:
   1.1.   Malpensa exports A.
   1.2.   Malpensa produces only B.
   1.3.   Malpensa produces more B than in autarky, but some A also.
   1.4.   Malpensa produces some B, but less than in autarky.
   1.5.   None of the above.

2.   Why is the division of labor limited by the extent of the market?

Solution to Problem from the Text

2.10   *Suppose that scale economies are due to the division of labor, and that there are two countries. Discuss the relation between the production possibility frontiers of the two countries and the world.*

   The shape of each country's production possibility frontier would depend upon actual production in the other country.

Answers to Self-Test

1.   1.5

2. The divison of labor is limited by the extent of the market because each individual operation must be performed by an entire unit of labor.

5. PRODUCT DIFFERENTIATION

Basic Ideas

1. Many consumer goods are characterized by *product differentiation*: individual sellers endow their products with distinct features to distinguish them from competing products and to appeal to particular consumers.

2. Each variety of a differentiated good may have national, internal, increasing returns to scale in its production process. If so, there is a conflict between variety and production efficiency.

3. International trade allows consumers to choose from a greater variety of differentiated goods.

4. Trade due to product differentiation is very similar to trade due to the division of labor. But whereas the division of labor involves *vertical* disintegration (the production of a single final good is split up into distinct stages), product differentiation involves *horizontal* disintegration (a single final good is produced in alternative distinct varieties).

5. Terms to know: **division of labor; product differentiation; monopolistic competition.**

Self-Test

1. If international trade is generated by product differentiation,which is likely to gain more from the trade: big countries or small countries?

2. In the presence of differentiated products, is trade between similar countries or trade between dissimilar countries more likely to lead to larger gains?

Additional Problem

1. Many economists believe that free trade generates more domestic political opposition when it causes large reallocations of resources between sectors. (This will come up in more detail later in the book.) If this is so, which type of trade is more likely to generate opposition: scale-economies trade with differentiated products, or comparative-advantage trade? Would you expect free-trade policies to be more likely between similar economies or between dissimilar economies?

Answers to Self-Test

1. Small countries

2. We can't say. Similar countries are more likely to exchange differentiated products and dissimilar countries are more likely to conduct comparative-advantage trade, but both types of trade are gainful.

6. REVIEW QUESTIONS

1. Explain how scale economies may form a basis for international trade.

2. What is *intraindustry* trade and how prevalent is it? Give alternative possible explanations for its existence. Do the alternatives have different welfare implications?

3. This and the preceding chapter discussed two alternative reasons for trade. What do the two imply about policy regarding North-South trade?

4. Make a table listing as many examples as you can of scale ecnomies displayed by the automobile industry. Identify each example as internal or external to the firm and as national or international in origin.

CHAPTER 3

Imperfect Competition

KEY IDEAS of Chapter Three

1. Imperfect competition could motivate countries to engage in trade *to subject their firms to more competition and thereby cause them to perform more efficiently.*

2. Imperfect-competition trade *need not inherently assign countries to specific industries,* as comparative-advantage trade does.

3. Imperfect competition introduces the possibility that the international distribution of economic *profit* can be an important determinant of the international distribution of gains from trade.

4. Scale-economies trade *may possibly leave a country worse off than it would be in autarky.*

5. Imperfect competition may induce intraindustry trade in *identical* products.

1. IMPERFECT COMPETITION

Basic Ideas

1. A market displays *imperfect competition* if some agent can influence the price at which he or she can buy or sell.

2. A *monopoly* is a market with a single seller.

3. An *oligopoly* has several sellers. Each firm can influence the price at which it sells, but it must also take note of *strategic interaction* with its rivals.

4. A *monopolistically competitive* market contains many sellers, each with a unique, differentiated good. Since its product is differentiated, each seller can influence its price; because there are many other sellers, no single one is significant enough to strategically interact with.

Self-Test

1. True or false: A market with several sellers approximates perfect competition if the sellers aggressively try to take customers from each other.

2. "In order to survive in today's bamboozle market, you have to keep a close watch on what each of your competitors is doing." The bamboozle market must be:
    1.1. Perfectly competitive.
    1.2. A monopoly.
    1.3. Oligopolistic.
    1.4. Monopolistically competitive.
    1.5. Any of the above

Solution to Problem from the Text

3.3* *A market demand curve shows the amount of a good that consumers will purchase at each hypothetical price. Suppose that the demand for widgets is* downward sloping: *at higher prices consumers buy fewer widgets. A firm's demand curve shows how much a particular firm could sell at each price. How is the demand curve of an individual widget firm related to the market demand curve for widgets if the widget market is: a monopoly; perfectly competitive; a duopoly.*

The firm demand curve for a monopoly coincides with the market demand curve.
   The demand curve facing a single firm in a perfectly competitive market is a horizontal line with a height equal to the going market price.
   The demand facing a firm in a duopoly equals the market demand minus whatever is being met by the other firm in the duopoly. But what the other firm does depends on the strategic interaction between the two firms,

so until we know something about this interaction we can't describe the demand curve facing a single firm.

Additional Problem

1. Discuss what type of market structure we observe in the U.S. automobile market.

Answers to Self-Test

1. False

2. 1.3

2. MONOPOLY

Basic Ideas

1. A monopolist can choose the point on the market demand curve that maximizes his profit.

2. A monopolist will maximize her profit by supplying the quantity that causes marginal revenue to equal marginal cost.

3. A monopolistic market is inefficient because marginal cost equals marginal revenue, which is less than price—the value to society of an additional unit of output.

Self-Test

1. Multiple choice: Which of the following statements is *not* correct regarding a monopolist?
    1.1. Strategic interaction is especially important for a monopolist.
    1.2. Monopoly is socially inefficient.
    1.3   There are significant barriers to entry.
    1.4. A monopoly may (or may not) earn large profits for a long time.
    1.5. None of the above

2. If the market demand curve is linear, what does the monopolist's marginal revenue curve look like?

Solutions to Problems from the Text

3.4   *Show how Figure 3.1 on page 73 of the text and Figure 3.3 on page 75 would change if the firm's fixed cost were 0.*

In each figure, setting the fixed cost equal to 0 would cause the *AC* curve to coincide with the (unchanged) *MC* line. Thus, in Figure 3.1, points *f*, *a*, and *c* would all coincide, and in Figure 3.3 profit would be indicated by the area of the rectangle having points *p* and *r* at its corners.

3.5   *The text distinguished between variable costs, which depend on how much is produced, and fixed costs, which arise simply from operating at all. But a firm might also have* sunk *costs, which have already been made or committed to, and which therefore cannot be avoided even if the firm does not operate at all. How do sunk costs change Figure 3.1 and Figure 3.2?*

Since sunk costs cannot be avoided no matter what the firm does, they will not influence the firm's behavior. Figure 3.1 is unchanged, but now the sunk costs must be added to the area of the shaded rectangle to find total cost. In Figure 3.3, sunk cost must be subtracted from the area of the shaded rectangle to determine total profit.

3.6   *Suppose that the production of fried clams entails a fixed cost of $6 and a marginal cost of $2 per pint. Draw the MC and AC curves of a fried-clam firm.*

3.7   *In the isolated hamlet of Marbletoe, residents would consume 10 pints of fried clams if they were free, and each dollar's price would reduce demand below 10 by 1 pint; that is, if a pint costs p, residents of Marbletoe would demand 10 – p pints of fried clams. Draw this hamlet's demand curve for fried clams and its associated MR curve.*

3.8   *The supply of fried clams in Marbletoe is controlled by a lucky monopolist, Rufus. What should Rufus do to maximize his profit, and how much would that profit be? How many pints of fried clams would Marbletoe enjoy, and what price would they pay for them?*

Rufus should sell 4 pints at $6 each, earning a profit of $24 – $14 = $10.

3.9   *How does your answer to the previous problem change if the fixed cost of producing fried clams falls from $6 to $3? Who gains from this? What happens if instead the marginal cost falls from $2 to $1?*

If the fixed cost falls, Rufus will not change his price or the amount that he sells, but his profit will rise by $3. Consumers are unaffected.
    If instead marginal cost falls, Rufus will lower his price to $5.50, and his sales will rise to 4.5 pints. In this case the customers benefit, because they face a lower price. But Rufus also benefits, because his profit rises to $24.75 – $10.50 = $14.25.

Answers to Self-Test

1.   1.1

2.   Linear, and twice as steep as the market demand curve

3. IMPERFECT COMPETITION AS A BASIS FOR TRADE: INTERNATIONAL OLIGOPOLY

Basic Ideas

1. If an industry is an oligopoly, international trade can increase the degree of competition, relative to autarky. This is a distinct reason to trade.

2. Oligopoly can generate two-way trade in identical commodities.

3. International trade is likely to lower oligopolistic profit and to benefit consumers.

4. Terms to know: **oligopoly, duopoly; Nash; Cournot; best-response curve; quantity competition; profit shifting.**

Self-Test

1. Multiple choice: Which of the following happens with *Cournot* competition?
    1.1. Firms collude to maximize their joint profit.
    1.2. Each firm decides the quantity it will sell and allows the market to determine the price.
    1.3. Each firm decides what price to charge and allows the market to determine how much it can sell at that price.
    1.4. Entry and exit of firms drives profits to zero.
    1.5. None of the above

2. Multiple choice: Which of the following is true in a *Nash* equilibrium?
    2.1. Firms collude to maximize their joint profit.
    2.2. Firms agree on market shares and then act to maximize individual profits.
    2.3. Output is the same as it would be if there were a monopoly.
    2.4. Entry and exit of firms drives profits to zero.
    2.5. None of the above

3. Multiple choice: With oligopoly, international trade might conceivably make a country worse off under which circumstance?
    3.1. Foreign firms succeed in capturing a large enough share of the profit in the oligopolistic market.
    3.2. Home and foreign firms compete so vigorously that profit disappears.
    3.3. Home firms try too hard to make the foreign market profitable.
    3.4. Too much is sold in the domestic market.
    3.5. Never

Solutions to Problems from the Text

3.10 *Suppose, as in **Problems 3.6 and 3.7**, that the production of fried clams, by the supplier Rufus, entails a fixed cost of $6 and a marginal cost of $2 per pint, and that, if a pint costs p, residents of Marbletoe would demand 10 - p pints of fried clams. Suppose now that there is a second supplier of fried clams, Violet, who has the same costs as Rufus. Violet is selling 2 pints. Given this strategy by Violet, what is the best that Rufus can do. Does your answer tell you anything about Rufus' best-response curve? Does it tell you anything about Violet's?*

With Violet selling 2 pints, Rufus faces a demand curve of $8 - p$. The best he can do is to charge a price of $5, selling 3 pints, for a profit of $15 - $12 = $3. Violet, selling 2 pints at the price of $5, just breaks even.

   This gives a point on Rufus's best-response curve: if Violet sells 2, Rufus's best response is to sell 3. This tells us nothing about Violet's best-response curve.

3.11 *Given that Rufus sells the quantity of fried clams you found in your answer to **Problem 3.10**, should Violet continue to sell 2 pints? If so, why; if not, what should she sell? Does your answer tell you anything about Rufus' best-response curve? Does it tell you anything about Violet's?*

With Rufus selling 3 pints, Violet faces a demand curve of $7 - p$. The best she can do is to charge a price of $4.50, selling 2.5 pints, for a profit of $11.25 - $11 = $.25. Rufus, selling 3 pints at the price of $4.50, now earns a profit of $13.50 - $12 = $1.50.

   This gives a point on Violet's best-response curve: if Rufus sells 3, Violet's best response is to sell 2.5. This tells us nothing about Rufus's best-response curve.

3.12* *Draw Rufus' best-response curve and Violet's best-response curve. Describe the duopoly equilibrium and compare this with the monopoly equilibrium you described in **Problem 3.8**.*

Violet and Rufus each sell 2⅔ pints of clams at a price of \$4⅔.

Answers to Self-Test

1.   1.2

2.   2.5

3.   3.1

4.* *EXPLORING FURTHER:* PRICE-SETTING INTERNATIONAL OLIGOPOLY

Basic Ideas

1.   In a Nash equilibrium, each firm chooses its best strategy, given the strategy choice of each other firm. However, behavior may vary, depending on what the *strategy variable* happens to be.

2.   In a price-setting oligopoly the strategy variable is *price*. That is, each firm chooses in equilibrium the price that will maximize its own profit, given the price charged by each of its rivals.

Solutions to Problems from the Text

3.13   *The previous section made seven basic points about trade and oligopoly when firms compete in quantities. Discuss in detail how valid each of these points remains if instead the firms compete in prices.*

You should be able to argue that the seven basic points are likely to remain true if the firms compete in prices rather than in quantities.

3.14*   *Suppose, as in Problems 3.10 and 3.11, that the production of fried clams by the supplier Rufus entails a fixed cost of $6 and a marginal cost of $2 per pint. Suppose now that Violet, who has the same costs as Rufus, sells steamed clams. If Violet charges q for a pint of steamed clams and Rufus charges p for a pint of fried clams, residents of Marbletoe would demand $10 - p + \frac{1}{2}q$ pints of fried clams. Violet is charging q = $4. Given this strategy by Violet, what is the best price that Rufus can set? Does your answer tell you anything about Rufus' best-response curve? Does it tell you anything about Violet's?*

Rufus should charge $7, which would enable him to sell 5 pints, earning a profit of $35 – $16 = $19. This reveals that p = $7 is Rufus's best response to q = $4, and so gives a point on Rufus's best-response curve. It tells us nothing about Violet's best-response curve.

3.15*   *Suppose that, if Rufus charges p and violet charges q, residents of Marbletoe would also demand $10 - q + \frac{1}{2}p$ pints of steamed clams. Draw Rufus' best-response curve and Violet's best-response curve. Describe the duopoly equilibrium and compare this with the monopoly equilibrium you described in Problem 3.8 and the duopoly equilibrium you described in Problem 3.12*.*

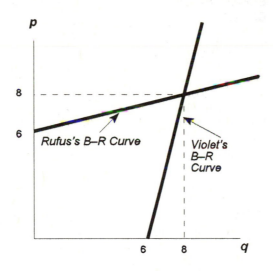

Rufus and Violet each charge a price of $8, each sells 6 pints of clams, and each earns a profit of $48 – $18 = $30.

3.16*   *This section supposed that the duopolists sold differentiated products. Try to discuss what might happen if instead they sold identical products.*

If the products are identical, price will equal marginal cost in a Nash equilibrium.

5.   MONOPOLISTIC COMPETITION

Basic Ideas

1.   In a monopolistically competitive industry firms produce differentiated products so each firm, as the sole producer of its unique variety, can act as a monopolist.

2.   There are many firms and entry is easy, so the profit of the representative firm is driven to zero.

3.   International trade allows consumers to choose from more varieties, and may allow the realization of economies of scale.

Self-Test

1. Multiple choice: The intraindustry trade of differentiated goods may be explained by:
   1.1.   Comparative advantage.
   1.2.   Economies of scale.
   1.3.   Oligopoly.
   1.4.   All of the above
   1.5.   None of the above

2. Multiple choice: The intraindustry trade of identical goods may be explained by:
   1.1.   Comparative advantage.
   1.2.   Economies of scale.
   1.3.   Oligopoly.
   1.4.   All of the above
   1.5.   None of the above

Answers to Self-Test

1.   1.4

2.   1.3

6. REVIEW QUESTIONS

1. Explain how imperfect competition can serve as a basis for trade.

2. What is *intraindustry* trade and how prevalent is it? Give three alternative possible explanations for its existence. Do the alternatives have different welfare implications?

3. This chapter discussed three alternative reasons for trade. What do the three imply about policy regarding North-South trade?

Part Two

How Nations Trade

CHAPTER 4

International Equilibrium

KEY IDEAS of Chapter Four

1. A country's *import demand curve* records, for each relative price of importables in terms of exportables, the excess of national demand for importables over the national supply of importables.

2. A country's *export supply curve* records, for each relative price of exportables in terms of importables, the excess of national supply of exportables over the national demand for exportables.

3. The world relative price adjusts to bring the home import demand into equality with foreign export supply.

4. The *price elasticity of import demand* is a critical parameter in determing how well international markets function. Generally, high elasticities contribute toward a smoothly operating system and low elasticities spell trouble.

5. Elasticities tend to be higher for manufactures than for primary products; elasticites pertaining to trade between developed countries tend to be higher than those pertaining to trade between developed countries and less developed countries.

1. THERE'S NO SUCH THING AS A FREE LUNCH

Basic Ideas

1. A demand for a good, service or asset is at the same time an offer to exchange something of equal value for it. Thus the total value of everything demanded by any individual must always equal the total value of everything supplied.

2. Since the above is true for every individual, it must also be true for collections of individuals, such as a country or group of countries.

3. This is Walras's Law: the aggregate value of all excess demands always equals zero.

4. If the only markets are for importables and exportables, Walras's Law says that the demand for imports is always equal in value to the supply of exports.

5. Terms to know: **equilibrium condition; identity; excess demand; excess supply**.

Self-Test

Next to each sentence write an **I** if what is described is analogous to an identity or an **E** if it is more like an equilibrium condition.

1. Price adjusts to equilibrate supply and demand.

2. Price is how much money you must pay for something.

3. A ball is a smooth, spherical plaything.

4. An undisturbed ball will not begin to roll on a level surface.

Solutions to Problems from the Text

4.1 *Suppose that in addition to apples and butane there are 9,998 other markets in the French economy. Then what does an excess demand for wine imply? If the other 9,999 markets are in equilibrium, what must be true of the apple market?*

An excess demand for wine implies that the total value of the excess supply of machinery and the other 9,998 goods is positive. If the other 9,999 markets are in equilibrium, the wine market must be also.

4.2 *Fill in the blanks in the following table.*

Price of Apples in Terms of Butane	Excess Demand for Apples	Excess Demand for Butane
1/10	*1000*	
1/5		*-80*
1/2		*-20*
2/3	*0*	
1	*-10*	
3/2		*30*
2		*50*
5		*100*
10	*-15*	

Price of Apples in Terms of Butane	*Excess Demand for Apples*	*Excess Demand for Butane*
1/10	1000	-100
1/5	400	-80
1/2	40	-20
2/3	0	0
1	-10	10
3/2	-20	30
2	-25	50
5	-20	100
10	-15	150

4.3 *A man sold a bond for $10,000, bought a $7,000 automobile, and put the remaining $3,000 in the bank. Since the value of the bond supplied exceeded the value of the car demanded, did he not violate Walras's Law?*

Walras's Law is satisfied because the value of the bond supplied ($10,000) equals the sum of the values of the car demanded ($7,000) plus that of the bank deposit demanded ($3,000).

Additional Problem

Answer **Problem 4.2** above if the first column is changed to "Price of Butane in Terms of Apples" and the second column to "Excess Supply of Apples."

Answers to Self-Test

1. E

2. I

3. I

4. E

2. IMPORT DEMAND CURVES

Basic Ideas

1. An import demand curve records how much a country would be willing to import at each hypothetical price of imports in terms of exports.

2. The volume of exports that a country would wish to trade at any particular point on its import demand curve is given by the product of imports times price at that point.

3. Because it merely summarizes what a single country would do under all conceivable circumstances, an import demand curve depends only upon information pertaining to that country, and it itself cannot indicate what international prices will be.

Self-Test

1. True or false: A country's import demand curve cannot tell us what relative prices are because the curve describes only the demand side of the economy and says nothing about the supply side.

2. True or false: A country's import demand curve cannot tell us what relative prices are because the curve describes only the supply side of the economy and says nothing about the demand side.

3. How is a country's import demand curve affected by each of the following?
    3.1. Domestic residents develop an increased dislike for foreign goods.
    3.2. Foreign residents develop an increased dislike for domestic goods.
    3.3. Foreign labor becomes more efficient.

Solutions to Problems from the Text

4.4   *Graph the observations in the completed table from* **Problem 4.2** *and "connect the dots" to draw an import demand curve.*

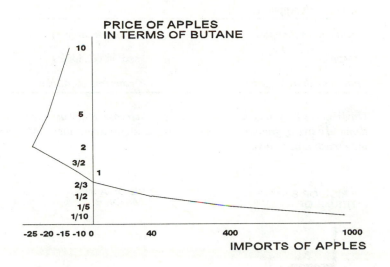

[Not drawn to scale.]

4.5   *use the completed table from* **Problem 4.2** *to graph an "export supply curve" showing the supply of exports of butane corresponding to each price of butane in terms of apples.*

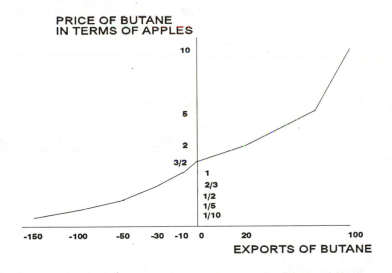

[Not drawn to scale.]

4.6   *Suppose France has 100 apples and no butane. The French tastes are such that
the country would wish to behave as follows:*

If the Price of Butane in Terms of Apples is:	The French Wish to:
greater than 3 Apples	*consume only Apples*
3 Apples	*export 60 Apples*
not more than 2 Apples	*consume 20 Apples*

*Use Walras's Law to deduce M^F and X^F for each case. Draw the French import
demand curve by graphing the observations and connecting them. Also draw
the French export curve.*

4.7   *Suppose you have the following data for Germany:*

P_B/P_A	B Demand	B Supply	A Demand	A Supply
4		120	140	20
4/3	80	110		30
1	100	100	50	
	140	80	45	85

*Fill in the blanks. Draw Germany's import demand curve for apples by graph-
ing the observations and connecting the dots.*

P_B/P_A	B Demand	B Supply	A Demand	A Supply
4	90	120	140	20
4/3	80	110	70	30
1	100	100	50	50
2/3	140	80	45	85

Germany's import demand curve for apples

4.8* *Suppose that in England 5 units of labor are required to produce either a bolt of cloth or a cask of wine, that England has 100 units of labor, and that each Englishman always consumes one cask of wine for each bolt of cloth that he consumes. Derive England's import demand curve exactly.*

4.9* *Suppose that in Portugal 4 units of labor can produce a bolt of cloth, 1 labor unit can produce a cask of wine, 100 labor units are available, and each Portuguese always spends one-half of her income on each good. Derive Portugal's import demand curve exactly.*

PRICE OF C IN TERMS OF W

1/4

-50   0   50

CLOTH

Additional Problems

1. Trade in commodities can be regarded as indirect trade in the services of the primary factors embodied in the goods. Derive the exact shapes of the "factoral" import demand curves for the English and Portuguese economies described in **Problems 4.8*** and **4.9***.

2. using the data from **Problem 4.7**, draw Germany's export supply curve for butane, export supply curve for apples, and import demand curve for butane.

Answers to Self-Test

1. False

2. False

3. The effect on the import demand curve will be:
    3.1. It shifts toward the price axis, as domestic residents become less willing to import at each price.
    3.2. No effect.
    3.3. No effect.

3.* EXPLORING FURTHER: INCOME AND SUBSTITUTION EFFECTS

Basic Ideas

1. An improvement in the terms of trade—a reduction in the relative price of imports —influences a country in two basic ways.

2. Since imports are cheaper relative to exports, consumers substitute importables for exportables in their consumption patterns, and producers substitute exportables for importables in their production patterns. Thus this substitution effect raises both imports and exports.

3. Since the country can now buy the same quantity of imports as before at a lower price, its income has, in effect, risen. This income effect will normally raise imports and lower exports.

4. Thus the income and substitution effects reinforce each other with respect to imports but work at cross purposes with regard to exports.

Solutions to Problem from the Text

4.10* *Discuss the roles of income and substitution effects in Problems 4.8* and 4.9*.*

The flat parts of both curves reflect substitution in production. When the countries specialize in the production of exportables there are no longer any production substitution effects; in the case of England there is no consumption substitution effects because, by assumption, the residents of this country are unwilling to substitute one good for the other. Thus the backward-bending part of England's curve reflects pure income effects. The vertical and downward-sloping parts of the Portuguese import demand curve, on the other hand, illustrate an income effect exactly neutralized by a consumption substitution effect with regard to exports.

Additional Problems

1. Discuss the significance of income and substitution effects in the response of oil importers to the oil price rises of the 1970s, and with respect to the oil price declines of the 1980s.

2. Discuss the influence of income and substitution effects on the shape of the import demand curve if exports are inferior. If imports are inferior. *(Note: An inferior good is one that we consume less of as our incomes rise, like gruel and second-hand clothes.)*

4. THE VOLUME AND TERMS OF TRADE

Basic Ideas

1. International equilibrium is described by the intersection of one country's import demand curve with the other country's export supply curve, because only at that intersection is the amount one country wants to import just equal to what the other wants to export while at the same time what the former wants to export is what the latter wants to import.

2. The two curves must be drawn consistently. That is, if positive movements on an axis measure off imports for one country they must measure exports for the other, etc.

Solutions to Problems from the Text

4.11 *Draw Figure 4.3 from page 99 in the textbook as it would look if France had the comparative advantage in butane.*

PRICE OF B IN TERMS OF A

German export supply

French import demand

BUTANE

4.12 *Suppose that France and Germany, as described in* **Problems 4.6** *and* **4.7**, *enter into free trade. By drawing the French import demand and German export supply curves find the terms of trade and volume of goods exchanged. Do the same with French export and German import curves.*

France exports 70 apples to Germany for 30 butane, so that $P_B/P_A = 7/3$.

4.13* *Suppose that the England and Portugal described in* **Problems 4.8*** *and* **4.9*** *engage in free trade. What will the terms of trade between these countries be? Who exports how much of what? What are the wages and prices in the two countries? Now suppose that England's labor force increases to 1,000 units and nothing else changes. Which curves shift? What are the new terms of trade and* *pattern of trade? What size must England's labor force be if that country is to export wine?*

England specializes in cloth production and exports 4 to Portugal in exchange for 16 casks of wine. If England's wage $= 1$, $P_C = 5$ and Portugal's wage is 5/4, so that $P_W = 5/4$ (these prices and wages can be any common multiple of these numbers, so long as they maintain the same relation to each other). If England's labor force increases to 1,000, its import demand curve shifts out from the origin by a factor of ten, and Portugal's import demand curve is unaffected. In the new equilibrium, England now produces both goods, exporting 50 cloth to Portugal for 50 wine. England would never export wine, since it has a comparative advantage in cloth.

Additional Problem

1. Draw Figure 4.3 from page 99 of the text as it would appear if neither country had a comparative advantage in anything, that is, if autarky prices in the two countries were equal.

5. ELASTICITY

Basic Ideas

1. The shape of an import demand curve at a point can be described by its import elasticity: the percentage increase in imports caused by a one percent improvement in the terms of trade.

2. The shape can alternatively be described by the export elasticity and by the elasticity of exports with respect to imports. Since they describe the same thing in different ways, these elasticities are all related to each other.

3. Things to know: **how to measure e geometrically;** $f = e - 1$; $g = f/e$.

Self-Test

1. Micronia is so small that nothing it could conceivably do would influence world prices. What can you say about the elasticity of the rest-of-the-world's import demand curve?

2. Petrolia produces one billion barrels of oil each and every year but has no use for the stuff. The country accordingly exports the oil for whatever it will fetch on world markets. What can you say about the elasticity of Petrolia's export supply curve?

Solutions to Problems from the Text

4.14 *Suppose you have the following observations:*

p	M	X
100		100,000
99	1,030	

Fill in the blanks. Calculate e, f, and g for the change from the first observation to the second.

p	M	X
100	1,000	100,000
99	1,030	101,970

$e = (100/1000)(30/1) = 3$;

$f = (100/100,000)(1970/1) = 1.97 \approx 2 = e\text{-}1$;

$g = (1000/100,000)(1970/30) = .66 \approx 2/3 \approx f/e$.

4.15 *In Problem 4.2 calculate e, f, and g for each pair of successive observations, using the definition of each elasticity. Also calculate f and g from your values of e using the relationships derived above. Try to explain any discrepancies.*

From the definitions, when the price of apples in terms of butane falls from 1/5 to 1/10: $e = [(1000 - 400)/400]/[\{(1/5) - (1/10)\}/\{1/5\}] = [3/2]/[1/2] = 3$; $f = [(100 - 80)/80]/[1/2] = [1/4]/[1/2] = 1/2$; $g = [1/4]/[3/2] = 1/6$. The formula $e = f - 1$ is an approximation that becomes more accurate for smaller changes in prices.

4.16* *What can you say about the elasticities of the curves you derived in Problems 4.8* and 4.9*?*

On those parts of the English and Portuguese import demand curves that are horizontal, e and f are infinite and g is unity. On the other parts of the Portuguese import demand curve, $f = g = 0$ and $e = 1$. On the other parts of the English import demand curve, $f < 0$, $g < 0$, and $e < 1$.

Additional Problems

1. In view of the description of trade between the DCs and the LDCs given in Chapter 1 of the textbook, speculate about the elasticities of the import

demand curves of these country groups.

2. Draw Figure 4.3 from page 99 in the textbook as it would look if there were several alternative international equilibria, rather than just one. What seems to be the role of elasticities?

Answers to Self-Test

1. e and f are infinite, and g is unity

2. $f = 0$, and so $e = 1$ and $g = 0$

6.   CASE STUDY: SOME INTERNATIONAL ECONOMIC PROBLEMS OF THE LESS DEVELOPED COUNTRIES

Basic Ideas

1.   Trade between the DCs and the LDCs seems to be characterized by low elasticities, and these are relevant to several issues involving that trade which are the subject of much concern and debate.

2.   These issues are: fluctuations in LDC export earnings; potential control over the terms of trade; an alleged secular deterioration in the LDCs' terms of trade.

3.   Attempts to come to grips with these issues on a multilateral basis have suffered from the "free rider" problem with regard to LDCs and from a divergence of national interests between DCs and LDCs.

4.   Be sure that you understand: the nature of the **free rider problem**.

Solutions to Problems from the Text

4.18   *The alleged secular decline in the LDCs' terms of trade was explained by low elasticities and the relative shifts of import demand curves. How would the argument be affected by elastic curves? What is the role of elasticity?*

The argument is qualitatively the same when elasticities are high, but it would not be as serious because the relative shifts of the import demand curves would cause more modest price changes.

4.19   *Unilateral action is unlikely to be effective, because an individual LDC faces a much more elastic import demand curve than do LDCs in the aggregate. But if so, how could the three issues ever arise for individual countries?*

They arise for individual countries because they arise for the entire
aggregate.

4.22   *Suppose that the LDCs succeed in improving their terms of trade by interfering*
with free trade in world markets. This makes the DCs worse off. Suppose the
latter are considering using foreign aid as a bribe to induce the LDCs to return
to free trade. Is it possible for the DCs to offer a tempting bribe, that is, one
large enough so that the LDCs are at least as well off as they are now, but not
so large that the DCs are worse off? Why?

Yes. Free trade is efficient for the world as a whole, so that a movement to
it will benefit the DCs by more than it harms the LDCs. This means that the
former can afford to fully compensate the latter and still be better off
themselves.

7.   "ELASTICITY OPTIMISM" AND "ELASTICITY PESSIMISM": EMPIRICAL ESTIMATES

Basic Ideas

1.   The basic idea behind our description of international equilibrium is that
the international economy works through relative price adjustments.

2.   Elasticity is basically a measure of how effective relative price changes are.
Accordingly, it is not surprising that low elasticities are associated with
problems.

3.   "Elasticity optimists" believe that price elasticities are high and "elasticity
pessimists" believe that they are low.

4.   Manufactures tend to be more price elastic than primary products. Thus
trade among the DCs, which involves a lot of intraindustry exchange of
manufactures, seems to be characterized by relatively high elasticities, and
DC–LDC trade, where manufactures are typically exchanged for primary
products, seems to feature lower elasticities.

5.   A "small" country is one that cannot influence the international prices at
which it trades. It thus faces an infinitely elastic (import demand or export
supply) curve from the rest of the world.

Self-Test

1.   True or false: A small country has an infinitely elastic import demand curve.

2.   What is the "identification problem?"

Solutions to Problems from the Text

4.23 *Suppose we represent a restrictive national trade policy by a shift in a country's import demand curve that causes it to demand fewer imports at each price, or by a shift of its export supply curve that causes it to supply fewer exports at each price. Discuss the effects of such a policy shift by each of the countries depicted in Figure 4.7 on page 111 of the textbook.*

    a.   Such a shift by Luxembourg reduces the volume of trade but has no effect on price.

    b.   Such a shift by the importer reduces both the volume of trade and the price; if done by an exporter it also reduces the volume of trade but raises the price.

    c.   Same as in **b**, except that the volume effects are relatively smaller and the price effects relatively larger.

4.24 *When is a shift in a country's import demand curve that causes it to demand fewer imports at each price the same as a shift of its export supply curve that causes it to supply fewer exports at each price?*

    Always

Answers to Self-Test

1. False

2. The problem of fitting data-points to estimate a curve when it is not known whether the data reflect movements along the curve or shifts of the curve.

8.* *EXPLORING FURTHER:* HOW TO DERIVE IMPORT DEMAND AND EXPORT SUPPLY CURVES

Basic Ideas

1. This section shows how to derive geometrically a country's import demand curve from its production possibility frontier and a set of community indifference curves.

2. The technique allows you to see the relation between a country's import demand and export supply curves, and how each relates to the *offer* curve: a third method of recording exactly the same information.

3. Be sure you understand: **offer curve.**

Solutions to Problems from the Text

4.25   *In Figure 4.10 on page 119 of the textbook, derive a French export supply curve of butane and import demand curve for apples.*

The respective answers are the same as panels (a) and (b) of Figure 4.11 on page 120 of the text, except that the horizontal axis is measured in the opposite direction, *i.e.*, each curve should be "flipped over" the vertical axis.

4.26   *What would the offer curve in Figure 4.11 on page 120 of the textbook look like if exports were measured on the butane axis and imports on the apple axis?*

The curve would have the opposite curvature. If an offer curve is imagined to be a bowl, it will "hold" its import axes; thus in this problem the curve should bend so that it "holds" the positive part of the apple axis and the negative part of the butane axis.

4.27   *Suppose that in England 5 units of labor are required to produce either a bolt of cloth or a cask of wine, that England has 100 units of labor, and that each Englishman always consumes 1 cask of wine for each bolt of cloth that he consumes. Use the techniques of this section to derive England's import, export and offer curves.*

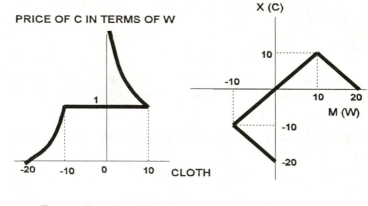

Export Supply of Cloth   **Offer Curve**

[See **Problem 4.8*** for the import demand curve of wine.]

Additional Problems

1.   Using indifference curves, production possibility frontiers, and import demand curves, show that:
   1.1.   Free trade is always better for a country than autarky;
   1.2.   Free trade is efficient in the sense that it is impossible to make one country better off without harming the other; and

      1.3.   Limited trade may be better or worse than free trade for a single country.

2.   Show geometrically that the income effect is very small near the origin on the import demand curve.

3.   Use the techniques of this section to derive the import demand curve of Portugal, as described in **Problem 4.9*** on page 96 of the text.

9. REVIEW QUESTIONS

1.   Explain the basic idea of international equilibrium.

2.   Write an essay on the concept of elasticity of import demand. Be sure you discuss: what it is, why it matters, empirical evidence.

3.   Discuss international economic problems facing the LDCs.

4.   Many of the international economic issues confronting the LDCs are also of concern to the DCs. For some of these, the interests of the two blocs coincide, and for others they are in conflict. Give examples of each and discuss the importance of this consideration for policy measures.

5.   Research attempts to establish and maintain international coffee agreements. Describe the details of actual agreements and their histories. Interpret in terms of the theory presented in this chapter.

Factor Endowments

KEY IDEAS of Chapter Five

1. The *factor-endowments approach* hypothesizes that a country has a comparative advantage in goods that make relatively intensive use of factors in which the country is relatively abundantly endowed.

2. The *Heckscher-Ohlin-Samuelson model* is a restrictive example of the factorendowments approach, making strong assumptions.

3. Because of its strong assumptions, the Heckscher-Ohlin-Samuelson model is able to make strong predictions regarding: (1) the pattern of comparative advantage and trade; (2) the effect of trade on the domestic distribution of income; (3) the effect of economic growth on trade; and (4) the relation between trade in goods and international factor mobility.

4. The price of the strong predictions is the strong assumptions. The predictions are relevant if: (1) trade is significantly due to comparative advantage (rather than to economies of scale or imperfect competition), (2) comparative advantage is largely explained by differences in relative factor endowments (rather than by differences in technology or in preferences), and (3) the Heckscher-Ohlin-Samuelson model adequately describes the role of relative factor endowments.

1.   THE HECKSCHER-OHLIN-SAMUELSON MODEL

Basic Ideas

1.   The Heckscher-Ohlin theory postulates that differences in relative factor endowments between countries is the cause of the pattern of comparative advantage.

2.   The principal theoretical tool used to expound, investigate, and apply this hypothesis is the Heckscher-Ohlin-Samuelson model.

3.   This abstract structure assumes: two countries, goods and factors; the two countries are identical in every respect except factor endowments; factors are immobile between countries but mobile between industries within a country; technology is characterized by constant returns to scale and is available to the two countries equally.

4.   Be sure you know: **constant returns to scale; factor abundance; factor intensity**.

Self-Test

1.   Multiple choice: Which of the following is inconsistent with the Heckscher-Ohlin-Samuelson model?
     1.1.   The home country trades with three others.
     1.2.   Technology has increasing returns to scale.
     1.3.   America has more land per worker than Europe, but about the same amount of capital per worker.
     1.4   Increasing opportunity cost
     1.5.   England exports cloth and machines and imports wine.
     1.6.   Italians are more fond of wine than the residents of the rest of the world.

2.   Suppose that there is only one known combination of capital and labor that can produce a unit of butane, but there are many ways to produce apples (that is, the two factors can easily be substituted for each other). What does this imply about the relative capital intensity of the two industries?

Solutions to Problems from the Text

5.1   *Recall the discussion of U.S. trade patterns in Section 10 of Chapter 1 of the textbook. Try to explain the apparent U.S. comparative advantage in terms of relative factor endowments (do not confine yourself to capital and labor—try to think of other relevant factors).*

U.S. exports could suggest an abundance of highly skilled labor and temperate-zone agricultural land. Imports could suggest a relative scarcity of other labor and mineral-laden land

5.2 *Suppose that England has 100 workers and 160 units of capital, whereas Portugal has 100 workers and 70 units of capital. Also suppose that each cask of wine requires 4 workers and 1 unit of capital to produce, whereas each bolt of cloth requires 5 units of capital and 2 workers. Apply the definitions of factor abundance and factor intensity.*

Since 160/100 > 70/100, England is capital abundant relative to Portugal; since 5/2 > 1/4, cloth is capital intensive relative to wine.

Additional Problem

1. In view of what you have learned about trade between the DCs and the LDCs, speculate about the relative factor abundance of these two groups of countries. About the relative factor intensities of their export industries.

Answers to Self-Test

1. All except 1.4

2. The relative capital intensity of the two industries would depend upon which technique was actually in use in the apple industry, and that would presumably depend upon the cost of capital and labor.

2. A BASIC RELATIONSHIP

Basic Ideas

1. An increase in wages relative to rents raises the cost of producing the labor-intensive good relative to the cost of producing the capital-intensive good.

2. The relation between relative factor prices and relative commodity costs is a technological one and so is identical for both countries, in the context of the Heckscher-Ohlin-Samuelson model.

3. The cost of a commodity must equal its price if that good is actually produced, in equilibrium, but might exceed price in a country that does not produce the good.

Self-Test

1. How is the relation between wages relative to rents and the cost of the labor-intensive good relative to that of the capital-intensive good affected by each of the following?
    1.1. An increase in population.
    1.2. A movement from free trade to autarky.

1.3.   An increase in wages relative to rents.

1.4.   A uniform increase in labor efficiency.

1.5.   An increased demand for the capital intensive good.

2.   In Figure 5.1 on page 129 of the textbook, suppose that the price of butane in terms of apples is equal to the distance *OB*. What must be true if the wage-rental ratio is less than the distance *OA*? If greater than *OA*?

Solutions to Problems from the Text

5.4   *Draw Figure 5.1 on page 129 of the textbook as it would appear if butane production were capital intensive. What would the curve look like if, by a fluke of nature, butane and apples used exactly the same technique of production?*

5.5   *Derive a curve, like that in Figure 5.1 on page 129 of the textbook, for England, where each cask of wine requires 4 workers and 1 unit of capital to produce and each bolt of cloth requires 2 workers and 5 units of capital. What could you conclude about English production if the wage and the rent in England both equaled 1, and the price of cloth in terms of wine was 2?*

$$\frac{(wine\ cost)}{(cloth\ cost)} = \frac{(4w + r)}{(2w + 5r)} = \frac{4(w/r) + 1}{2(w/r) + 5}$$

If $w = r = 1$, then $(wine\ cost)/(cloth\ cost) = 5/7 > 1/2$, so England would produce only cloth.

5.6 *Suppose that, as a result of some innovation, it is now possible to produce butane with fewer workers per unit of capital than before. No change occurs in the apple technology. What is the effect on the curve in Figure 5.1 on page 129 of the textbook?*

It becomes flatter.

5.7* *What would the curve in Figure 5.1 on page 129 of the textbook look like if butane were relatively capital intensive at low wage-rental ratios but relatively labor intensive at high wage-rental ratios, with apples and butane using exactly the same technique at some intermediate wage-rental ratio? What circumstances could cause two industries to have this relation?*

The curve would be U-shaped, reaching a minimum at the intermediate wage rental ratio. This could happen if it were much easier to substitute capital for labor in the apple industry than in the butane industry.

Additional Problem

1. Each poobah requires 1 unit of land and 1 unit of labor in its production, whereas a zingo requires a total of 3 units of land and labor in any combination (including fractions). Draw the curve relating the relative cost of poobahs and zingoes to the relative prices of land and labor.

Answers to Self-Test

1.   1.1.   No effect.
     1.2.   No effect.
     1.3.   No effect: a movement along the curve.
     1.4.   It would shift the curve down.
     1.5.   No effect.

2.   If less than OA the country must be producing only butane, if greater than OA only apples.

3. THE HECKSCHER-OHLIN THEORY: COMPARATIVE ADVANTAGE AND FACTOR PRICES

Basic Ideas

1.   This section discusses two of the four basic propositions developed in the Heckscher-Ohlin-Samuelson model.

2.   The *Heckscher-Ohlin theorem* states that a country has a comparative advantage in the good making relatively intensive use of the country's relatively abundant factor.

3.   The *factor-price equalization theorem* states that free trade will make the prices of each factor more nearly equal across countries, with complete equality taking place if both countries produce both goods.

4.   These propositions share the property that each is demonstrated using the technological relation between relative costs and relative factor prices.

5.   Things to know: **how to demonstrate each proposition geometrically.**

Self-Test

1.   Multiple choice: Which of the following observations is inconsistent with the others?
     1.1.   France and Germany engage in free trade.
     1.2.   France is relatively capital abundant.
     1.3.   French firms employ more capital-intensive techniques than their German counterparts.
     1.4.   Both countries produce both goods.
     1.5.   It's raining everywhere.

2.   True or false: Free trade causes wages to equal rents if both countries produce both goods.

3.   True or false: Labor-abundant countries export labor-intensive goods instead of labor.

Solutions to Problems from the Text

5.9   *Agricultural trade between the U.S. and Europe is not free. The yield per acre*
on a French farm is typically much higher than on an American farm devoted
to the same crop. Does this indicate relative American inefficiency or
backwardness? Explain in terms of the theory. What would you expect to be true
of relative French and American prices of the relevant factors? What do you
think would be the effect of a movement to free trade?

France is obtaining higher yields per acre by using more capital and labor
per acre than America; this indicates a relative abundance of land in
America. Free trade would tend to equalize factor prices and so cause the
two countries to utilize more similar techniques.

5.10   *Suppose each cask of wine requires 4 labor units and 1 capital unit in its*
production, and each bolt of cloth requires 2 and 5 units respectively; the wage
and the rent each equal 100. What is the cost of wine and cloth? Suppose the
wage and rent both increase to 110. By what percentage have they risen? What
are the new costs of the two goods and by what percentages have they changed?
Answer the same questions if instead the wage increases from 100 to 120 and
the rent from 100 to 105. If instead the wage falls from 100 to 90 while the rent
rises from 100 to 120.

Wine cost = 4 x 100 + 1 x 100 = 500 and cloth cost = 2 x 100 + 5 x 100 =
700. Both w and r rise by 10 percent. Now: wine cost = 4 x 110 + 1 x 110 =
550 and cloth cost = 2 x 110 + 5 x 110 = 770. Thus the cost of wine has increased by 10%, as has the cost of cloth. If instead the wage increases to 120
and the rent to 105, wine cost goes up to 585 and cloth cost to 765; thus the
percentage increases are: 20 percent (wages) > 17 percent (wine) > 9.3
percent (cloth) > 5 percent (capital). If the wage falls to 90 and the rent
rises to 120, wine cost falls to 480 and cloth cost rises to 780. Thus the
percentage increases are: 20 percent (wage) > 11.4 percent (cloth) > -4
percent (wine) > -10 percent (rent).

5.11*   *Discuss in detail the Heckscher-Ohlin and factor-price equalization theorems in*
the context of Problem 5.7*.

Both propositions can be violated in such a case. This is illustrated below.
Germany is labor-abundant, and autarky relative factor prices in the two
countries are indicated at F and G respectively. Note that Germany has a
comparative advantage in apples, even though apples are capital-intensive
in Germany. (However France has a comparative advantage in butane
which is capital-intensive in France, the capital abundant country.) The
free-trade relative price is indicated by p, with both countries producing
both goods at factor prices indicated by F' and G' respectively. Not only has
free trade failed to completely equalize factor prices, it has actually made
them more unequal.

BUTANE COST/APPLE COST

5.12*   *Suppose that we retain all of the assumptions of the Heck-
         scher-Ohlin-Samuelson model, except that we assume that all French citizens
         have a much greater relative preference for apple consumption than all German
         citizens (who therefore have a much greater relative preference for butane
         consumption). How is the Heckscher-Ohlin theorem affected?*

         No effect

Additional Problems

1.   Suppose that England and Portugal share the technology described in
     Problem 5.10 above, and that the other assumptions of the
     Heckscher-Ohlin-Samuelson model are satisfied. Suppose that in autarky
     the wage and rent each equal 100 in England, while in Portugal the wage is
     90 and the rent is 120. What does this indicate about the relative factor
     abundance of the two countries? Show that the Heckscher-Ohlin theorem is
     demonstrated.

2.   Suppose that Portugal and England, as described in the preceding problem,
     enter into free trade. The international price of wine is 550 and that of cloth
     is 770. Both countries continue to produce both goods. Show how the
     factor-price equalization theorem is demonstrated.

3.   How is the factor-price equalization theorem affected in the context of
     Problem 5.12* above?

Answers to Self-Test

1. 1.3

2. False

3. True

4. THE HECKSCHER-OHLIN THEORY: INCOME DISTRIBUTION AND GROWTH

Basic Ideas

1. This section discusses the remaining two of the four basic propositions derived from the Heckscher-Ohlin-Samuelson model.

2. The *Stolper-Samuelson theorem* says that an increase in the relative price of a good will cause the price of the factor used intensively in the production of that good to rise relative to both commodities, and the price of the other factor to fall relative to both commodities.

3. The *Rybczynski theorem* says that an increase in the relative endowment of a factor, at constant prices, increases the output of the good making intensive use of that factor relative to both factor endowments, and reduces the output of the other good relative to both endowments.

4. The two theorems are proved by a very similar logic.

5. Points to know: **how to prove the two theorems; how they relate to income distribution and growth; real income; how to spell "Rybczynski."**

Self-Test

1. Multiple choice: The Heckscher-Ohlin-Samuelson model makes several strong assumptions. Which of the following is not required for either the Stolper-Samuelson or the Rybczynski theorem to be valid?
    1.1. The two countries share the same technology.
    1.2. There are two goods and two factors.
    1.3. Tastes are identical in the two countries.
    1.4. Within each country the two factors are freely mobile between the two industries.

2. Multiple choice: If the price of apples rises by 10 percent and the price of butane falls by 10 percent, while factor prices do not change, Crazy Harry's real income:
    2.1. Rises.
    2.2. Falls.
    2.3. Is unchanged because the average price change is 0 percent.

2.4. Rises if, and only if, Crazy Harry spends more than half his income on butane.

Solutions to Problems from the Text

5.13 *What do you think is the consequence of the historic rise in the American wage, relative to other factor prices, for the cost of a college education? The consequence for the cleanliness of city streets? Specifically relate your answers to the theory.*

Since both activities are relatively labor-intensive, their prices should have increased more rapidly than prices generally.

5.14 *Show how your answers to* **Problem 5.10** *illustrate the Stolper-Samuelson theorem.*

When the cost of labor-intensive apples rose relative to that of capital-intensive cloth, the wage rose proportionally more than both and the rent proportionally less than both.

5.15 *The savings rate in Japan since the Second World War has been much higher than in most other countries. What is the likely effect on relative Japanese factor abundance? use the theory of this section to predict the likely consequences.*

The high savings rate should allow much capital accumulation, causing Japan to become relatively more capital abundant compared to the rest of the world. This would likely cause an even more rapid rise in the production of capital-intensive goods, and therefore lead to increases in their exports of these goods.

5.16 *Suppose that the country described in* **Problem 5.10** *above produces 200 casks of wine and 200 bolts of cloth. How much capital and labor is this economy using? Suppose wine output falls to 80 casks. What are the changes in percentage terms? How much capital and labor is now required? What are these changes in percentage terms? How does this illustrate the Rybczynski theorem?*

The 200 casks of wine require 800 labor and 200 capital whereas the 200 cloth require 400 labor and 1000 capital, for a total of 1200 labor and 1200 capital. If the output of wine falls to 80, 480 less labor and 120 less capital will be required. Thus wine output falls 60 percent labor usage falls 40 percent capital usage 10 percent, and cloth output 0 percent.

5.17 *Calculate the outputs of wine and cloth in Portugal and England if the countries have the technology described in* **Problem 5.10** *above, if England has 100 workers and 160 capital units, and if Portugal has 100 workers and 70 capital units. (Do this either by trial and error or by setting up and solving two simultaneous equations in two unknowns.) Show how a comparison of Portugal and England illustrates the Rybczynski theorem. Show how it also* demonstrates the Heckscher-Ohlin theorem, if the two countries are freely trading.

In England: $W + 5C = 160$ (capital) and $4W + 2C = 100$ (labor). These have the solution $W = 10$ and $C = 30$.

In Portugal: $W + 5C = 70$ (capital) and $4W + 2C = 100$ (labor). These have the solution $W = 20$ and $C = 10$.

Thus: ([(30-10)/10] = 3) > ([(160-70)/70] = [9/7]) > ([(100-100)/100] = 0) > ([(10-20)/10] = -1), which illustrates the Rybczynski theorem.

5.19* *The Stolper-Samuelson and Rybczynski theorems apply to situations in which both goods are actually produced. Suppose instead that France specializes completely in the production of apples. How would French wages and rents be affected by a rise in the price of apples? By a rise in the price of butane? How are real wages affected? How would French outputs respond to a change in factor endowments, with the prices of apples and butane unchanged?*

A rise in the price of apples would raise both wages and rents in the same proportion, thereby increasing the real wage of anyone who spent any part of her income on butane, and holding constant the real wage of any person consuming only apples. A rise in the price of butane would leave wages and rents unchanged, thereby lowering the real wage of anyone who spent any part of his income on butane and holding constant the real wage of any person consuming only apples. An increase in either factor endowment would increase the output of apples.

5.20* *The Stolper-Samuelson theorem assumes that both factors are freely mobile between industries within a country. But in fact this is not true, at least for substantial time periods. Suppose, for example, that labor is freely mobile between apple and butane production but that capital is immobile, so that each industry's capital stock is fixed. Discuss the Stolper-Samuelson theorem in this case.*

For the answer to this problem, read Section 10 of Chapter 6 of the textbook.

Additional Problems

1. Suppose that we depart from the Heckscher-Ohlin-Samuelson model by allowing three factors of production (land, labor, and capital), rather than just two, all of which are used in the production of each of the two goods. Suppose that both goods are in fact being produced, and that one of them rises in price. Go through the proof of the Stolper-Samuelson theorem in the textbook, noting exactly how the argument is changed or not.

2. Suppose that we depart from the Heckscher-Ohlin-Samuelson model by allowing three goods (apples, butane, and cloth), rather than just two, each of which uses both factors. Suppose that the endowment of one of these

factors increases, all prices remaining unchanged. Go through the proof of the Rybczynski theorem in the textbook, noting exactly how the argument is changed or not.

Answers to Self-Test

1.   1.1 and 1.3.

2.   2.4

5.* EXPLORING FURTHER: ANALYSIS OF THE HECKSCHER-OHLIN-SAMUELSON MODEL—THE FIRM

Basic Ideas

1.   This section gives a geometric treatment of the behavior of a competitive firm.

2.   Such a firm will minimize its costs if it chooses the technique of production where the marginal rate of technical substitution equals (minus) the ratio of the respective factor prices.

3.   Things to know: **isoquant; constant returns to scale; marginal rate of technical substitution.**

Solutions to Problems from the Text

5.21   *Suppose that the production of each bushel of apples requires 4 (or more) units of capital together with 2 (or more) units of labor. Draw the one-bushel isoquant.*

What can you say about the $MRTS_{KL}^A$ in this case?

What techniques of production would an apple producer choose if $w/r = 5$? If $w/r = 1$? For other values of w/r?

The technique $K = 4$, $L = 2$ would be chosen in all cases (where both w and r are positive).

5.22 *Suppose that each bolt of cloth requires 1 unit (or more) of capital plus 4 units (or more) of labor to produce. Answer the same questions as in **Problem 5.21** above.*

The technique $K = 1$, $L = 4$ would be chosen in all cases (where both w and r are positive).

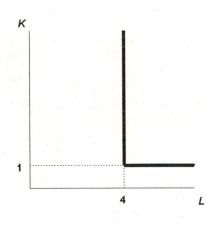

5.23 *Suppose that cloth can be produced either as described in **Problem 5.22** or by using 7 (or more) units of capital plus 1 (or more) units of labor. Answer the same questions as in **Problem 5.21** above.*

To the right of point B, the $MRTS_{KL}$ equals 0, above point A it is infinite, between the two points it equals 2, and at the points itself it is undefined. If $w/r = 5$, technique A would be used; if $w/r = 1$, B would be used; if $w/r = 2$, any technique between A and B inclusive could be used.

Additional Problems

1. Redraw Figure 5.8 on page 140 of the textbook as it would look with both a butane isoquant and an apple isoquant drawn in the proper relation to each other when apples are relatively capital-intensive.

2. Suppose that K units of capital and L units of labor can always produce $(K/L)^{1/2}$ bushels of apples. Answer the questions of **Problem 5.21** above.

6.* *EXPLORING FURTHER:* ANALYSIS OF THE HECKSCHER-OHLIN-SAMUELSON MODEL—THE GENERAL EQUILIBRIUM OF PRODUCTION

Basic Ideas

1. This section presents a geometric method for finding the factor prices and production pattern in an economy, given commodity prices and endowments.

2. Thing to know: **how to use Figure 5.9 on page 142 of the textbook.**

Self-Test

1. Suppose that the technology for producing apples is identical to that for producing butane. Draw a diagram like that of Figure 5.9 on page 142 of the textbook for each of the following cases. using your diagrams, say what will be produced in each case.
   1.1. The price of apples exceeds that of butane.
   1.2. The price of butane exceeds that of apples.
   1.3. The prices of apples and butane are equal.

Solutions to Problems from the Text

5.25 *Suppose each wine cask requires 4 units of capital and 2 of labor while each bolt of cloth requires 1 unit of capital and 4 of labor. What will be produced if the economy has 10 units of labor and 6 of capital? What will factor prices be if the price of wine is Fr2 and that of cloth is Fr1?*

$4W + C = 6$ (capital) and $2W + 4C = 10$ (labor) have the solution $W = 1$ and $C = 2$.

$4r + 2w = 2$ (price of wine) and $r + 4w = 1$ (price of cloth) have the solution $r = 3/7$ and $w = 1/7$.

5.26 *What will happen to the outputs of the two goods if, in **Problem 5.25**, the capital stock increases to 8 units? What happens to factor prices if the price of cloth increases to Fr2?*

W increases to $11/7$ and C falls to $12/7$. w increases to $3/7$ and r falls to $2/7$.

5.27 *The discussion in the textbook assumed that the economy-wide capital-labor ratio was between the least-cost capital-labor ratios in the two sectors, that is, that G in Figure 5.9 on page 142 of the textbook was between the rays OA and OB. What would happen if instead the economy's endowment were as indicated in Figure 5.9 by point H? By J?*

If the endowment point were H, the economy would specialize in apples and relative factor prices would be given by the slope of the apples isoquant passing through H. If the endowment point were J, the economy would specialize in butane and relative factor prices would be given by the slope of the butane isoquant passing through J.

5.28* *How do your answers to **Problem 5.25** change if a bolt of cloth can be produced either by the technique described in that problem, or by 7 units of capital plus 1 of labor?*

No change, because the original technique would still be the cheapest way to produce cloth.

5.29* *Use isoquants to illustrate, in a diagram like Figure 5.9 on page 142 of the textbook, the situation described in **Problem 5.7*** above.*

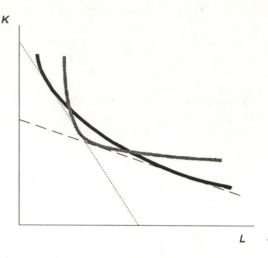

Additional Problems

1. How would the general equilibrium depicted in Figure 5.9 on page 142 of the textbook be altered if P_A were to double?

2. How would the general equilibrium depicted in Figure 5.9 in the textbook be altered if the capital stock K were to double?

3. Suppose that an economy is producing both goods, as in Figure 5.9 in the textbook. Now introduce a third good, cloth, with its own distinctive iso-quants. If the prices of apples and butane do not change, under what circumstances will cloth actually be produced instead of one of the other goods? When will all three goods be produced? Complete the parallelogram in this latter case.

Answers to Self-Test

1. The economy will:
    1.1. Specialize in apple production.
    1.2. Specialize in butane production.
    1.3. Produce an indeterminate combination of apples and butane.

7.* *EXPLORING FURTHER:* ANALYSIS OF THE HECKSCHER-OHLIN-SAMUELSON MODEL—BASIC PROPOSITIONS

Basic Ideas

1. This section uses the geometry developed in the two preceding sections to demonstrate explicitly the four basic propositions of the Heckscher-Ohlin theory.

2. You should, of course, understand and be able to repeat the proofs of the propositions. Test your understanding by constructing numerical examples.

Additional Problems

1. Using the technology described in **Problems 5.21** and **5.22,** illustrate the four propositions with specific numerical examples.

2. In Figure 5.11 on page 145 of the textbook, complete the parallelograms from point *G* to find the allocations of capital and labor to the industries both before and after the price change. Compare the two situations.

3. With your answer to **Problem 5.29*** as a starting point, draw a situation where two countries produce both goods while freely trading with each other, but nevertheless have unequal factor prices.

4. Because of identical tastes, two countries freely trading together will consume the two goods in identical proportions. If factor prices are equalized, the same production techniques will be used in the two countries, so they will "consume" factors in the same proportions (*i.e.* the factors used to produce the goods they actually consume). using the geometry developed in this and the preceding sections, depict the pattern of factor trade (in this indirect sense of the factors used to produce the goods actually traded) between two countries who continue to produce both goods.

8. REVIEW QUESTIONS

1. What are the basic assumptions of the Heckscher-Ohlin-Samuelson model?

2. What are the basic results of the Heckscher-Ohlin-Samuelson model?

CHAPTER 6

Explaining Trade

KEY IDEAS of Chapter Six

1.   The *Leontief Paradox* refers to Leontief's finding that the United States utilized more capital per worker in the production of importables than in the production of exportables. This was an enduring feature of U.S. trade for many years.

2.   The Leontief Paradox stimulated an enormous amount of research, both theoretical and empirical.

3.   The most successful attempts to explain Leontief's findings remained within a factor-endowments framework but allowed more than just two goods and factors, allowed consideration of the roles of natural resources, human capital, and so on. Also, casual attempts to interpret actual trade seem to be most fruitful when they adopt a factor-endowments perspective.

4.   The basic theorems of the 2 x 2 x 2 Heckscher-Ohlin-Samuelson model retain considerable validity in the context of many goods and factors. However, a version of the Heckscher-Ohlin theorem itself, sufficiently simple to be useful, has not yet been found to be supported by the data. Thus it is not clear to what extent differences in relative factor endowments determine trade.

5.   The fact that attitudes toward trade policy often seem determined by the sectors with which people are affiliated rather than by the factors from which they earn incomes has also cast doubt on the relevance of the Stolper-Samuelson theorem. This has renewed interest in *specific-factors models*: models in which some factors are not mobile between industries, at least in the short run.

1. THE LEONTIEF PARADOX

Basic Ideas

1. In perhaps the most influential empirical study in economics, Leontief muscled actual data into the straightjacket of the two-factor (capital and labor), two-commodity (exports and importables), two-country (the United States and the rest of the world) Heckscher-Ohlin-Samuelson model.

2. Leontief employed data on the U.S. technology and U.S. trade to calculate that the U.S. employed significantly more capital per worker in the production of import-competing goods than in the production of exports.

3. In light of the Heckscher-Ohlin theorem, Leontief's finding is inconsistent *either* with the prior belief that the United States was relatively capital abundant *or* with the view that the 2 x 2 x 2 model adequately approximates reality.

2. POSSIBLE EXPLANATIONS OF THE LEONTIEF PARADOX

Basic Ideas

1. This section investigates two minor modifications of the Heckscher-Ohlin-Samuelson model that could conceivably reconcile it with both the casual empiricism that the U.S. is relatively capital-abundant, and the Leontief Paradox (that U.S. import-competing goods are more capital-intensive than U.S. exports).

2. A factor intensity reversal is present if the commodity which is capital-intensive at some factor prices becomes labor-intensive at other factor prices. This could potentially explain the paradox, if U.S. imports are labor-intensive abroad but capital intensive in the U.S.

3. A demand reversal is present if a country has a sufficiently pronounced demand (relative to that of the rest of the world) for the good which uses intensively that country's relatively abundant factor, so that the country imports that good.

4. There is a lack of clear empirical evidence that factor intensity reversals do, in fact, explain the Leontief Paradox, and the evidence seems to indicate that demand reversals do not explain it.

Self-Test

1. Suppose that a capital-abundant country engages in free trade and specializes completely in the production of the good that, at that country's factor prices, is labor-intensive. Which of the following could not account for this state of affairs?
   1.1. A demand reversal
   1.2. A factor intensity reversal
   1.3. International differences in technology

Solutions to Problems from the Text

6.3 *Draw a diagram showing the relation between the wage-rental ratio and the ratio of butane cost to apple cost if a factor intensity reversal is present. If the relative factor intensities of the two industries reverse themselves twice.*

BUTANE COST/APPLE COST   BUTANE COST/APPLE COST

w/r   w/r

One Reversal   **Two Reversals**

6.4 *If the Leontief Paradox were indeed due to a factor intensity reversal, what would Leontief have found if, instead of calculating the capital and labor used to produce a bundle of U.S. import substitutes, he had calculated the capital and labor actually used in the rest of the world to produce a bundle of U.S. imports? What would he have found if he had performed his actual calculation for the rest of the world rather than for the U.S.?*

He would not have obtained the paradox in either case.

6.5* *What can you say about factor-price equalization if a demand reversal is present?*

Factor-price equalization must take place with free trade, that is, neither country will specialize in production.

6.6*   *Discuss the factor-price equalization, Rybczynski, and Stolper-Samuelson
       theorems in the presence of a factor-intensity reversal.*

The factor-price equalization theorem no longer applies, but the
Rybczynski and Stolper-Samuelson theorems are unaffected, as long as the
change in endowments or commodity prices does not carry the country
across such a reversal.

Additional Problems

1.   It has been suggested that relative factor abundance be determined on the
     basis of relative autarky factor prices instead of on the basis of physical
     factor endowments. That is, a country would be classified as labor abundant
     if, in autarky, w/r were lower in that country than abroad, rather than if K/L
     were lower in that country than abroad. Discuss how factor intensity
     reversals and demand reversals affect the Heckscher-Ohlin theorem when
     this notion of relative factor abundance is used.

2.   If we were interested in the factor content of trade rather than its
     commodity composition, we might revise the Heckscher-Ohlin theorem to
     state: the capital abundant country will on balance "export" capital and
     "import" labor, if the factors used to produce its exports are compared to
     the factors used by the rest of the world to produce that country's imports.
     Discuss how factor intensity reversals and demand reversals affect this
     version of the theorem.

3.   Discuss the factor-price equalization, Rybczynski, and Stolper-Samuelson
     theorems in the presence of a demand reversal.

Answer to Self-Test

1.   1.1.   A demand reversal

3.   EXTENSIONS OF THE HECKSCHER-OHLIN-SAMUELSON MODEL

Basic Ideas

1.   This section examines more substantive departures from the Heckscher-
     Ohlin-Samuelson model. They share the property that trade is still viewed
     as the consequence of relative factor endowments, and that the model is
     altered essentially by the addition of more factors and, sometimes, goods.

2.   One potential explanation of the Leontief Paradox adds a third factor,
     natural resources, to capital and labor. This could explain the paradox if:
     capital and natural resources are complements in production; the U.S. is
     scarce in natural resources.

3.   Another explanation adds *human capital*—the value of education, training, etc. Human capital might either be regarded as a third factor or added to physical capital to obtain a revised measure of total capital.

4.   The third explanation looks at *skill groups*. This involves viewing labor as a number of different factors, rather than just one, and allowing many commodities which utilize the various skills.

5.   These modifications to the Heckscher-Ohlin-Samuelson model seem to posses considerable explanatory power.

Solutions to Problems from the Text

6.7   *Sometimes human capital is added to physical capital to obtain a measure of total capital, and sometimes the two types of capital are treated as separate factors. Physical capital itself can take many forms (different types of buildings, different equipment, inventories of different goods), and the form it takes depends upon the sector in which it is employed. If the purpose of the theory is to explain trade in a long run perspective where capital is completely flexible, how should the two types of capital be treated (added together, or separate)? What difference does it make? Can you think of any reasons to distinguish between human and physical capital but not between forms of the latter?*

The fact that in the long run capital can be reallocated between physical form and human form as well as between different physical types suggests that a single aggregate measure should be used. If this were not done, and a study seemed to "explain" trade patterns by relative endowments of the two types of capital (and perhaps other factors), this could simply be a confusion of cause and effect. But one possible reason for distinguishing human capital from physical capital is that their market structures differ: there are markets in which physical capital goods can be bought and sold, but slavery is prohibited.

6.8   *Suppose you were to discover that in nearly all countries wages are generally higher in export industries than in import competing industries (there is some factual support for this). What would this imply about the empirical relevance of the human capital explanation? Would this cause you to prefer one method of measuring human capital over another?*

This suggests that the wage differentials could reflect something other than human capital, motivating one to try to measure the latter by its cost rather than by wage differentials. It also adds to the reasons for testing the theory with data from trading partners as well as domestic data.

6.9   *Specific skills are due in part to innate ability and in part to training (or human capital). If innate abilities are distributed in about equal proportions in the populations of different countries, should the skill groups and human capital explanations be distinct?*

In principle, no

6.10*   *Some commodities, because of high transportation costs, do not enter into*
international trade at all. Personal services are often of this sort. Suppose we
alter the basic model by adding a third, nontraded good. Does this change the
model in any way beyond increasing the number of goods from two to three? If
nontraded goods consist mainly of service industries, what effect would they
have on calculations such as Leontief's? Try to deduce the implications of the
presence of a nontraded good on the four basic propositions derived from the
Heckscher-Ohlin-Samuelson model.

Besides increasing the number of goods, adding a nontraded commodity
causes tastes to exert a different influence. The quantity of factors to be
allocated between the traded goods, in response to international prices,
necessarily equals the country's endowment, minus the quantity of factors
used to produce nontraded goods. But because the latter are nontraded, the
quantity produced domestically must equal the quantity demanded, and this
depends upon tastes. Thus tastes help to determine the quantity of factors
available for the production of traded goods. This is not the case, of course,
in the Heckscher-Ohlin-Samuelson model.

4. ALTERNATIVES TO FACTOR ENDOWMENTS

Basic Ideas

1.   This section and the next discuss explanations of trade—and of the Leontief
Paradox—that are not based on a factor endowments approach, though
they may or may not be consistent with such an approach.

2.   The alternative explanations considered in this section are all special cases
of comparative advantage, even though they differ from the factor-
endowments theory, which is also such a special case. The next section, by
contrast, considers possibilities that are distinct from comparative
advantage.

3.   *Technological theories* assert that a country may have a comparative
advantage in the activity of research and development, and consequently
export a changing mix of new goods, because of the R&D that they embody.

4.   *Tariffs* and other governmental policies could influence trade enough so
that the underlying pattern of comparative advantage is not reflected in
actual trade flows.

5.   *S. B. Linder* hypothesized that countries tend to export goods which also
have a strong domestic market, because those are the goods a country
knows the most about, and that per capita incomes largely determine which
goods have strong domestic markets. If so, similarities in per capita incomes
would generate trade.

Self-Test

1. Multiple choice: The product cycle refers to:
   1.1. The changing location of production of a particular good over time.
   1.2. The changing location of consumption of a particular good over time.
   1.3. The changing nature of a particular good over time.
   1.4. The changing pattern of comparative advantage over time.
   1.5. A particular type of dog food.

2. True or false: Linder's theory is more concerned to explain DC-DC trade than DC-LDC trade.

3. Multiple choice: Which of the following ideas is relevant to *both* the product cycle theory and Linder's hypothesis?
   3.1. That differences in tastes are important determinants of the pattern of trade.
   3.2. That innovation is an activity that some countries have a comparative advantage in.
   3.3. That firms can best learn how to produce a good if they have close contact with their customers.
   3.4. All of the above
   3.5. None of the above

Additional Problems

1. For each of the explanations discussed in this section, explain either how that explanation could in fact be a manifestation of international differences in relative factor endowments, or else how it has nothing to do with thi

2. What are the two basic assumptions on which Linder's theory is based?

Answers to Self-Test

1. 1.1

2. True

3. 1.3

5.   INCREASING RETURNS TO SCALE AND IMPERFECT COMPETITION

Basic Ideas

1.   National economies of scale suggest that countries trade to specialize and reap the rewards of large scale production. In this case the pattern of trade need not be determinate, or at all significant, so no theory could hope to explain it.

2.   International scale economies suggest that intraindustry trade—as opposed to interindustry trade—could be generated by similarities in relative factor endowments, rather than by differences.

3.   Imperfect competition provides a basis for interindustry trade that may either reinforce or counteract the influence of factor endowment differences.

4.   Though the theories discussed in this section suggest that intraindustry trade might be negatively related to factor endowment differences, this cannot explain the Leontief Paradox because the latter has to do with the factor content of trade.

Self-Test

1.   Multiple choice: In the presence of product differentiation or international economies of scale, international factor mobility and
   1.1.   Interindustry trade are complements.
   1.2.   Intraindustry trade are substitutes.
   1.3.   Intraindustry trade are complements.
   1.4.   All of the above
   1.5.   None of the above

2.   When do differences in relative factor endowments and the presence of oligopoly tend to promote the *same* pattern of interindustry trade?

Answers to Self-Test

1.   1.3

2.   When each country's relatively competitive sector makes relatively intensive use of that country's relatively abundant factor.

6.   TESTING THE FACTOR-ENDOWMENTS THEORY

Basic Ideas

1.   The two-factor, two-commodity version of the theory is too simple to accommodate reality in a useful way.

2.   The factor-endowments approach helps us to understand the world economy, which can be usefully and instructively approached with only a moderate number of goods and factors.

3.   The empirical work discussed in this section is concerned with the relation between three sets of variables: endowments, technology and trade flows. Until recently most studies, like Leontief's, employed data on only two of these three sets of data and, guided by the theory (to varying degrees), made inferences about the third.

4.   A version of the Heckscher-Ohlin theorem simple enough to be useful has not yet been found to be supported by the data.

5.   Concept to understand: **Heckscher-Ohlin-Vanek theorem.**

Solution to Problem from the Text

6.12   *Table 6.1 on page 166 of the text shows illiterate labor to be very abundant in India and very scarce in the United States. What does Table 6.2 imply about the consequences for each country's trade of a migration of one unit of illiterate labor from India to the United States? Suppose that at the same time 2 units of capital move from the United States to India. What happens to each country's trade in this case?*

The entries in the fourth row of Table 6.6 (the row labeled ILLIT L) show the estimated effect on the United States's net exports of the immigration of illiterate labor from India, and the same row, *with the signs reversed,* shows the effects on India's net exports.

The entries in the first row of Table 6.6 (the row labeled CAP), *when doubled in magnitude*, show the estimated effect on India's net exports of the inflow of capital from the United States, and the same row, *again doubled in magnitude and with the signs reversed*, shows the effects on the United States's net exports.

7.* *EXPLORING FURTHER:* MANY GOODS AND FACTORS

Basic Ideas

1.   The four basic propositions derived from the Heckscher-Ohlin-Samuelson model are based upon that model's assumption that there are just two goods and two factors.

2.   Empirical work seems to indicate, on the whole, that while relative factor endowments may indeed be crucial determinants of trade patterns, the latter cannot be adequately understood within a two-good, two-factor framework. Thus the relevance of the four basic propositions is intimately related to the degree to which they generalize to models with more goods and factors.

3.   This section argues that, although the propositions must be qualified in some significant ways when there are more than two goods and factors, their essential messages retain much validity.

Solutions to Problems from the Text

6.20   *What does the Heckscher-Ohlin-Vanek theorem deduced in the previous section imply about the validity of the natural resources explanation of the Leontief Paradox if factor-price equalization takes place?*

If factor-price equalization took place and if the United States were abundant in capital and scarce in natural resources, the country would have to be trading an assortment of goods such that the former was on balance exported and the latter imported (in the sense of the factors used in the production of imports and exports), regardless of whether or not those two factors tended to be complementary in individual industries.

6.21   *Go through the reasoning of Section 7* of Chapter 5, as best as you can, if there are three goods and two factors. If there are two goods and three factors.*

This is discussed in section A.5 of Appendix I in the textbook.

8.   THE SPECIFIC-FACTORS MODEL

Basic Ideas

1.   The Heckscher-Ohlin-Samuelson model assumes that both factors are freely mobile between industries within a single country. But limits to internal mobility are often important in practice.

2.   The specific-factors model is a variant of the Heckscher-Ohlin-Samuelson model in which only one of the factors is mobile between industries. The

other factor is specific to the industry in which it is located (that is, it cannot move between industries), but it is mobile between firms within that industry.

3.   Factors are more likely to be mobile the more time they have to move. Thus the Heckscher-Ohlin-Samuelson model can be regarded as a long run version of the specific-factors model. Also a model in which both factors are specific can be regarded as a short run version of the specific-factors model.

4.   If a factor, say capital, is sector-specific it is really two factors, since apple capital can't be substituted for butane capital. Thus the specific-factors model can also be thought of as differing from the Heckscher-Ohlin-Samuelson model by having three factors rather than just two, and therefore by having more factors than goods.

5.   An increase in the price of a commodity will cause the reward of the factor specific to that sector to rise even more, and the reward of the other specific factor will decline absolutely. Thus the specific factors play the same role as in the Stolper-Samuelson theorem. But the effect on the reward of the mobile factor is ambiguous.

Self-Test

1.   Multiple choice: In the specific-factors model, a small change in factor endowments, with commodity prices unchanged
    1.1.   Is impossible, because the factors are specific.
    1.2.   Will alter factor prices.
    1.3.   Will have no effect on factor prices, by the factor-price equalization theorem.
    1.4.   Will have no effect on outputs, because the factors are specific.
    1.5.   None of the above.

2.   For each of the following, write *S* if the property is a characteristic of the specific-factors model, *H* if it is characteristic of the Heckscher-Ohlin-Samuelson model, *B* if it is characteristic of both models, and *N* if it is characteristic of neither.
    2.1.   There are more goods than factors.
    2.2.   There are more factors than goods.
    2.3.   Relative price changes cause unambiguous changes in all real factor rewards.
    2.4.   Relative price changes cause unambiguous changes in all nominal factor rewards.
    2.5.   There are two goods.

Solution to Problem from the Text

6.22   *Show how the effects of an increase in the supply of labor can be described geometrically by a shift of point* H *and the* AA *curve in our figure to the left. Compare with Figure 6.2(a) on page 179 of the text.*

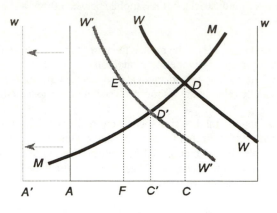

Additional Problems

1. Discuss the usefulness of trying to explain the pattern of comparative advantage on the basis of endowments of specific factors.

2. Suppose that, in contrast to both the Heckscher-Ohlin-Samuelson model and the specific-factors model, *all* factors are sector specific. Discuss the effect of an increase in the price of apples on all factor rewards.

Answer to Self-Test

1. 1.2

2. 2.1. *N*
    2.2. *S*
    2.3. *H*
    2.4. *H*
    2.5. *H*

9. REVIEW QUESTIONS

1. What is the Leontief Paradox? Describe attempts to explain it.

2. What were the most important results to come from the attempts to explain the Leontief Paradox?

3. What can you say about how important relative endowment differences really are in explaining international trade?

4. Discuss the factor-endowment basis of the international trade of the United States.

5. What is the *specific-factors* model? Why are we interested in it?

Part Three

Using Trade Theory

CHAPTER 7

Tariffs and Trade Theory

KEY IDEAS of Chapter Seven

1. A tariff, by taxing imports, causes domestic relative prices to differ from international relative prices.

2. A country which levies a tariff suffers a *production cost* because its firms make decisions on the basis of domestic relative prices rather than on the basis of the international relative prices at which the country actually trades.

3. A country which levies a tariff suffers a *consumption cost* because its consumers make decisions on the basis of domestic relative prices, rather than on the basis of the international relative prices at which the country actually trades.

4. A large country can *improve its terms of trade* with a tariff.

5. A tariff normally increases the *domestic* relative price of imports. This affects the domestic allocation of resources and distribution of income.

6. Other forms of protection produce results analogous to those of tariffs.

7. When trade is due to economies of scale, protection can induce *scale effects*.

8. When trade is due to imperfect competition, protection may induce *profit shifting* between countries.

1.   THE TARIFF

Basic Ideas

1.   A tariff is a tax on imports.

2.   Although tariffs take many different forms, their central feature, common to all the forms, is that they cause the relative prices of imports to be higher in domestic markets than on world markets.

Self-Test

1.   Suppose the world price of an imported good rises. Which of the following forms of a tariff on that good would cause the actual degree of protection to rise the most (or fall the least) as a result: specific tariff, ad valorem tariff, variable levy? Which would rise the least (or fall the most)?

Solutions to Problems from the Text

7.1   *In the example of the specific tariff on sparkling wine in the textbook, calculate the equivalent ad valorem rates on both Asti-Spumante and Champagne and compare the two. Suppose instead that sparkling wine is subject to a 10 percent ad valorem rate. Calculate the equivalent specific tariffs on both products. Suppose that both export prices rise by 50 percent. Calculate the changes in tariff payments in all cases.*

Asti Spumante: $t = (5.17 - 4.00)/4.00 = .29$, or 29 percent.
Champagne: $t = (31.17 - 30.00)/30.00 = .04$, or 4 percent.

7.2   *Explicitly derive expression (7.5) on page 187 of the textbook from expression (7.4).*

$q = p(1+t) = p + tp$, so that $q - p = tp$, or, dividing both sides by p,
$t = (q - p)/p$.

Additional Problems

1.   Countries sometimes subsidize exports. Deduce the differences between a specific subsidy and an ad valorem one. Derive a formula, analogous to (7.5) in the textbook, which shows the relation between q and p produced by an export subsidy of s percent.

2.   The text discussed some ways in which it would matter in practice whether a tariff is specific or ad valorem. Try to think of some ways in which a variable levy could in practice differ from the other two.

3.   The United States has always had many specific tariffs and many ad valorem tariffs. By contrast, European tariffs became largely specific during the 1920s and have become largely ad valorem since the Second World War. Can you think of any reasons for this change?

4.   Examine the actual United States tariff structure (see Appendix II of the textbook for data sources). Write a report on U.S. tariffs, covering such aspects as: the different types of tariffs and their relative prevalence, the average size of tariffs, differences between tariffs on different goods, etc.

5.   Do the previous problem for Canada. What significant similarities are there between U.S. and Canadian tariffs? Significant differences?

Answer to Self-Test

1.   Rise the most: ad valorem tariff
      The least: variable levy

2.   COMPARATIVE ADVANTAGE AND TARIFFS

Basic Ideas

1.   A tariff causes relative prices to differ between domestic and world markets. As this is just the situation to which the principle of comparative advantage applies, the latter can be used to deduce basic consequences of tariff protection.

2.   Tariffs are globally inefficient.

3.   A nation levying a tariff suffers a *production cost* because its GNP is lower, when evaluated at actual world prices, as a consequence.

4.   A nation levying a tariff suffers a *consumption cost* because it consumes a collection of goods less desirable than what it could afford to buy, at actual world prices.

5.   The production and consumption costs do not imply that a nation necessarily harms itself by levying a tariff, since actual world prices might be different from what they would be in the absence of the tariff.

6.   Things to understand: **how the principle of comparative advantage implies the existence of production and consumption costs.**

Solutions to Problems from the Text

7.5   *Suppose you have the following data for Germany.*

P_B/P_A	B Demand	B Supply	A Demand	A Supply
4/3	80	110		30
1	100	100	50	

Suppose the international price of butane is one apple, and that Germany imports butane with a tariff of one-third. What is the production cost to Germany in terms of apples? In terms of butane?

$p = 1$ and so $q = 4/3$. Then Germany supplies 110 butane and 30 apples, which are worth 140 apples at $p = 1$. With free trade, Germany would supply 100 butane and 50 apples, worth 150 apples. Thus the production cost is 10 apples (or 10 butane).

7.6   *Industries often request tariff protection from foreign competition. But if a tariff protects* industry, *how can it cause a production cost?*

The protection is for the industry—and its vested interests—but the cost is borne by the economy as a whole.

7.8*   *As in* **Problem 4.8***, *5 labor units are required to produce a unit of either cloth or wine in England, 100 labor units are available, and the English always consume the two goods in equal quantities. Suppose the world price of wine is one-third bolts of cloth, and that England imports wine with a 100 percent tariff. What are the production and consumption costs to England?*

The production cost is 0, because England produces 20 cloth both with and without the tariff. With free trade England would trade 5 cloth for 15 wine, consuming 15 of each good. With the tariff England exports 4 cloth for 12 wine, thereby having 16 cloth and 12 wine for consumption. But this is no better than 12 wine and 12 cloth since the two goods are always consumed in equal amounts. Thus the consumption cost of the tariff is in effect 3 wine plus 3 cloth.

Additional Problems

1.   The argument in the textbook concluded that a home tariff harmed the world because the MRT_{XM} and MRS_{XM} at home were larger than abroad. Go through the argument again under the assumption that the home and foreign countries both tax their imports.

2.   Redraw Figure 7.1 on page page 189 of the textbook to show a country that is better off as a result of levying a tariff, in spite of the production cost.

Self-Test

1. True or false: The production cost of a tariff arises from the fact that protected industries have no incentive to adopt efficient techniques.

2. True or false: The consumption cost arises from the fact that, one way or another, consumers must in the end provide the tariff revenues collected by the government.

Answers to Self-Test

1. False

2. False

3.* *EXPLORING FURTHER:* THE GEOMETRY OF TARIFF COSTS

Solutions to Problems from the Text

7.9 *In Figures 7.3 and 7.4 on pages 192 and 193 of the textbook, the dotted line through E is inside the parallel dotted line through N: the combinations of goods equal in value, at domestic prices, to actual production are smaller than the combinations equal in value to actual consumption. Why is this the case? How can you interpret the distance between the two dotted lines?*

The amount consumers spend to buy goods exceeds the amount producers receive by the tariff revenue paid to the government. This revenue is equal to the distance between the two lines.

7.10 *Prove that point N in Figures 7.2 and 7.3 in the textbook must lie northwest of M, that is, the consumption distortion of a tariff reduces trade instead of increasing it. On what does your proof depend?*

Since an indifference curve is tangent to the *AC* line at point *M*, points between *A* and *M* must be intersected by steeper indifference curves, and points between *M* and *C* by flatter curves. Since the domestic relative price of imports exceeds the world price, point *N* must lie at a steeper point on an indifference curve than does *M*. Thus *N* must be between *A* and *M*.

Additional Problem

1. Demonstrate that a small country can only harm itself by levying a tariff.

4. TARIFFS AND PRICES

Basic Ideas

1. The imposition of a tariff shifts a country's import demand curve down by a proportion equal to the tariff rate.

2. A tariff will improve a country's terms of trade if that country is large enough to influence world prices.

3. A tariff will increase the relative domestic price of importable goods, unless the country faces a backward-bending foreign export supply curve.

Self-Test

1. What is the Metzler Paradox?

2. Multiple choice: A tariff will bring about a greater improvement in a country's terms of trade,
    2.1. The more elastic its import curve.
    2.2. The less elastic its import curve.
    2.3. The more elastic the rest of the world's export curve.
    2.4. The less elastic the rest of the world's export curve.
    2.5. None of the above

Solutions to Problems from the Text

7.11 *If you did **Problem 4.7** correctly, you obtained the import demand curve below. How is it affected by a 50 percent German tariff on apple imports?*

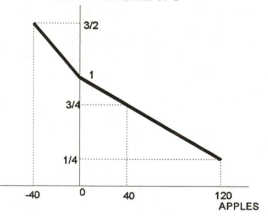

Germany's import demand curve for apples

The curve is shifted as follows.

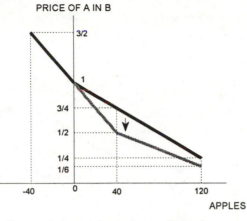

Germany's import demand curve for apples

7.12 *If you did Problem 4.6 correctly, you obtained the export supply curve below. Suppose that France levies no tariff and engages in trade with the Germany of Problem 7.11 above. Show the effect of the German tariff on the trade between the two countries. What is the effect on the terms of trade and on the domestic relative prices in both countries?*

With the tariff, France exports 66.67 apples to Germany for 25.93 butane. Before the tariff 80 apples were exchanged for 40 butane, so Germany's terms of trade have improved from one-half to seven-eighteenths. The relative price of an apple in Germany is now seven-twelfths.

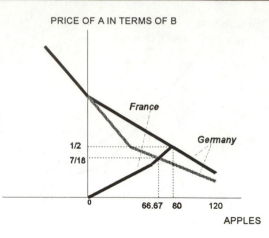

7.13* *Show how a tariff on imports shifts a country's export supply curve. use the export curve to show the effect of a tariff on international and domestic relative prices. How does a 10 percent French tariff on butane affect the curve in Problem 7.12?*

The export supply curve shifts to the left in proportion to the tariff, and it also shifts up in proportion to the tariff.

In the above figure, $t = AB/AE = AC/DC$. The other points shift in a similar way.

7.14* *The discussion in the textbook implicitly assumed that the government spends all tariff revenues on exportables. In Figure 7.5(a) on page 194, for example, domestic citizens pay OECD to the rest of the world, for the import OD, and they pay ABCE to their government as tariff revenue. If some of this revenue, however, is spent on imports, total imports will equal, not OD, but OD plus the imports that are bought with the tariff revenue. Suppose, contrary to the discussion in the text, that the government always spends all tariff revenues on additional imports. Show how a tariff affects the home import demand curve in* *this case. Under these circumstances, will a tariff still improve the terms of trade? When will it increase the relative domestic price of imports?*

The figure below shows a country's free trade import demand curve. Now suppose that the country levies an ad valorem tariff at the rate *BC/CD*. If the terms of trade are, say, *EO*, the country would trade at point *A*. But now, at those same terms of trade, domestic residents face a relative price of imports equal to *FO*. Thus they purchase *OD* imports, paying for them with *OFBD* exportables, of which *EFBC* is collected by the government as tariff revenue and *OECD* is exported to pay for the imports.

Now, however, the government's revenue is spent on additional imports. At the supposed terms of trade, the tariff revenue of *EFBC*, in terms of exportables, will buy the quantity *DG* of importables, where *DCHG = EFBC*. Thus the country now trades at *H*. Total imports equal *OG*, of which *OD* is done by the private sector and *DG* is done by the government spending its revenues. The quantity *OEHG = OFBD* is exported to pay for the total imports. Thus the tariff-ridden import-demand curve goes through *H* rather than *C*.

A tariff now shifts the import demand curve down and to the right just enough so that the area under the new curve at any point is just equal to the area under the corresponding point on the original curve. Any inelastic part of the offer curve will now be shifted out, rather than in, as a result of a tariff. This is because, as we move down an import demand curve, the area corresponding to each point becomes larger if the curve is elastic but smaller if it is inelastic. Since the curve in the above figure is elastic, the area determined by *A* is larger than that determined by *B*, and therefore larger than that determined by *H* also, so *A* must be to the right of *H*. If the curve had been inelastic, *A* would have determined a smaller area than *H* and so been to the left of it.

The following figure shows the effect of a tariff on a country's offer curve if all revenue is spent on importables, and if the curve has both elastic and inelastic portions.

EXTRA QUESTION:

Suppose that a country is trading on the inelastic part of its import demand curve, that it imposes a tariff on imports, and that its government spends all tariff revenues on imports. What is the effect on that country's terms of trade? On its relative domestic price of imports?

Additional Problems

1. Suppose that the France of **Problem 7.12** above retaliates against the German tariff by levying its own tariff of 20 percent on imports of butane. Depict this geometrically. What is the effect on the terms of trade and domestic relative prices in both countries? Compare each country's consumption with what it would consume with free trade.

2. Suppose, in **Problem 7.14***, that, instead of spending all tariff revenues on imports, the government spends the revenues exactly as the people would spend them or, equivalently, that all tariff revenues are redistributed to the population. (This doesn't sound like governments we know, but it could capture the idea that tariff revenues substitute for other taxes that would be levied if the tariff revenues did not exist.) Answer the questions of **Problem 7.14*** in this case.

Answers to Self-Test

1. A tariff causes the domestic relative price of imports in terms of exports to fall.

2. 2.4

5.   TARIFFS AND THE FACTOR ENDOWMENTS THEORY

Basic Ideas

1.   A tariff raises the relative domestic price of imports, unless the foreign export supply curve bends back. The application of this conclusion to the basic results of the Heckscher-Ohlin-Samuelson model has implications for the domestic effects of a tariff.

2.   The Heckscher-Ohlin theorem implies that a tariff protects the industry that makes relatively intensive use of the country's relatively scarce factor.

3.   The Stolper-Samuelson theorem implies that a tariff increases the real reward of the country's relatively scarce factor and lowers that of the country's relatively abundant factor.

4.   If factors are specific, a tariff will increase the real reward of those factors specific to the import competing sector and reduce the real reward of those factors specific to the export sector.

Self-Test

1.   True or false: A tariff benefits the relatively abundant factor at the expense of the relatively scarce factor.

2.   Multiple choice: Assuming that the terms of trade do not significantly improve, a tariff will:
      2.1.   Benefit the scarce factor more than it harms the abundant factor.
      2.2.   Harm the scarce factor more than it harms the abundant factor.
      2.3.   Benefit the abundant factor more than it harms the scarce factor.
      2.4.   Benefit the scarce factor less than it harms the abundant factor.
      2.5.   Benefit the abundant factor more than it benefits the scarce factor.

Solutions to Problems from the Text

7.15   *On the basis of the discussion in this section of the textbook, the owners of which factors of production in the American economy would you expect to favor protection?*

       Labor that is not highly skilled and mineral-rich land.

7.17   *What is the effect of a tariff upon the domestic distribution of income if the foreign export supply curve bends back?*

       A tariff reduces the relative domestic price of importables thereby lowering the real income of the relatively scarce factor and raising that of the relatively abundant factor.

7.18* *Deduce how the factor-price equalization theorem would be affected by the presence of a tariff in one or both countries.*

A tariff in either or both countries would prevent relative commodity prices from being equal in the two countries. This means that factor prices could not be made equal by (tariff ridden) trade, even if both countries produce both goods.

Additional Problems

1. Discuss how commercial policy could help explain the differences in agricultural yields shown in Table 5.1 on page 147 of the textbook. How could changes in such policy help explain the relative wage movements shown in Table 5.2 on page 149 of the textbook?

2. Discuss the domestic effects of a tariff if the government spends all tariff revenues on imports and if equilibrium occurs on the inelastic part of the home country's import curve. Prepare a table showing the various effects of a tariff under different assumptions about home and foreign elasticities and about government disposal of tariff revenues.

Answers to Self-Test

1. False

2. 2.4

6.   NONTARIFF BARRIERS

Basic Ideas

1. There are many distinct tools of protection, but the basic conclusions of tariff theory apply to most of them.

2. A general tax on exports has exactly the same effect on the relative price of imports in terms of exports as does an equal import tariff.

3. A quota is potentially equivalent to a tariff.

Self-Test

1. Multiple choice: A tariff at the rate t is equivalent to:
    1.1.   An export subsidy at the rate t.
    1.2.   An import subsidy at the rate t.
    1.3.   An export tax at the rate t.
    1.4.   An export subsidy at the rate $2t$.
    1.5.   None of the above

2. True or false: An import quota is not generally equivalent to a tariff if the government does not, in effect, sell the quota rights for what they can fetch.

Solutions to Problems from the Text

7.19 *Show how your answers to **Problems 7.11** and **7.12** could be duplicated by an appropriate quota.*

A German import quota of 66.67 apples does the trick, provided that the German government sells import licenses for what they will fetch.

7.21 *The Indian government has established import quotas on many goods used as productive inputs by that country's industry. In some cases these quotas have been allocated among importing firms in proportion to the output capacities of the firms. What is the effect of such an allocation system on economic incentives? Discuss the long-run implications and compare them to those of a tariff.*

Firms would have an incentive to expand output capacity beyond what they actually intend to produce, in order to obtain import quota allotments.

7.22 *Suppose that a certain economy uses three goods: importables, exportables, and nontraded goods. There are therefore two relative commodity prices: the price of imports in terms of exports and the price of nontraded goods in terms of exports. Show how a tariff on imports affects both relative prices (as equations 7.4 and 7.10 do on page 187 of the textbook) and do the same for a tax on exports. What do you conclude about the Lerner symmetry theorem?*

A tariff: $Q_X = P_X$, $Q_M = P_M(1+t)$, and let Q_N denote the domestic price of nontraded goods (there is no world price since the goods are not traded). Let q and p denote the domestic and world relative prices of imports in terms of exports, and let q' and p' denote the relative price of nontraded goods in terms of the domestic price of exports and in terms of the world price of exports, respectively. Then:

$$q = p(1+t) \text{ and } q' = p'.$$

An export tax: $Q_X(1+t) = P_X$ and $Q_M = P_M$, so that

$$q = p(1+t) \text{ and } q' = p'(1+t).$$

The two policies are no longer equivalent.

4.23 *Consider a quota and its equivalent tariff, as in Figure 7.8 on page 202 of the textbook. Show how each form of protection causes equilibrium to respond to*
  a. An outward shift of the foreign export curve.
  b. An outward shift of the home free trade import curve.

  a. A shift of the foreign export supply curve (H is before and J is after):

b.   A shift of the home free-trade import demand curve:

Additional Problems

1.   Show how your answers to **Problems 7.11** and **7.12** could be duplicated by an appropriate export tax.

2.   Suppose that a certain country exercises commercial policy solely through an export quota. Discuss the economic effects, and draw the analog to

Figure 7.8 on page 202 of the textbook. To what extent are import quotas and export quotas related to each other in the way that the Lerner symmetry theorem relates import taxes and export taxes?

3.   A certain country imposes a binding quota on imports and auctions off the quota rights. The resulting revenue is then used by the government to purchase additional imports (above the quota amount). Analyze the effects of this policy and compare to the discussion in the text. Also compare to your answer to **Problem 7.14***.

Answers to Self-Test

1.   1.3

2.   True

7.   TARIFFS WITH SCALE ECONOMIES

Basic Ideas

1.   With national increasing returns to scale, a tariff can inflict a *scale cost*: average costs increase if the tariff causes a good to be produced in several locations rather than in just one, where scale economies could be maximized.

2.   If scale economies in some industry are external to the firm, a tariff might benefit the home economy at the expense of the rest of the world by inducing the industry to locate in that country.

Self-Test

1.   Multiple choice: The scale cost of a tariff:
    1.1.   Is a special case of the production cost.
    1.2.   Has the production cost as a special case.
    1.3.   Involves producing in the wrong location rather than in too many locations.
    1.4.   Involves producing in too many locations rather than in the wrong location.
    1.5.   Is a special case of the consumption cost.

Solution to Problem from the Text

7.24   *The textbook discussed the effects of a tariff if, with free trade, France and Germany both produced butane, which has increasing returns to scale, but only France produced apples, subject to constant returns. How does the argument change if initially only Germany produces butane, but both countries produce apples? What do you conclude from this?*

If both countries produce apples and engage in free trade, wages must be the same in the two countries, because otherwise apple producers in the country with the higher wage would be driven out of business. In this case a moderate French tariff would have no effect on French production, though it would subject French consumers to the consumption cost. It could also harm German consumers if it causes butane production to fall, thereby raising costs. However, only if the tariff is large enough to be prohibitive could it cause the establishment of a French butane industry.

Additional Problems

1. The textbook's discussion of external economies of scale considered a free trade equilibrium where France produced both apples and butane, but Germany produced only butane. Compare the welfare of both countries in such an equilibrium with what their welfare would be in autarky. Do the same if the free trade equilibrium instead had France specialized in apple production and Germany producing both goods.

2. How would the textbook's discussion of the effects of a tariff in the presence of external economies of scale be altered if the economies were instead *internal* to the firm?

Answer to Self-Test

1. 1.4

8.   TARIFFS WITH IMPERFECT COMPETITION

Basic Ideas

1. With an oligopolistic import market, a tariff *shifts profit* to domestic firms from their foreign rivals.

2. With an oligopolistic import market, a tariff harms domestic consumers by its *anticompetitive effect*.

3. In an oligopolistic export market where firms compete by setting quantities, an export subsidy *shifts profit* from foreign firms to domestic firms.

4. In an oligopolistic export market where firms compete by setting quantities, an export subsidy *makes domestic firms compete more* with each other, which reduces their combined profit.

5. In an oligopolistic export market where firms compete by setting *prices*, an export subsidy shifts profit from domestic firms to foreign firms.

Self-Test

1. Multiple choice: Which of the following was shown to give rise to the possibility that a tariff might have a great effect even if it might soon become superfluous?
   1.1. External economies of scale
   1.2. Internal economies of scale
   1.3. Oligopoly where firms compete in quantities
   1.4. Oligopoly where firms compete in prices
   1.5. None of the above

Solution to Problem from the Text

4.25 *Suppose that the French butane market is a duopoly, with one French firm and one German. What would be the effects of a French tariff on butane if the two firms compete with prices rather than with quantities, as discussed in the text?*

The French tariff would shift the German reaction curve out, raising the equilibrium prices charged by both firms, with the German price increasing more than the French. French consumers would be worse off. The German firm would lose profit, which would be shifted to the profit of the French firm and to the tariff revenue of the French government.

Additional Problems

1. What can you say about the Lerner symmetry theorem if both markets are oligopolistic?

2. With oligopoly, could a country ever be tempted to tax imports and exports of the *same* good simultaneously?

Answer to Self-Test

1. 1.1

9. REVIEW QUESTIONS

1. List all the separate welfare effects of a tariff. For each effect, indicate:
   a. Whose welfare is influenced and how;
   b. When the effect is relevant (size of country, perfect or imperfect competition, type of scale economies, and so on).

2. In what ways does the presence of imperfect competition alter the analysis of the effects of a tariff?

3. What are the implications of comparative advantage for the effects of a tariff?

CHAPTER 8

Why Nations Restrict Trade ·

KEY IDEAS of Chapter Eight

1. A country may impose tariffs in order to influence its *international* economic relations or to influence its *internal* economic performance.

2. A tariff is usually a *first-best* method to attain an international objective, from a national point or view. From a cosmopolitan perspective, it may or may not be first-best.

3. A tariff is usually a *second-best* method to attain an internal objective. This means that, although a tariff may be useful in attaining such an objective, other policies can do so at lower cost.

4. In practice, the most important reason for protection, in the industrial countries at least, is to respond to demands by pressure groups for special treatment.

1.   MOTIVES FOR PROTECTION: INTERNATIONAL ECONOMIC OBJECTIVES

Basic Ideas

1.   This section discusses those reasons that a country might levy tariffs which have to do with the economic relations of that country with the rest of the world.

2.   If a country is large enough to influence world prices it can use a tariff to exert its monopoly power and make itself better off. But there is a limit to this, since free trade is better than autarky.

3.   The "optimum tariff" is the best a single country can do. It is optimum from a purely nationalistic perspective, since it harms the rest of the world more than it benefits the tariff-levying country. From a cosmopolitan perspective the optimum tariff is zero.

4.   If a country wishes to limit the volume of imports *per se*, for non-economic reasons, a tariff is an efficient way to do so.

5.   In an oligopolistic market, trade policy can be used to shift profit from foreign firms to home firms. It does this by making more aggressive home-firm behavior credible. Depending on circumstances, optimum policy for this purpose could involve either taxes or subsidies.

6.   Profit-shifting trade policy in an oligopolistic market is optimal from a nationalistic perspective because it benefits the home country by hurting foreign firms. But it may also be beneficial from a cosmopolitan viewpoint, since an oligopoly is inefficient to begin with.

Self-Test

1.   Some primary product exporters attempt to influence their terms of trade by means of an export tax. Write the formula for the optimum export tax.

2.   What is the optimum tariff from the point of view of the entire world, rather than from that of the tariff levying country?

3.   Multiple choice: An export subsidy:
     3.1.   Involves subsidizing foreign consumers.
     3.2.   May shift profit from domestic firms to foreign firms in an oligopolistic market.
     3.3.   May shift profit to domestic firms from foreign firms in an oligopolistic market.
     3.4.   All of the above
     3.5.   None of the above

Solutions to Problems from the Text

8.1 *Some people urged that the United States use the "wheat weapon" against OPEC: force up the price that OPEC must pay for our agricultural exports just as they forced up the price of their oil exports. Discuss the feasibility of such a policy.*

Feasibility is limited by the fact that wheat, and its substitutes, is exported (or can be exported) by many countries.

8.2 *We shall see that tariffs are often second-best policy tools. That is, they are inferior in some ways to alternative methods of achieving whatever goals the tariffs are being used for. Examine each of the three motives discussed in this section to see if you can think of some other, superior, policy.*

An optimum tariff policy is first-best from the point of view of the levying country, but dominated by international transfer payments from a global perspective. A tariff is a first-best way to limit trade for noneconomic reasons. If an international market is an oligopoly, first-best policy involves eliminating the oligopolistic distortions (in the home market, from a nationalistic perspective, and in the world market, from a cosmopolitan perspective).

8.3 *The optimum tariff policy $t = 1/f^*$ would seem to indicate that when on the backward-bending part of the foreign export curve ($f^* < 0$), a subsidy to imports ($t < 0$) is best. But we concluded that tariffs should be increased in such a case. Reconcile.*

The formula $t = 1/f^*$ holds only if t is actually the optimum tariff; if $f^* < 0$ the tariff can't be an optimum one, so the formula is irrelevant.

8.4 *How would the discussion in the textbook of an optimal export subsidy (or tax) change if the home and foreign oligopolists competed in the home market rather than in a foreign one?*

If the home and foreign oligopolists competed in the home market the effect of commercial policy on domestic consumers would also have to be taken into account. For example, a tariff that shifted profit from the foreign firm to the domestic firm would increase home welfare by doing so. But if it raised prices it would make domestic consumers worse off. Thus the tariff would have a *distributional* effect (helping firms partly at the expense of consumers), and the overall effect on national welfare would be the sum of these two component effects.

Additional Problems

1. Draw Figure 8.1 on page 223 of the textbook as it would appear if the home country were small in world markets.

2. Suppose that the home and foreign countries both pursue optimum tariff policies, and that each country ends up imposing a tariff that is optimum, given the tariff of the other country. What is the relationship between the home domestic relative price of imports, q, and the relative price, q^*, of the same two goods prevailing in the foreign country? Draw the analog to Figure 8.1 on page 223 of the textbook.

3. Suppose that the foreign export curve shifts outwards, as a result either of a reduction in foreign tariffs or of economic growth abroad. Show geometrically what this implies about an optimum tariff levied by the home country.

Answers to Self-Test

1. $t = 1/f^*$

2. Zero

3. 3.4

2. MOTIVES FOR PROTECTION: INTERNAL ECONOMIC OBJECTIVES

Basic Ideas

1. Governments use tariffs to raise revenue. Because they are relatively simple taxes to administer, tariffs are frequently important revenue sources in LDCs. They are no longer so important in most DCs, although they were historically.

2. Because they influence relative domestic prices, tariffs can be used to deal with external economies, market imperfections, and other distortions. But because they introduce distortions of their own, tariffs are second-best, relative to more direct measures. The infant industry argument—that temporary tariffs are necessary to establish an industry which will be viable on its own in the long run—is an important example of this class of motives.

3. Because they influence consumption and production, tariffs can be used to attain noneconomic objectives with regard to these two activities. But again they are in principle second-best methods.

4. Terms to understand: **external economies and diseconomies; domestic distortions; second best.**

Self-Test

1. True or false: "External economies" refer to cost reductions that can be achieved if goods are produced abroad rather than at home.

2. True or false: Tariffs are second-best because they are usually imposed for questionable motives.

3. True or false: Although tariffs are in principle a second-best way of raising government revenue, alternative methods could, in practice, be so difficult to administer that tariffs are in fact best.

Solutions to Problems from the Text

8.5 *This section showed that a tariff was a second-best way of attaining a non-economic objective because other methods can do the same without the consumption cost. Does this argument apply to the motive of trade limitation for noneconomic reasons discussed in the previous section of the textbook? What is the essential difference between the two motives?*

With trade limitation for noneconomic reasons the policy objective is to discriminate against imported goods, and the tariff is a direct way of doing this. If the objective is instead to achieve a production target, or a consumption target, a tariff is an indirect method and the discrimination against imported goods which it introduces is an unnecessary side effect.

8.6 *Is the tariff a second-best method of raising government revenue? If so, what methods are better?*

Yes. Lump-sum taxes, for example, do not introduce the distortions that tariffs do.

Additional Problems

1. The government would like to reduce the domestic consumption of horned winglaks which, as all the world knows, are imported but also produced domestically. For this purpose a tariff on horned winglaks is under consideration. Would a consumption tax be preferable? Why? If a tariff is cheaper to administer than is a consumption tax, how much cheaper must it be for the tariff to be as good a method as a consumption tax?

2. Based on your investigation of U.S. tariffs for **Additional Problem 4** on page 103, do any U.S. tariffs seem to be due to any of the motives discussed in this section of the textbook?

3. Based on your investigation of Canadian tariffs for **Additional Problem 5** on page 103, do any Canadian tariffs seem to be due to any of the motives discussed in this section of the textbook?

Answers to Self-Test

1. False

2. False

3. True

3. MOTIVES FOR PROTECTION: PRESSURE GROUPS

Basic Ideas

1. Because tariffs influence relative domestic prices, they can be used to alter the domestic distribution of income.

2. In the long run, a tariff will raise the real earnings of a country's relatively scarce factor and reduce the real earnings of the relatively abundant factor.

3. In the short run factors can be quite industry specific. In this case tariffs raise the earnings of factors employed in the import competing sector and lower the real earnings of factors employed in the export sector.

4. A tariff is again a second-best method: the gainers gain less than the losers lose.

5. Terms to understand: **specific factors; long run versus short run.**

Self-Test

1. Multiple choice: In the long run, the owner of a certain factor of production will be better off if:
    1.1. Not very much of her income is spent on imports.
    1.2. That factor is the one which the export sector employs intensively.
    1.3. She uses her factor in the import competing sector.
    1.4. Not very much of her income is spent on exportables.
    1.5. None of the above

2. Multiple choice: In the short run the owner of a certain factor of production will be better off if:
    2.1. Not very much of his income is spent on imports.
    2.2. That factor is the one which the export sector employs intensively.
    2.3. He uses his factor in the import competing sector.
    2.4. Not very much of his income is spent on exportables.
    2.5. None of the above.

Solution to Problem from the Text

8.7 *The optimum tariff argument supplies a motive where the tariff is a first-best tool from a* nationalistic *perspective. But from a* cosmopolitan *perspective is it a first-best method for redistributing income between countries? Why? If it is not, what methods are better and why?*

A tariff is second-best from a cosmopolitan perspective because it reduces world income, whereas direct international transfer payments would not, and are thereby first-best.

Additional Problems

1. The nation of Upper Arrogancia finds its import-competing industries mired in a worldwide recession, and its leaders are considering a dramatic rise in tariff protection as a method of stimulating employment in the import sector. But they are concerned about the possibility of foreign retaliation. What circumstances would make retaliation more likely? Less likely?

2. If a tariff causes losers to lose more than gainers gain, how could a democracy ever end up imposing tariffs?

Answers to Self-Test

1. 1.5

2. 2.3

4.* *EXPLORING FURTHER:* THE SECOND-BEST NATURE OF THE TARIFF

Basic Ideas

1. A tariff is a second-best method of dealing with domestic distortions because it cures the latter by introducing distortions of its own.

2. A small tariff will introduce less harmful distortions than it neutralizes and so is better than free trade.

3. It never pays to levy a tariff large enough to completely neutralize the domestic distortion.

4. An intermediate tariff could be better, or worse, than free trade.

Solutions to Problems from the Text

8.8 *This section suggested two possible first-best ways of dealing with the trade association example of a distortion. Are those two ways equivalent? What would determine which should be used?*

The differences are in implementation. A production subsidy would have to be financed by a tax of some sort, and so requires the administrative costs of the *tax-cum-subsidy* plus any distortions introduced by the tax. Breaking down the trade association would presuppose some policy of economic intervention.

8.10 *Formulate analogs of this section's four conclusions that apply to the use of a tariff to improve the terms of trade.*

If a country is able to influence its terms of trade, a tariff is a first-best way of doing so (from that country's point of view; it is a second-best method of international income redistribution from a global standpoint). A small tariff is definitely better for such a country than is free trade, but a prohibitive tariff (that is, a retreat into autarky) is worse than free trade. An intermediate tariff may be either better or worse than no tariff at all.

Additional Problems

1. Go through the analysis of this section in detail as if the motivation for tariff policy were not a domestic distortion, but rather a desire to limit domestic consumption of importables for noneconomic reasons.

2. Prove each of the four conclusions of this section of the textbook *without* using community indifference curves.

5. EFFECTIVE PROTECTION

Basic Ideas

1. A tariff on an intermediate good, such as steel, raises the cost of goods, such as automobiles, that use that intermediate good. Thus a tariff on steel reduces the degree of protection given to the activity of producing automobiles.

2. The *effective rate of protection* of a particular activity measures the net effect of a country's tariff structure on that activity.

3. Industrial countries typically levy higher tariffs at later stages of production, resulting in even higher effective rates at those later stages.

4. Be sure to understand: **how to derive and to use the effective rate formula; the difference between nominal and effective tariff rates.**

Self-Test

1. True or false: Effective rates of protection are always at least as high as nominal rates, and often very much higher.

2. True or false: The fact that many effective tariff rates are much higher in industrial countries than are the (typically modest) nominal rates indicates that the production and consumption costs of those countries' tariff structures are actually significantly greater than the nominal rates would seem to indicate.

Solutions to Problems from the Text

8.11 *Suppose that shoes have a 25 percent nominal tariff rate, leather a 15 percent rate, and two thirds of the cost of a pair of shoes is due to the leather they contain, and one third to value added. What is the effective rate of protection of the activity of making shoes from leather?*

The effective rate of protection of making shoes from leather: $e = .25 + (.25 - .15)[(2/3)/(1/3)] = .25 + .2 = .45$. Thus the effective rate is 45 percent.

8.12 *Suppose that, in a refinery, a_o barrels of crude oil, a_c tons of coal, and a_m units of materials are combined with value added to yield b_g gallons of gasoline and b_a gallons of aviation fuel. If P_o, P_c, P_m, P_g, and P_a denote the world prices of oil, coal, materials, gasoline, and aviation fuel respectively, if t_o, t_c, t_m, t_g, and t_a denote the corresponding nominal tariff rates, derive a formula, analogous to (8.4) on page 242 of the textbook, for the effective rate of protection of refining, e_R.*

e_R equals:

$$\left[\left(\frac{P_g b_g}{Q}\right)t_g + \left(\frac{P_a b_a}{Q}\right)t_a\right]$$

$$+\left(\left[\left(\frac{P_g b_g}{Q}\right)t_g + \left(\frac{P_a b_a}{Q}\right)t_a\right] - \left[\left(\frac{P_0 a_0}{[Q-v]}\right)t_0 + \left(\frac{P_c a_c}{[Q-v]}\right)t_c + \left(\frac{P_m a_m}{[Q-v]}\right)t_m\right]\right)\left(\frac{[Q-v]}{v}\right)$$

where $Q = P_g b_g + P_a b_a$, so that

$$Q - v = P_0 a_0 + P_c a_c + P_m a_m.$$

8.13* *Consider the example of steel and autos in the textbook. Gross output, denoted X_A and X_S for autos and steel respectively, refers to the total output of an industry. Net output (Y_A and Y_S) refers to gross output less that part of output used as an input in other industries (that is, that part of gross output available for consumption or export). Thus, $Y_A = X_A$ and $Y_S = X_S - aX_A$. Chapter 1 of the textbook showed that relative commodity prices equal the marginal rate of*

*transformation between any two goods that are actually produced. Show that
this refers to the* MRT *between* net *outputs. Will the ratio of values added per
unit equal the* MRT *between* gross *outputs? Why? What do you conclude
about the significance of effective rates of protection?*

Let *MRTN* denote the marginal rate of transformation of steel for
automobiles between net outputs, and let *MRTG* denote that between gross
outputs. Net output is what a country actually has available to consume or
to sell. Thus if $P_a > P_s MRTN$, where P_s and P_a denote the respective prices
of steel and automobiles, the country (or a firm) could increase its income
by producing less steel and more automobiles. Thus $p = MRTN$, where $p =$
P_a/P_s. Now, with the assumed production structure, $MRTN = MRTG - a$.
Thus $MRTG = MRTN + a = p + a = (P_a + aP_s)/P_s$, which is the ratio of
values added per unit.

Additional Problems

1. In Table 8.2 on page 244 of the textbook, suppose that the output of each
    stage of processing is produced only from value added plus the output of
    the immediately preceding stage (that is, stage 3 uses value added plus stage
    2 output, but does not directly use any stage 1 or stage 4 output). For each
    stage, calculate the shares of total cost accounted for by value added and by
    intermediate inputs.

2. In the preceding problem, suppose that stages 3 and 4 of processing are
    performed in a single plant. Calculate the effective rate of protection
    accorded to the activity of that plant.

Answers to Self-Test

1. False

2. False

6.   REVIEW QUESTIONS

1. List the major reasons for protection. For each, state who gains and who
    loses, and state whether a tariff is first-best or not, from the perspective of
    the tariff levying country, and from that of the world as a whole.

2. In what way(s) do the international motives for protection differ
    systematically from the internal motives?

3. Exactly what does it mean when we say that tariffs are a second-best way of
    dealing with non-economic objectives or domestic distortions?

4. What is effective protection?

CHAPTER 9

How Nations Restrict Trade

KEY IDEAS of Chapter Nine

1. Tariff policy often seems to be the result of political conflict between *special interest groups* within countries

2. During the last half century, the General Agreement on Tariffs and Trade (GATT) has been associated with the development of *historically low protection* with regard to the trade of manufactured goods between industrial economies.

3. GATT *multilateralism* is being supplemented (and perhaps threatened) by *regionalism* and by the "New Protectionism."

4. The most important tool of the "New Protectionism" is the voluntary export restraint (VER).

1.   THE POLITICAL ECONOMY OF PROTECTION

Basic Ideas

1.   Since tariffs are only second-best with regard to most of the motives examined, it is curious that protection has been so widespread.

2.   Protection is often justified on the basis of fallacious economic arguments.

3.   Since protection generally helps some groups while hurting others, it has often been examined in terms of pressure group politics.

4.   Studies of the characteristics of protected industries have had mixed success, but there is some evidence that industrial nations tend to protect most heavily the industries that use unskilled labor most intensively.

Self-Test

1.   What is the "scientific tariff?"

2.   True or false: The industrial nations tend to give relatively high protection to industries making relatively intensive use of unskilled labor.

Additional Problem

1.   Describe several common but fallacious arguments for protection, and show exactly why they are fallacious. Are there circumstances under which one or more of them might actually be valid?

Answers to Self-Test

1.   A tariff equal to the excess of domestic production cost above foreign production cost

2.   True

2.   COMMERCIAL POLICIES AFTER THE SECOND WORLD WAR

Basic Ideas

1.   The General Agreement on Tariffs and Trade (GATT) is the primary vehicle for international cooperation on commercial policy.

2. The basic GATT agreement prohibits quantitative restrictions on trade and mandates use of the Most Favored Nation (MFN) clause, though there are exceptions.

3. GATT has also sponsored a series of multilateral tariff reduction negotiations, and it helps to settle trade disputes between nations.

4. The GATT rounds of tariff reductions have reduced tariffs on the trade of manufactured goods among industrial nations to historic lows.

5. There has been relatively little success in liberalizing agricultural trade, trade involving the LDCs, and nontariff trade barriers.

6. The most recent GATT negotiations, the Uruguay Round, was the first to deal with trade in services and counterfeiting, both of great concern to the U.S. It also established a new international body, the World Trade Organization (WTO), which will assume the GATT's administrative functions.

7. In recent years there has been an apparent resurge of protectionism in the DCs, emphasizing the application of discretionary nontariff trade barriers in response to the demands of special interests.

Self-Test

1. What did ITO stand for?

2. What has GATT stood for?

3. What does WTO stand for?

4. Multiple choice: The GATT rounds of tariff negotiations:
   4.1. Were a major advance because they abandoned the reciprocity principle emphasized earlier by the United States.
   4.2. Were bilateral rather than multilateral, thus allowing the negotiators to get down to the nitty gritty.
   4.3. Focused upon across-the-board reductions, rather than item-by-item negotiations, starting with the Kennedy Round.
   4.4. None of the above
   4.5. All of the above

5. True or false: Despite the threats, both real and imagined, of the "new protectionism," tariffs on the trade between the industrial nations remain by and large at historically low levels.

Answers to Self-Test

1. International Trade Organization

   2.   General Agreement on Tariffs and Trade

   3.   World Trade Organization

   4.   4.3

   5.   True

3.   THE "NEW PROTECTIONISM"

Basic Ideas

   1.   Contemporary trade policy is being driven by four distinct, but related
            forces:

       a.   Multilateralism (e.g., the GATT and the Uruguay Round)

       b.   Regionalism (e.g., NAFTA)

       c.   Unilateralism (or the "New Protectionism")

       d.   Outsiders coming inside the world trading system (i.e., reform in
            many LDCs and in the former communist countries).

   2.   The "New Protectionism" is usually implemented by means of several *ad
            hoc* measures, instead of by permanently increasing tariffs.

4.   TOOLS OF THE "NEW PROTECTIONISM"

Basic Ideas

   1.   International agreements (notably the GATT) restrict the ability of nations
            to conduct trade policy by the comprehensive revision of tariff laws (the
            historical method.) Thus various discretionary methods are more important.

   2.   Prominent U.S. measures, also used by many other nations, include: the
            escape clause (safeguard provisions), anti-dumping and countervailing duty
            laws, and measures to deal with unfair trade practices.

   3.   Trade Adjustment Assistance, the national security clause and provisions
            for agricultural trade measures are other U.S. policy tools.

   4.   Be sure you understand: **the way the various measures work.**

Self-Test

1. Multiple choice: The escape clause:
   1.1. Allows countries to escape from foreign tariffs, if they are too high.
   1.2. Safeguards domestic export industries from the threat of a sudden increase in foreign tariffs.
   1.3. Provides for financial relief to domestic firms and workers hurt by foreign tariffs.
   1.4. None of the above
   1.5. All of the above

2. True or false: In practice, the measures discussed in this section have often been powerful influences inducing the negotiation of voluntary export restraints.

3. What does TAA stand for?

4. Why do you think that the countervailing duty law generates little government revenue, even when it is rigorously enforced?

Additional Problem

1. What are *results-oriented* trade policies? How do they differ from traditional policies? Can you point to any examples? What are their pros and cons?

Answers to Self-Test

1. 1.4

2. True

3. Trade Adjustment Assistance

4. Because when countervailing duties seem likely to be imposed, foreign governments often drop their subsidies, so that the latter will not simply be appropriated by the U.S. government.

5. CASE STUDY: THE VER SYSTEM

Basic Ideas

1. The *voluntary export restraint* is the most prevalent way that new protection is implemented involving the imports of industrial countries.

2. Voluntary export restraints are:

   a. sector specific

      b.   quantitative

      c.   voluntary, to a significant degree, on both sides

      d.   discriminatory

      e.   temporary responses to established import positions.

3.   A major reason for the prevalence of voluntary export restraints is that they allow countries to violate the spirit of the GATT without directly challenging it.

Self-Test

1.   Which of the following features of voluntary export restraints fundamentally violate the spirit of the GATT?
     1.1.   They are sector specific.
     1.2.   They are quantitative.
     1.3.   They are voluntary.
     1.4.   They are discriminatory.
     1.5.   They are temporary responses to established import positions.

Answers to Self-Test

1.   1.2 and 1.4

6. REVIEW QUESTIONS

1.   Compare and contrast U.S. tariff history with that of Canada. What are the major similarities and differences? Explain each.

2.   Discuss the "new protectionism." What is it and how does it differ from the old? What are its most important tools?

3.   Discuss attempts since the Second World War to reach multilateral agreements on trade policy.

CHAPTER 10

International Factor Movements

KEY IDEAS of Chapter Ten

1. Trade will reflect *comparative* advantage when factors are immobile internationally and *absolute* advantage when factors are mobile.

2. Trade due international differences in relative factor endowments *substitutes* for international factor mobility, but trade due to other causes may well be *complementary* with factor mobility.

3. Modern international labor mobility often involves the *temporary* movement of unskilled labor—sometimes legally and sometimes illegally.

4. International capital mobility is actually *intertemporal* trade.

1. THE BASIC THEORY: ABSOLUTE ADVANTAGE VERSUS COMPARATIVE ADVANTAGE

Basic Ideas

1. This and the following two sections examine aspects of international factor movements common to all factors.

2. If factors of production are mobile internationally, absolute advantage replaces comparative advantage as the basic determinant of production and trade patterns.

Self-Test

1. Multiple choice: The pattern of international commodity trade is determined by:
   1.1. Absolute advantage if factors are internationally mobile and comparative advantage if they are not.
   1.2. Absolute advantage if factors are not internationally mobile and comparative advantage if they are.
   1.3. Comparative advantage in either case.
   1.4. Absolute advantage in either case.
   1.5. None of the above.

Solutions to Problems from the Text

10.1 *In the simple Ricardian example of Table 10.1 and Table 10.2 on pages 277 and 288 of the textbook, is it meaningful to talk of the French and German production possibility frontiers once labor becomes internationally mobile? What about the world frontier? Draw such a curve, if you can, and compare it with Figure 1.2(a) on page 13 of the textbook. (Assume, as in Chapter 1, that, initially, France has 600 workers and Germany 500.)*

The world frontier:

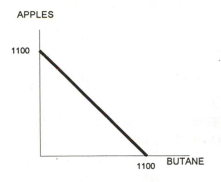

10.2   *Our discussion of the simple Ricardian model tacitly assumed that French and German laborers were identical and that the productivity differences in Table 10.1 on page 287 of the textbook reflected differences in climate. Suppose, instead that Table 10.1 shows each country's labor productivity at home, but that 3 French laborers are always required to do the same work that could be done in the same country by 1 German worker (thus 2 German workers can produce 1 unit of butane in France, and so forth). Derive the world production possibility frontier in this case. Describe who produces what, where, at various points along this curve.*

The world frontier:

10.3   *In Problem 10.2, suppose that everyone in the world always consumes equal amounts of apples and butane. Fully describe international equilibrium.*

In equilibrium the world produces 420 apples and 420 units of butane. French workers in France produce apples, German workers in France produce the remaining 120 apples, and German workers in Germany produce the 420 units of butane.

Answer to Self-Test

1. 1.1

2. THE BASIC THEORY: FACTOR MOBILITY AND THE FACTOR-ENDOWMENTS THEORY OF TRADE

Basic Ideas

1. If international trade is due to differences in relative factor endowments across countries, trade and factor movements are substitutes.

2. International factor mobility expands the world production possibility frontier.

3. Factor mobility, like trade, redistributes income from a country's relatively scarce factor to its relatively abundant one

Self-Test

1. True or false: In the Heckscher-Ohlin-Samuelson model, if international capital mobility, as well as trade, is free, wage rates will become equalized across countries.

Solutions to Problems from the Text

10.4   *Figure 5.6 on page 137 of the textbook used the Rybczynski theorem to show the effect of economic growth on international trade. In similar fashion, depict the effects of international factor movements on international trade.*

The basic argument is the same, since an inflow of capital is just one particular cause of the growth of a country's capital stock. The main difference is that capital which flows into one country necessarily flows out of the other country, from which it came, so that the shift of one import curve in the figure should now be accompanied by an opposite shift of the other country's export curve.

10.5* *How is our discussion of international factor mobility and the Heckscher-Ohlin-Samuelson model affected if, before either factor is internationally mobile, the two countries are separated by a factor-intensity reversal?*

Once either factor becomes mobile the two countries will not be separated by a factor-intensity reversal, since they will have the same factor prices. Thus such a reversal can affect only the pre-factor mobility situation, which we studied in Chapter 5 of the textbook.

10.6*   *Discuss how our treatment of factor mobility and the Heckscher-Ohlin-Sam-uelson model changes if technology is different in the two countries.*

International mobility of one factor, say capital, will still cause its rent to be equalized across countries, but wages need not be. Therefore free trade in goods and one factor no longer renders international mobility of the second factor superfluous. If both factor prices are equalized, as they would be if both factors were mobile, the international trade of goods would not be superfluous but would proceed on the basis of absolute advantage.

10.7*   *Suppose two countries, each resembling the specific factors model, engage in free trade. Discuss the results, for factor-price equalization and other possible properties, if the* intersectorally *mobile factor, labor, also becomes* internationally *mobile. What happens if, instead, one of the sector-specific factors becomes internationally mobile (but remains intersectorally immobile)? Discuss how international factor mobility can substitute for intersectoral factor mobility.*

Suppose that two countries engage in free trade, with all the assumptions of the Heckscher-Ohlin-Samuelson model holding except that one factor, say capital, is not mobile across industries. If labor, the intersectorally mobile factor, also becomes mobile across countries, wages will become equal in the two nations. *This means that the rent of each type of capital must also be equal across countries.* To see why this is so, suppose that instead the rent of apple capital were higher in Germany than in France. Since the German apple industry would have to pay exactly the same as the French apple industry for labor and more for capital its costs would necessarily be higher. Therefore German apple producers would be unable to compete with the French and would be driven out of business. This would leave German apple capital unemployed, since it is unable to move into the butane industry. Thus the rent paid to German apple capital would fall until it equaled the rent paid to French apple capital, so that German apple producers could stay in business and employ the German apple capital.

Thus international mobility of the intersectorally mobile factor causes factor-price equalization. The pattern of trade would then be determined by the two countries' relative endowments of apple capital and butane capital.

Suppose now that it is instead one of the *specific* factors that is internationally mobile. Imagine that apple capital can freely move between France and Germany, but must always be used by an apple firm. Labor and butane capital remain immobile between countries. The rent received by apple capital will therefore become equal in the two countries. Then the wage must also be equal, if both countries continue to produce apples. This is because, if wages were in fact unequal, the country with the higher wage could not possibly compete in the world apple market, with both countries paying the same rent for apple capital. By the same reasoning, the fact that wages are equal in the two countries requires the rent of butane capital to be equal also. Thus all factor prices are again equalized, if both countries continue to produce apples. It is possible, however, that all of the now internationally mobile apple capital will locate in one country, causing the other country to specialize in butane. In such a case factor prices need not be equal. This will in fact happen if the two countries' relative endowments of labor and butane capital are sufficiently dissimilar. If they are not, factor-price equalization must ensue.

The general conclusion, then, is that the international mobility of one specific factor plus international trade in goods produces factor price equalization, and completely substitutes for mobility of the other two factors, provided that relative endowments of those two factors are not too different across countries. International mobility of the intersectorally mobile factor, on the other hand, is (if accompanied by free trade in goods) a perfect substitute for international mobility of the other two factors regardless of relative factor endowments.

Additional Problems

1. Suppose that we modify the Heckscher-Ohlin-Samuelson model by assuming that the French apple industry is uniformly more efficient than the German (that is, any combination of capital and labor can produce more apples in France than the same combination could produce in Germany), and that the German butane industry is uniformly more efficient than the French. Initially the two countries are equally capital abundant (they have the same endowment of capital per worker), their tastes are identical, and apple production is the capital-intensive industry. Starting from a state of autarky, the two countries begin free trade in both goods and also allow the free international movement of capital. What will happen?

2. In the preceding problem, is the amount of international trade greater or less than what it would be if capital were not internationally mobile? If an economist were to apply Leontief's procedure to post trade data what would she find? What do you conclude from all this?

Answer to Self-Test

1. True

3. FACTOR MOVEMENTS AND TRADE: SUBSTITUTES OR COMPLEMENTS?

Basic Ideas

1.   If international trade is due to differences in relative factor endowments across countries, trade and factor movements are substitutes.

2.   If trade is due to some other cause, trade and factor movements are likely to be complements.

3.   Factor movements and intraindustry trade are complements.

Self-Test

1.   Multiple choice: International labor mobility can be expected to:
     1.1.   Increase interindustry trade and reduce intraindustry trade.
     1.2.   Increase both interindustry and intraindustry trade.
     1.3.   Reduce both interindustry and intraindustry trade.
     1.4.   Increase intraindustry trade and reduce interindustry trade.
     1.5.   None of the above

Solution to Problem from the Text

10.8   *Suppose that France and Germany are as in the standard Heckscher-Ohlin-Samuelson model,* except *that they have identical factor endowments* but *different tastes: France has a greater relative preference for butane than does Germany, which has a greater relative preference for apples. What will happen if there is free trade but no factor mobility. Discuss the possible consequences of also allowing factors to migrate. Are trade and factor mobility substitutes or complements in this case?*

   In autarky, the greater French preference for butane, the labor-intensive good, would produce a higher wage-rental ratio in France than in Germany. With free trade but no factor mobility, France imports butane from Germany, and factor prices are equalized internationally. If instead factors can move but there is no trade, labor would migrate to France and/or capital would move to Germany. Trade and factor mobility are substitutes.

Additional Problem

1.   Whether trade and factor mobility are substitutes or complements seems like an arcane, academic question. Why should any reasonable, well-balanced, non-geek care in the slightest?

Answer to Self-Test

1. 1.4

4.   LABOR MIGRATION

Basic Ideas

1.   This section examines aspects of international factor movements characteristic of labor.

2.   The temporary migration of unskilled workers is the most prominent contemporary form of international labor mobility.

3.   This migration is sometimes legal, as with European guest workers, and sometimes illegal, as with much of the temporary migration of Caribbean and Central American workers into the United States.

4.   Countries who welcome temporary unskilled migrants do so to help shield themselves from the business cycle and other changes, and to preserve their own labor-intensive industries.

5.   The U.S. immigration law was revised in the 1980s to deal better with the problem of illegal immigration. Notable changes include penalties for firms that knowingly employ illegal immigrants and amnesty for migrants that had been in the country for an extended period.

6.   Be sure you can explain: **guest-worker systems**.

Solution to Problem from the Text

10.9   *In Chapter 8 we saw that a small tariff would improve the welfare of any country large enough to influence its terms of trade. How is this argument affected if the importable sector is relatively intensive in the use of unskilled (migrant) labor, and if the incomes of such migrants are not counted as part of national welfare?*

The Stolper-Samuelson theorem implies that the real incomes of migrants will rise while that of the other factor falls. So, if migrant incomes are not counted as part of national welfare, the country would be worse off, despite the improvement in its terms of trade.

Additional Problems

1. Find some countries with significant income in the form of remittances from migrants working abroad (see Appendix II of the textbook for data sources). Why do you think that remittances are so important for these particular countries? Where do you think that most of their migrants have gone?

2. The textbook discussed several instances where labor mobility and trade seem to be substitutes. The preceding section of the textbook, however, pointed out that sometimes trade and factor mobility can be complementary. Think of some concrete cases where this is perhaps true with regard to labor.

5.   INTERNATIONAL CAPITAL MOVEMENTS

Basic Ideas

1. This section examines aspects of international factor movements characteristic of capital.

2. International capital movements refer to borrowing and lending between countries, not to the international trade of capital goods.

3. Because a country pays for what it buys from the rest of the world, the capital balance and the current balance always sum to zero.

4. In the early 1980s, the United States had the largest net creditor position in the world. But then very large current account deficits transformed the country into the world's largest debtor in just a few years.

5. Be sure you can explain the following: **capital inflow and outflow; current balance; capital balance; stocks versus flows; official transactions; long term versus short term; direct versus portfolio investment.**

Self-Test

1. The nation of Polonia has thus far neither a borrower nor a lender been. In 1990 Polonia buys $1 billion of foreign bonds, in 1991 Polonia receives 10 percent interest on the bonds, and in 1992 the issuer of the bonds defaults. No other capital movements take place. What is Polonia's *trade* balance in 1990, 1991 and 1992?

2. If the foreign subsidiary of an American firm issues bonds to its parent, is it portfolio or direct investment?

Solutions to Problems from the Text

10.10   *For each of the following transactions, tell, from the point of view of each*
country, whether the transaction contributes to the current balance or the
capital balance and, if the latter is the case, what type of capital movement it is.

   a.   *New Yorkers use checks drawn on a New York bank to buy bonds from a*
Canadian corporation.

   b.   *Russia sends oil to Germany in exchange for oil drilling equipment.*

   c.   *Russia, in exchange for oil drilling equipment, promises to send Japan*
100 million barrels of oil from the new well in five years.

   d.   *An American firm issues six-month commercial paper in London to*
finance the purchase of a British department store.

   e.   *You use a check drawn on a Philadelphia bank to buy a vacation home*
on the Mediterranean.

   a.   NY checks: short-term capital; Canadian bonds: long-term (portfolio)
capital

   b.   Current transaction (trade)

   c.   Equipment: current transaction (trade); promise of future oil: capital
transaction

   d.   Commercial paper: short-term capital; purchase of department store:
long-term capital

   e.   Check: short-term capital; house: long-term capital

10.11   *In Section 4 of the textbook we saw that remittances from natives working*
abroad are important sources of income for some countries. How do you think
that such payments fit into the scheme of Figure 10.3 in the text?

   The current balance

Additional Problems

   1.   If the capital balance and the current balance must always just cancel, how
can trade and capital movements ever possibly be complements, as Section
3 of the textbook said they sometimes are?

   2.   The textbook argued that Walras's Law implies that the current and capital
balances always sum to zero. Why are labor movements not also included?

Answers to Self-Test

   1.   1990: +$1 billion; 1991: –$100 million; 1992: 0

   2.   Direct

6. INTERTEMPORAL TRADE

Basic Ideas

1. The two-commodity trade models developed in Parts One and Two of the text can be used to study intertemporal trade if the goods are thought of as "present goods" and "future goods."

2. The relative price of present goods in terms of future goods is one plus the rate of interest.

3. A net import of present goods in exchange for future goods constitutes a present current account deficit (or capital account surplus).

4. Our earlier trade theory (such as that of tariffs) can be applied straightforwardly to analyze the current account.

Self-Test

1. Multiple choice: The application of the principle of comparative advantage to intertemporal trade predicts that, when international capital movements are allowed:
    1.1. The country with the higher autarky interest rate will become a lender.
    1.2. The country with the higher autarky interest rate will become a borrower.
    1.3. The country with the higher autarky interest rate will develop a current account surplus.
    1.4. The country with the higher autarky interest rate will become poorer.
    1.5. None of the above

2. Suppose a country with a current account deficit imposes a tariff on the purchase of foreign goods. What happens if the analog of the *Metzler paradox* holds?

Solutions to Problems from the Text

10.12   *Draw Figure 10.5 on page 305 of the text as it would appear if France were in the international equilibrium depicted in Figure 10.6 on page 306. Do the same for Germany.*

PRESENT GOODS

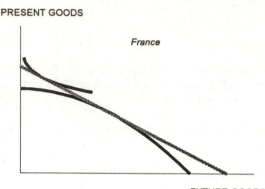

France

FUTURE GOODS

10.13   *Suppose that Figures 10.5 and 10.6 on pages 305 and 306 are generated by the Heckscher-Ohlin-Samuelson model of Chapter 5, where labor and land are the two primary factors, present goods are relatively labor intensive, and (as in the HOS model) both of these primary factors are immobile internationally. Discuss the meaning of the four basic HOS theorems in this context. Contrast this with the conclusions reached in Section 1 of this chapter, where one of the primary factors was internationally mobile, and both goods were "present" goods.*

The Heckscher-Ohlin theorem, for example, would predict that the relatively labor-abundant country would experience (in the present) a capital-account surplus and the land-abundant country would experience a capital-account deficit.

10.14*   *What happens to the equilibrium in Figure 10.6 on page 306 of the text if France imposes a tariff on the import of German goods, and spends the proceeds on future goods? Does it matter if France taxes exports instead? Suppose it taxes the sale of assets to foreigners? The payment of interest to foreigners?*

A tariff on German goods would shift the French current-account demand curve down, producing a fall in the rate of interest and a reduction in the French capital-account surplus. The equivalent export tax would be a tax on promises to repay in the future, not a tax on the export of present goods.

Answers to Self-Test

1.   1.1

2.   The domestic rate of interest and the foreign rate of interest both fall.

7. REVIEW QUESTIONS

1. In what ways is the international exchange of factors similar to the international trade of goods? In what ways is it different?

2. In what ways is the international movement of labor similar to the international movement of capital? In what ways is it different?

3. Discuss whether international factor mobility and international trade are likely to be substitutes or complements.

CHAPTER 11

The Multinational Firm

KEY IDEAS of Chapter Eleven

1. Direct investment is associated with the spread of multinational corporations.

2. Direct investment grew rapidly after World War II. Initially it was dominated by outflows from the United States, but is now much more *two-way* in nature.

3. The most prominent part of modern direct investment: is in the manufacturing and service sectors, involves horizontally-integrated firms, and occurs within the *triad* of the United States, western Europe, and Japan.

4. Theory suggests that direct investment will take place when there is a coincidence of *ownership* and *locational* and *internalization* considerations.

5. The evidence contrasts sharply with the implications of introducing direct investment in a straightforward way into models of international trade, whether based on comparative advantage, economies of scale, or imperfect competition.

6. Multinational firms have been controversial in both host and source countries. Though controversy remains, host countries have become more receptive in recent years.

1.   DIRECT INVESTMENT AND THE MULTINATIONAL CORPORATION

Basic Ideas

1.   About one-fourth of world trade actually takes place within multinational corporations.

2.   Direct investment has grown rapidly since World War II.

3.   While direct investment used to occur mainly in natural-resource industries, in recent decades it has grown the most in manufacturing and, more recently still, in services.

4.   While multinational firms used to be primarily vertically integrated, they are now more likely to be horizontally integrated.

5.   Terms you should understand: **vertical integration; horizontal integration.**

Self-Test

1.   True or false: Direct investment is much more important in the world economy now than it was before World War II.

2.   True or false: Because of technological advances in communications and other areas, direct investment is a much larger share of total us foreign investment than it was earlier in the century.

Answers to Self-Test

1.   True

2.   False

2.   WHY DO MULTINATIONAL ENTERPRISES EXIST?

Basic Ideas

1.   Any theory of the MNE must explain why a certain market is serviced by the subsidiary of a foreign corporation rather than by independent domestic firms, by domestic firms under license to the foreign corporation, or by imports from the foreign corporation.

2.   The predominant explanation for the existence of MNEs consists of three parts.

a. The firm possesses some unique attribute that can be exploited for profit in a foreign market.

b. Because of comparative cost considerations it is advantageous to exploit this attribute by means of foreign production.

c. It is cheaper to internalize the transfer of the attribute than to transfer it through markets.

3. Terms you should understand: **ownership advantage; locational considerations; internalization of transactions; joint venture.**

Self-Test

1. True or false: Direct investments by U.S. firms in Europe constitute movements of capital from the U.S. to Europe.

2. Which of the following modes of servicing a foreign market might be chosen if the *locational* conditions for going multinational are met?
    a. Exports
    b. Joint venture
    c. Licensing a foreign firm.
    d. Establishing a foreign subsidiary.

3. Which of the following modes of servicing a foreign market might be chosen if the *locational* and *internalization* conditions for going multinational are met?
    a. Exports
    b. Joint venture
    c. Licensing a foreign firm.
    d. Establishing a foreign subsidiary.

Solutions to Problems from the Text

11.1 *Give an example of a vertically integrated MNE in a natural-resource industry. Why is it "natural" for firms in such industries to integrate vertically? Can you explain this in terms of our general theory of why firms go multinational?*

Consider large oil firms.

11.3 *Many years ago, IBM decided to close down its operations in India rather than to comply with a law requiring substantial local ownership. Can you think of any reasons why IBM would prefer doing no business at all to participating in a joint venture?*

A joint venture could easily have resulted in disclosing technical secrets to the partners in the venture. Also, IBM may have wished to demonstrate to other countries contemplating similar local ownership requirements that it would, in fact, pull out entirely in response. Then again, who knows why IBM does what it does?

Additional Problems

1. Try to reconcile the observation, that the larger part of direct investment is within the group of countries that trade the most with each other, and the argument of Chapter 10 of the textbook that trade and factor movements are substitutes.

2. Pick one MNE from Table 11.2 on page 316 of the textbook and research its global operations in detail. Try to interpret what you uncover in terms of the theory of this section of the text.

3. Suppose that you are an executive in a firm with a valuable patent to be exploited in a foreign market. You must choose whether to do so by setting up a foreign subsidiary or by licensing the patent to a foreign firm. What concrete factors would you consider?

Answers to Self-Test

1. False

2. b, c, d

3. b, d

3.   INTERNATIONAL TRADE THEORY AND THE MULTINATIONAL FIRM

Basic Ideas

1. Comparative-advantage trade theory says nothing about direct investment because it has no explicit theory of the firm.

2. Identifying direct investment with international capital mobility in the Heckscher-Ohlin-Samuelson model focuses only on locational considerations and ignores the fact that direct investment often does not correspond to an international movement of capital.

3. If direct investment is nevertheless identified with the introduction of international capital mobility into the Heckscher-Ohlin-Samuelson model, there are two implications: *(1)* international differences in relative factor endowments should cause direct investment; *(2)* direct investment and international trade should be negatively correlated.

4. Direct investment can be introduced into the monopolistic competition model of trade in differentiated products by allowing firms to use capital in one country with labor in another. This adds ownership considerations, is consistent with the fact that imperfect competition and scale economies seem important where multinational firms are concerned, and does not

require that direct investment be linked to an international movement of capital.

5. If direct investment is introduced into the monopolistic competition model of trade in differentiated products by allowing firms to use capital in one country with labor in another, there are three implications: *(1)* international differences in relative factor endowments should cause direct investment; *(2)* direct investment and international trade should be negatively correlated; *(3)* two-way direct investment can never take place.

4. THE EVIDENCE

Basic Ideas

1. Most of the largest MNEs are U.S. based, and the U.S. is both a heavy net creditor with regard to direct investment, and the source of a large part of world direct investment. However, foreign MNEs and foreign direct investment in the U.S. are growing rapidly.

2. The larger share of world direct investment takes place between those parts of the globe (DCs) that also trade the most with each other.

3. The evidence is dramatically at odds with the predictions that followed above from introducing direct investment into comparative-advantage trade theory and into a model of trade due to imperfect competition and economies of scale.

4. This motivates one or more of the following approaches: *(1)* adding transport costs or trade barriers to the above models; *(2)* investigating internalization considerations; *(3)* considering distinctive features of the service sector.

Self-Test

1. Multiple choice: Which of the following statements is *not* true?
    1.1. About one quarter of world trade is intrafirm.
    1.2. Most direct investment comes from the DCs, and nearly half of it has come from the U.S.
    1.3. Nearly three-quarters of world direct investment has been directed towards the DCs.
    1.4. All of the above
    1.5. None of the above

Answer to Self-Test

1.   1.4

5.   PUBLIC POLICY TOWARD THE MULTINATIONAL ENTERPRISE

Basic Ideas

1.   Because political integration has not proceeded in step with the economic integration embodied in MNEs, the latter pose problems for national governments.

2.   MNEs can erode the ability of national governments to conduct policy, can help generate conflict between governments, and can become the vehicles for already existing international conflict.

3.   Source countries have problems regarding the taxation of MNEs, and labor in these countries often sees the MNE as an exporter of jobs.

4.   Host countries sometimes feel exploited by MNEs and often complain that the latter do not bring in enough capital and new technology.

5.   Host countries have become much more receptive to multinational firms in recent years.

Self-Test

1.   What are transfer prices?

2.   Multiple choice: Which of the following is true?
     2.1.   U.S. MNEs pay no taxes on foreign earnings.
     2.2.   The foreign tax bill of U.S. MNEs is reduced by the amount of any U.S. taxes that they pay.
     2.3.   MNEs mU.S.t pay taxes on foreign earnings when those earnings are repatriated.
     2.4.   All of the above
     2.5.   None of the above

3.   Multiple choice: Which of the following countries has not screened foreign direct investment projects before allowing them to take place?
     3.1.   France
     3.2.   Germany
     3.3.   Japan
     3.4.   Canada
     3.5.   None of the above

4. True or false: Labor generally supports inward direct investment and opposes outward direct investment.

Answers to Self-Test

1. Prices that one part of an MNE charges to another part

2. 2.3

3. 3.2

4. True.

6. REVIEW QUESTIONS

1. In what ways is direct investment similar to the international exchange of factors? In what ways is it different?

2. What are the alternative ways in which a firm may service a foreign market? What determines which way the firm will choose?

3. Describe actual patterns of direct investment in the modern international economy. How well do they accord with the predictions of theory?

4. What are the pros and cons of direct investment from a host-country perspective? From a source-country perspective?

Monetary Mechanics

CHAPTER **12**

The Balance of Payments

KEY IDEAS of Chapter Twelve

1. A nation's balance of payments accounts measure economic transactions between the residents of that country and the rest of the world.

2. The accounts use a *double-entry* system that calls for any transaction to generate debit entries and credit entries, with the sum of the former equal to the sum of the latter.

3. In principle, the balance of payments accounts of every nation, and therefore of the world as a whole, should always sum to exactly zero. In practice, *errors and omissions* prevent the data from reflecting this.

1.   THE NATIONAL BUDGET IDENTITY

Basic Ideas

1.   The budget identity: buying something is *by definition* selling something of equal value in return.

2.   The national budget identity ensures that the total of a country's balance of trade surplus, net investment earnings from abroad, net transfers from abroad, and net sale of assets always equals zero.

2.   BALANCE OF PAYMENTS ACCOUNTS

Basic Ideas

1.   A country's balance of payments accounts are a record of transactions in a specific time interval between residents of that country and the rest of the world.

2.   Each transaction generates two equal entries in the accounts: a credit (+) for an export of a good, service, or asset or for the receipt of a unilateral transfer; and a debit (−) for an import of a good, service, or asset or for making a unilateral transfer.

3.   Be sure you know: **how to tell a credit from a debit; what the various detailed subaccounts refer to.**

Solutions to Problems from the Text

12.1   *A U.K. distillery sells an American firm 200 cases of whiskey in exchange for a $25,000 check drawn on an American bank. The distillery uses $15,000 of this to buy equipment in France, and the other $10,000 to retire bonds it issued years ago to a group of wealthy Italian investors. Write all the resulting entries in the balance-of-payments accounts of the U. S., France, U.K., Germany and Italy.*

U.S.:	$25,000 debit, merchandise imports; $25,000 credit, short-term capital
France:	$15,000 credit, merchandise exports; $15,000 debit, short-term capital
UK:	$25,000 credit, merchandise exports; $25,000 debit, short-term capital; $15,000 debit, merchandise imports; $15,000 credit, short-term capital; $10,000 debit, long-term capital; $10,000 credit, short-term capital
Germany:	No entries
Italy:	$10,000 credit, long-term capital; $10,000 debit, short-term capital

12.2   *Write all balance of payments entries resulting from each of the following*
transactions.

   a.   *The U.S. Army gives $1 million in pay to American soldiers stationed in*
          Germany.
   b.   *Ford Motor Company (U.S.) pays $1 million to Ford's German subsid-*
          iary for automobile parts.
   c.   *An American automobile dealer pays $1 million, by check, to the Ger-*
          man firm BMW for automobiles.
   d.   *BMW pays $1 million to the Bundesbank for DM1.6 million.*
   e.   *Daring Danny of Denver, sky-diving champion of all Colorado west of*
          the Rockies, pays Lloyds of London $10,000 for a life insurance policy.
   f.   *Lloyds of London pays Daring Danny's widow $1 million in settlement of*
          a life-insurance policy claim.
   g.   *A Japanese firm sends Russia $2 million worth of drilling equipment in*
          return for $2 million worth of oil.
   h.   *A Japanese firm sends Russia $2 million worth of drilling equipment in*
          return for a promise of $4 million worth of oil in five years.
   i.   *You visit Singapore and have $1,000 stolen by a local pickpocket.*
   j.   *You visit Singapore and lose $1,000 worth of American traveler's checks,*
          for which you receive a refund from the local bank.

   a.   No entries
   b.   U.S.: $1 million debit for merchandise imports; $1 million credit, short
        term capital. The reverse for **Germany**.
   c.   Same as part **b**
   d.   U.S.: $1 million debit, short term capital; $1 million credit, liabilities
        to foreign official institutions. The reverse for **Germany**.
   e.   U.S.: $10,000 debit, $10,000 credit, short term capital. The reverse for
        the **U.K.**
   f.   U.S.: $1 million credit, transfers; $1 million debit, short term capital.
        The reverse for the **U.K.**
   g.   **Japan:** $2 million credit, merchandise exports; $2 million debit,
        merchandise exports. The same for **Russia**.
   h.   **Japan:** $2 million credit, merchandise exports; $2 million debit, long
        term capital. The reverse for **Russia**.
   i.   **U.S. (or whatever country you're a resident of):** $1,000 credit, short
        term capital; $1,000 debit, transfers. The reverse for **Singapore**.
   j.   U.S.: $1,000 credit, short term capital; $1,000 debit, short term capital

3.   CASE STUDY: THE U.S. BALANCE OF PAYMENTS

Solutions to Problems from the Text

12.3   *Generally, only transactions between American residents and foreign residents*
generate entries in the American balance of payments. But in one case, transac-
tions between two foreigners result in such entries. What is this case?

When foreign residents sell U.S. dollar assets to a foreign central bank.

12.4*   *Consider Canada's balance of payments, as described in the table below.*
   a.   Discuss each line, as the text did for Table 12.2. In what ways do Canada's payments differ from those of the United States? Why?
   b.   What is the item "Change in Value of Reserves?" To what is a negative number due?

Canadian Balance of Payments, 1993 (billions of Canadian dollars)

Merchandise trade	*9.8*
Services	*−14.2*
Goods and Services	*−4.4*
Private Unilateral Transfers	*0.7*
Official Unilateral Transfers	*−0.5*
Income	*−26.7*
Total Current Account	−30.9
Direct Investment	*−1.6*
Portfolio Investment	*27.1*
Other Nonofficial Capital	*11.5*
Total Nonofficial Capital	37.0
Net Errors and Omissions	*−6.6*
Change in Value of Reserves	*−0.1*
Official Reserve Assets	*0.6*
Net Official Reserve Transactions	0.5

Source: IMF, Balance of Payments Statistics.

A significant part of Canadian international reserves consists of assets denominated in U.S. dollars. If the exchange rate of the latter in terms of Canadian dollars changes, the value of these assets in terms of Canadian dollars likewise changes. This accounts for the item "Change in Value of Reserves." The negative entry in the table could be produced by a depreciation of the Canadian dollar relative to the U.S. dollar.

Additional Problems

1. Look up the most recent detailed presentation of U.S. balance of payments statistics (see Appendix II of the textbook for data sources). Be sure you can explain the meaning of each entry. Reorganize the data in the same form as Table 12.1 on page 345 of the textbook.

2. Look up the most recent detailed presentation of Canadian balance of payments statistics (see Appendix II of the textbook for data sources). Be sure you can explain the meaning of each entry. Reorganize the data in the same form as the table in **Problem 12.4*** above. Compare with that table.

4. REVIEW QUESTIONS

1. Discuss how the balance of payments accounts should treat the activities of multinational firms..

2. Why are official transactions in reserve assets recorded separately?

CHAPTER 13

International Financial Markets

KEY IDEAS of Chapter Thirteen

1. Currencies of different countries are exchanged for each other on the *foreign exchange* market.

2. The foreign exchange market allows individuals in countries with different currencies to buy each other's goods and assets.

3. *Forward* foreign exchange markets allow individuals who sign contracts in a foreign currency to hedge against the exchange-rate risk involved.

4. *Eurocurrencies* are bank deposits denominated in a currency other than that of the country in which the bank is located.

5. International financial markets appear to be highly efficient, but there is doubt that they are efficient in the sense that their prices fully reflect all available information.

1. THE FOREIGN EXCHANGE MARKET

Basic Ideas

1. The currencies of different countries are exchanged for each other on the foreign exchange market.

2. At the retail end, firms and individuals with foreign business transactions can buy or sell foreign exchange, for domestic currency, with their bankers.

3. In order to be able to service their customers, the international departments of large banks participate in the interbank market for foreign exchange.

4. There are such participating banks in the major financial centers of the world. These banks deal with other banks in the same center (usually through a broker) or with banks in foreign centers (with some of whom they are connected by direct telephone or telex lines).

5. Arbitrage keeps the exchange rates of different currency pairs in different centers mutually consistent.

6. The U.S. dollar is especially important because it is often a vehicle currency, a central-bank intervention currency, and an international unit of account.

7. In most foreign centers the most important foreign exchange transactions are those involving the local currency and the U.S. dollar, and New York is often an important alternative center for such transactions.

8. Be sure you understand: **Figure 13.2 on page 357 of the textbook; triangular arbitrage; vehicle currency; intervention currency.**

Self-Test

1. On the basis of the data in Table 13.1 on page 360 of the textbook what should be the price of the British pound in terms of the French franc?

2. True or false: If the New York foreign exchange market were officially abolished, the international trade of the United States would disappear, eventually if not at once.

Solutions to Problems from the Text

13.1   *Figures 13.1 and 13.2 on pages 356 and 357 of the textbook assumed that contracts were in terms of the currency of the exporter. How are the figures changed if contracts are in the importer's currency? If all contracts are in dollars?*

If contracts are in the importer's currency, Acme Spirits pays $20,000 for the whiskey to the Scottish distillery, which (instead of Acme) then sells the $20,000 to Bank A for pounds. Similarly, Coagulated Mush pays pounds to the American agricultural exporter, who then sells them to Bank B for dollars. Other transactions remain the same.

13.2   *In Figure 13.2 on page 357 of the textbook trade between the United States and the United Kingdom was assumed to be in balance. Suppose instead that, at the same prices, Acme Spirits imports 400 cases of whiskey, soybean exports remaining equal to 4,000 bushels. How is the figure changed?*

In this case Acme Spirits must pay $40,000 to the banking system for £20,000 to pay for the whiskey, the other transactions remaining the same. Thus there is an excess supply of $20,000 in the world and an excess demand of £10,000. These can be met by a depreciation of the dollar relative to the pound or by central-bank intervention and the consequent payments imbalances.

13.3   *The foreign exchange market described in this section of the textbook involves bank deposits, but exchanges of currencies also take place, though on a very much smaller scale. For example, a tourist might buy a few pound notes from her New York bank before leaving for London, and she might sell a few pound notes to that bank when she returns. Describe the influence of arbitrage on the relation between the dollar price of pound notes in New York and the pound price of dollars in London. How do you think this influence compares with that of arbitrage in the foreign exchange market as discussed in the textbook?*

The significant cost of actually transporting currency from country to country prevents arbitrage from equalizing exchange rates for notes around the world as closely as rates for bank deposits.

Additional Problem

1.   Find out from your local bank the current buying and selling prices for small quantities of U.K. currency. Compare these prices with the current exchange rate for the U.K. pound, as quoted in the financial pages of your newspaper.

Answers to Self-Test

1.   8.604 French francs per pound (on Wed.)

2.   False

2. THE FORWARD MARKET

Basic Ideas

1. The forward exchange market is one in which individuals agree *today* to exchange *at some specific date in the future* a certain amount of one currency for a certain amount of another currency.

2. Firms and individuals can use the forward exchange market to protect themselves against the risk of future exchange rate fluctuations.

3. One explanation of the relation between the spot and forward exchange rates is that of covered interest parity: the forward premium on foreign exchange must equal the interest differential.

4. Another explanation of the relation between the spot and forward exchange rates involves speculation: the forward premium must equal the expected rate of appreciation of the spot rate.

5. The two explanations are consistent in the sense that a high degree of capital mobility will cause the interest differential to equal the expected rate of appreciation of the spot rate.

6. Make sure you understand: **covered interest arbitrage and covered interest parity; how forward exchange allows international trade to proceed unimpeded by exchange risk; the potential consistency of the two explanations of the relation between spot and forward exchange rates.**

Self-Test

1. True or false: Interest arbitrageurs will buy forward exchange if the forward premium exceeds the differential of domestic interest rates relative to foreign rates.

2. True or false: Speculators will buy forward exchange if the forward premium exceeds the expected appreciation of the spot rate.

Solutions to Problems from the Text

13.5 *In the textbook, Acme Spirits covered itself against exchange risk by buying pounds forward. Another way of accomplishing this would be to borrow dollars from its bank, use the dollars to buy spot pounds, and deposit the pounds in a British bank until the time came to pay for the whiskey. What would be the cost of this second method? Which method would probably be cheaper and why?*

If R denotes the spot price of pounds and i_{US} and i_{UK} the relevant U.S. and U.K. interest rates, the total dollar cost of the second method would be:

$$\frac{R(1 + i_{US})}{(1 + i_{UK})} \cdot$$

13.6   *Suppose that the U.S. interest rate is 8 percent per annum, the U.K. rate is 12 percent per annum, the spot price of a pound is $2.06, and the one-year forward price is $2.00. Describe the interest arbitrage this should induce.*

$$1 + i_{US} = 1.08 < (1 + i_{UK})\left(\frac{R_F}{R_S}\right) = (1.12)\left(\frac{2}{2.06}\right) = 1.09$$

so arbitrageurs sell U.S. Treasury bills, buy pounds spot, buy U.K. Treasury bills, and sell pounds forward.

13.7   *Suppose in **Problem 13.6** that the 90-day forward price of a pound is $2.02. Describe the interest arbitrage that should be induced.*

The 90-day interest rate equals one-fourth of the per annum rate. Thus $1 + i_{US} = 1.02 > (1 + i_{UK})(R_F/R_S) = (1.03)(2.02/2.06) = 1.01$ so arbitrage is in the opposite direction to that in **Problem 13.6**.

13.8   *Can you think of any reason why capital movements should be less than perfect if traders are free to buy and sell spot and forward foreign exchange and the treasury bills of all countries?*

Forward cover can remove exchange risk, but there are other risks involved in investing in foreign treasury bills that are not present when investing in domestic treasury bills. The forward exchange contract is an obligation of a commercial bank, whereas treasury bills are obligations of national governments. Also there is a chance that exchange controls could be imposed before the foreign bills mature, making it impossible (or expensive) to repatriate funds. For these reasons, a bank may prefer to invest in the treasury bills of its own government, even when covered interest arbitrage promises a profit.

13.10*   *As we shall see later in the textbook, exchange depreciation may cause domestic inflation. Suppose Acme Spirits were confident that, should the dollar depreciate relative to the pound, the American price of Scotch whiskey would quickly rise in the same proportion. How should this influence the firm's decision on obtaining forward cover for its obligations to the U.K. distillery? What if Acme Spirits knew that dollar depreciation would raise the U.S. price of the whiskey, but was unsure about how much or how soon?*

If Acme Spirits knew that the American price of Scotch whiskey would quickly rise in the same proportion as any depreciation of the dollar relative to the pound, the company would incur no risk from dealing in pound-denominated contracts for its whiskey imports. Whatever it lost on buying the whiskey, as a result of a dollar depreciation, would be made up when it sold the whiskey domestically. Thus Acme Spirits would not enter the forward market to protect itself. If the firm were unsure about how much of a dollar depreciation would be translated into a higher domestic price, or about how soon it would occur, the firm would still be subject to exchange risk and so it would obtain some forward cover. But it would not cover completely, since the domestic price changes would still offer some protection.

13.11*   *Between 1973 and 1979 many controls on international capital movements were removed by the United Kingdom and Germany. Can you discern any effects of this in Tables 13.7 and 13.8 on pages 368 and 369 of the textbook? Explain.*

The failure of interest parity to hold in 1973, as revealed in Table 13.8 in the textbook, was due in good part to existing exchange controls and the threat of future controls. These were largely absent in 1979.

Additional Problems

1.   Using the data in Table 13.1 on page 360 of the textbook, calculate the difference between the U.S. and British 60-day interest rates that would have to have held on March 23, 1994 in order to maintain covered interest parity.

2.   Using the data in Table 13.1 on page 360 of the textbook, calculate the difference between the Canadian and British 60-day interest rates that would have to have held on March 23, 1994 in order to maintain covered interest parity.

3.   Work out the interest-arbitrage argument in the textbook if instead the trader is British and is concerned about the value of his assets in pounds rather than in dollars. Do the same for the speculation example in the textbook.

4.   Using the data in Table 13.1 on page 360 of the textbook, calculate the expected appreciation of the Canadian dollar in terms of the British pound for the ninety days following March 23, 1994, according to the speculation theory of the forward premium.

Answers to Self-Test

1.   False

2.   False

3.* *EXPLORING FURTHER:* EQUILIBRIUM IN THE FORWARD EXCHANGE MARKET

Basic Ideas

1. The *arbitrage schedule* records the demand for forward exchange—for the purpose of covered interest arbitrage—that would be forthcoming at each value of the forward premium.

2. With perfect capital mobility, the arbitrage schedule is infinitely elastic at the value of the forward premium equal to the interest differential. But transactions cost, exchange risk, and default risk can prevent capital mobility from being perfect.

3. The *speculation schedule* records the supply of forward exchange—for the purpose of speculation—that would be forthcoming at each value of the forward premium.

4. The speculation schedule is infinitely elastic at the value of the forward premium equal to the expected value of the spot rate if that expectation is held with complete certainty, or if speculators are indifferent toward risk.

5. The intersection of the arbitrage and speculation schedules shows the equilibrium forward premium, where the net demand for forward exchange for interest arbitrage just equals the net supply offered by speculators.

6. If the interest differential and the expected appreciation of the spot rate are unequal, the forward premium will lie somewhere between the two.

7. A high degree of international capital mobility will put pressure on the interest differential and the expected spot appreciation to coincide, and to thereby equal the forward premium as well.

Solutions to Problems from the Text

13.12   *Show graphically how the forward exchange market would likely react to each of the following events, and describe the consequences in words.*
   a.   An increase in domestic interest rates
   b.   An increase in the expected future spot rate
   c.   An increased fear that foreign banks may be unable or unwilling to honor their forward commitments
   Relate this to the situations described in Table 13.8 on page 369 of the textbook.

   a.   An increase in domestic interest rates would shift the arbitrage schedule up, so that equilibrium would move up along the speculation schedule.
   b.   An increase in the expected future spot rate would shift the speculator's supply schedule up so that equilibrium would move along the arbitrage schedule.

c.   Both schedules would become more inelastic.

13.13   *The text assumed that commodity trade between the United States and the United Kingdom was balanced. How would the analysis change if instead the United States had a large trade surplus with the United Kingdom?*

If merchants obtained forward cover, the large U.S. trade surplus would imply a large net supply of forward pounds by merchants. Thus equilibrium would not occur where the arbitrage and speculation schedules intersect, but rather at a forward premium for which the excess demand for forward pounds of arbitrageurs and speculators equaled the excess supply of merchants.

13.14   *Show geometrically the result of intervention by the Bank of England to support the spot exchange rate of the pound relative to the dollar. Do the same for intervention to support the forward rate.*

Intervention to support the spot pound would shift the speculation schedule down. Support of the forward rate, to be successful, would require the authorities to make up the difference between the speculation and arbitrage schedules at the forward premium corresponding to the forward rate being supported.

Additional Problems

1.   How would the diagrams of this section be affected if people suddenly thought that there was a very good chance that the U.K. authorities would prevent banks from honoring their commitments to buy sterling, but that there was very little chance of any other controls being established?

2.   What would happen if the authorities in the two countries decided to intervene in the spot and forward markets so as to maintain permanently a forward premium on the domestic currency that exceeded the expected appreciation of the spot rate?

4.   FOREIGN CURRENCY FUTURES AND OPTIONS

Basic Ideas

1.   A purchaser of a foreign currency futures contract pays now in exchange for a certain amount of a foreign currency at a certain date in the future.

2.   Foreign currency futures are standardized contracts traded on organized and regulated exchanges.

3.   Purchasers of foreign currency futures typically put up only a margin and close out their positions before actually taking delivery.

4. A foreign currency option gives the purchaser the right to buy (*call* option) or to sell (*put* option) a certain amount of a certain currency at a certain price for a certain time.

Self-Test

1. What is the "strike price" in an option contract? How is it related to the price of the option?

2. What combination of options transactions is equivalent to buying £100,000 ninety days forward at the forward price of $1.60/£?

Answers to Self-Test

1. The price at which an option can be exercised. A higher strike price reduces the price of a call option but increases the price of a put option. Be sure you can deduce why.

2. Write a European-style put option for £100,000 with a strike price of $1.60/£, and buy a European-style call option for £100,000 at a strike price of $1.60/£. If the spot price turns out to be below $1.60/£, the put option will be exercised by its buyer; if the spot price is above this, you will exercise the call option.

5. THE EUROCURRENCY MARKET

Basic Ideas

1. Eurodollars are U.S. dollars on deposit outside the United States.

2. The Eurodollar market has grown from virtually nothing in the 1950s to over five trillion dollars today. There are also large markets in several other Eurocurrencies.

3. Foreign banks in the Eurodollar market accept dollar deposits and make dollar-denominated loans. These deposits are "backed up" by dollars on deposit in the United States.

4. Some dollar depositors, such as Russia and some Arab governments, use the Eurodollar market because they wish to deal in dollars without exposing themselves to the jurisdiction of the United States.

5. The Eurodollar market is unregulated and thus free of legal reserve requirements and controls on interest rates. This has given it a competitive advantage, which at times has been substantial, over national money markets.

6. Be sure you understand: **Eurocurrency mechanics; the meaning of Eurodollar, Eurocurrency, Eurobank.**

Self-Test

1. Multiple choice: Eurodollars are:
    1.1. Dollars issued by European central banks.
    1.2. Dollars owned by European central banks.
    1.3. Foreign currencies owned by Americans.
    1.4. Deposits in American banks by foreigners.
    1.5. None of the above.

2. True or false: The U.S. money supply increases when an American resident borrows Eurodollars from a London bank.

Solutions to Problems from the Text

13.15 *Suppose that Bayer acquires $5 million drawn on an American bank and deposits it in the London branch of Chase Manhattan. Chase's New York office then borrows $4 million from its London branch. Show the balance sheet entries of both the home office and the branch. What are the effects on the sizes of the Eurodollar market and the U.S. and U.K. money supplies?*

New York		London	
Reserves:	*Demand Deposits:*	*Reserves:*	*Demand Deposits:*
$4 million	$4 million	$1 million *(deposit in some U.S. bank)*	$5 million
		Loans: $4 million	

The Eurodollar market increases by $5 million; there is no effect on either money supply.

13.16 *The text showed that U.S. reserve requirements gave Eurobanks a competitive edge over domestic banks. But Eurodollars are mostly time deposits, and U.S. reserve requirements for time deposits are quite low, whereas the requirements for demand deposits are much higher. Would you not therefore expect Eurodollars to consist mainly of demand deposits? Why do you think this has not happened?*

Many Eurodollar time deposits are simply overnight, and many more are a week or less. These are basically the same as demand deposits.

13.17   *The Depository Institutions Deregulation and Monetary Control Act phased out all U.S. ceilings on deposit interest rates by 1986. What do you think were the effects on the Eurocurrency markets?*

Deregulation eliminated the competitive advantage the Euromarkets enjoyed because of interest rate ceilings, but they still have an advantage because of reserve requirements. The interest rate ceilings were particularly important in the past when monetary conditions in the U.S. became very tight; thus deregulation will help prevent such tight money episodes from accelerating the growth of the Eurodollar market. But that market is by now sufficiently well developed so that it does not need a competitive advantage to survive.

13.18   *Measure what happens to: (1) U.S. liabilities to foreign official institutions; (2) German official holdings of dollars; and (3) the size of the Eurodollar market in the following series of transactions:*

  a.   *The Bundesbank switches $1 billion from its account at Morgan Guaranty New York to Morgan Guaranty London (MGL) in order to obtain a higher interest rate.*

  b.   *MGL lends $900 million to a German firm (which is facing tight monetary conditions inside Germany). The German firm in turn sells the dollars to the Bundesbank for DM in order to invest in Germany. The Bundesbank deposits the $900 million at MGL.*

  c.   *Another German firm borrows $810 million from MGL and trades the dollars for DM. In turn the Bundesbank deposits the $810 million at MGL.*

  d.   *The Bundesbank lodges a protest with the Federal Reserve Board complaining that it is impossible to maintain an anti-inflationary policy so long as the United States is flooding Europe with excess dollars. How should the Fed. reply?*

  a.   The Eurodollar market increases by $1 billion.

  b.   The Eurodollar market, U.S. liabilities to foreign official institutions, and German official dollar holdings increase by $900 million.

  c.   U.S. liabilities to foreign official institutions and German official dollar holdings increase by $810 million.

  d.   The Fed. could urge the Bundesbank not to deposit its dollars in the Eurodollar market. The latter would perhaps reply that it wouldn't matter if they were deposited in New York instead.

13.19*   *Suppose that Texaco and British Petroleum each make $500 million payments to the government of Kuwait:*

  a.   *Texaco makes payment by issuing a draft on its account with City Bank/New York (CBNY);*

  b.   *BP sells spot sterling for dollars causing the Bank of England to draw down its dollar reserves held with CBNY by $500 million in order to support the spot rate;*

  c.   *Kuwait deposits the $1 billion with CB London.*

  Show how these transactions affect:

    i.   *The U.S. and U.K. money supplies;*

    ii.   *The size of the Eurodollar market.*

In what way would these transactions tend to influence interest rates in the United States, the United Kingdom, and the Eurodollar market? How might this alter patterns of borrowing and lending?

The Bank of England's intervention has increased the U.S. money supply and reduced the U.K. money supply by $500 million (ignoring any subsequent sterilization); the Kuwaiti deposit has increased the Eurodollar market by $1 billion. This should reduce interest rates in the United States and in the Eurodollar market, and increase them in the United Kingdom.

13.20*   *During the mid-1960s many observers worried that the Eurodollar system would collapse in the face of widespread speculation against the dollar. Since that time we have witnessed several speculative episodes, and in each instance not only has the Eurodollar market survived, but it has actually increased in size. Explain why this should have been expected by analyzing the impact of the expectation of a dollar depreciation on:*
   a.   Nonbank demand for Eurodollar borrowing;
   b.   Non(commercial)bank supply of Eurodollar deposits.

Other things being equal, nonbank demand for Eurodollar borrowing could have been expected to rise, with the borrowers expecting to repay their loans with depreciated dollars. Those who had to hold dollars (such as central banks) would also have been more likely to deposit them in the Euromarkets, where the unregulated interest rates would be free to rise in anticipation of a dollar depreciation.

Additional Problem

1.   Investigate current activity in the Eurocurrency markets (see Appendix II of the textbook for data sources). Interpret in the light of the discussion in this section of the text.

Answers to Self-Test

1.   1.5

2.   False

6.   SHOULD THE EUROCURRENCY MARKETS BE REGULATED?

Basic Ideas

1.   It is frequently argued that the Eurocurrency markets should be regulated because:
   a.   They have caused a huge increase in the global money supply.
   b.   They prevent individual countries from controlling their own money supplies.

    c.   They allow deficit countries to borrow indefinitely and thus postpone painful adjustments until it is too late.

    d.   They furnish a large volume of liquid funds that can be easily moved around, causing global disruption of exchange and interest rates.

    e.   They are unregulated and so could collapse after a speculative bubble, bringing on a worldwide panic.

2.   Many of the alleged problems have to do with international capital mobility, of which the Eurocurrency markets are more a symptom than a cause.

3.   Regulation is very difficult in any case, because the Eurodollar market will simply move from any place where regulations are imposed to some other place where they are not.

Self-Test

1.   What does "IBF" stand for and what is it?

Answer to Self-Test

1.   International Banking Facility.

7.   THE EFFICIENCY OF THE FOREIGN EXCHANGE MARKETS

Basic Ideas

1.   A market is efficient if its prices fully reflect all currently available information.

2.   Market efficiency is important because economic agents base their actions on the prices they face.

3.   Covered interest parity is an aspect of exchange market efficiency, since the parity relationship holds when the spot and forward exchange rates reflect the available information about interest rates.

4.   Covered interest parity holds almost exactly in the Eurocurrency markets, and normally comes reasonably close to holding between national money markets as well.

5.   The forward premium is often an inaccurate predictor of future spot appreciation, but it comes close to being an unbiased predictor, and is nearly as good as any other predictor. Recent evidence does indicate, though, that the forward premium is not in fact completely unbiased. This could reflect a risk premium necessary to induce people to hold certain currencies.

6.   Be sure you understand: **market efficiency and why it matters; risk premium; joint hypothesis.**

Self-Test

1.   Multiple choice: Which of the following is an indicator of efficiency in the foreign exchange market?
      1.1.   High commissions
      1.2.   Low commissions
      1.3.   The fact that spot deliveries occur within two business days.
      1.4.   The ability to obtain forward cover for any date in the future.
      1.5.   None of the above

2.   True or false: A foreign currency pays a risk premium when its forward rate exceeds the spot exchange rate.

3.   True or false: If the forward rate is an unbiased predictor of the future spot rate, a speculator betting consistently against the former would almost certainly end up losing money, even though he could make large gains on occasion.

Solution to Problem from the Text

13.21   *German exchange controls on capital inflows were relaxed on January 30, 1974, but Figure 13.7 on page 391 of the textbook shows that the Euromark and German interbank interest rates actually moved together a few months earlier. Can you think of any reason for this?*

      Individuals anticipated in advance that exchange controls were about to be relaxed.

Answers to Self-Test

1.   1.5

2.   False

3.   True

8.   INTERNATIONAL CREDIT MARKETS

Basic Ideas

1.   Foreign bonds are bonds issued in the domestic bond market by foreign entities.

2. Many foreign bonds are issued in Switzerland. Other important centers include the U.S., Germany and Japan.

3. Eurobonds are denominated in a currency—or a combination of currencies—other than that of the country in which they are issued.

Self-Test

1. Multiple choice: Most Eurobonds are denominated in:
   1.1. U.S. dollars.
   1.2. Japanese yen.
   1.3. Swiss francs.
   1.4. Currency cocktails.
   1.5. None of the above.

2. Are Eurobonds typically bearer bonds or registered bonds?

Answers to Self-Test

1. 1.1

2. Bearer bonds

9. REVIEW QUESTIONS

1. Describe the basic international financial markets.

2. What do we mean by the *efficiency* of the foreign exchange markets? Describe relevant evidence.

3. Explain how spot and forward foreign exchange rates are related to each other.

Part Five

International Monetary Economics

CHAPTER 14

The Exchange Rate

KEY IDEAS of Chapter Fourteen

1. *International monetary equilibrium* requires that exchange rates be consistent with a willingness on the part of the public to hold various national monies in the proportions in which they are supplied.

2. International monetary equilibrium can be attained through variations in exchange rates, variations in money supplies, or some combination of the two. The method depends upon the *exchange-rate regime*.

3. In practice, a wide—and changing—variety of exchange-rate regimes is found in the world.

4. International capital movements constitute *intertemporal trade*.

5. *Expectations* about the future course of the exchange rate are important for international capital movements.

6. The degree to which international capital mobility is *imperfect* influences the operation of the international monetary system.

1.   MONEY

Basic Ideas

1.   Money serves as a medium of exchange, a unit of account, and a store of value.

2.   The demand for money is positively related to real national income and to the price level, and is negatively related to the rate of interest paid by alternative assets.

Solutions to Problems from the Text

14.1   *Suppose the money market is in equilibrium and that the central bank then increases the supply, G. If i and y do not change in response, what must happen to the price level P?*

P must rise.

14.2   *Suppose the money market is in equilibrium and that the economy experiences a growth in production, y. If the central bank does not change the money supply, G, and if P does not change in response, what must happen to the rate of interest i?*

i must rise.

14.3   *Suppose the money market is in equilibrium and that the central bank then increases the supply, G. If P and y do not change in response, what must happen to the rate of interest i?*

i must fall.

14.4   *Suppose the money market is in equilibrium and that the country experiences an inflationary rise in the price level P. If the central bank does not change the money supply in response, and if i does not change, what must happen to output y?*

y must fall.

2.   INTERNATIONAL MONETARY EQUILIBRIUM

Basic Ideas

1.   This chapter examines the operation of an international monetary system when exchange rates may vary.

2. Assuming the quantity theory of money, the equilibrium terms of trade determines the equilibrium relative values of various countries' money supplies.

3. The actual absolute sizes of various countries' money supplies then determine the equilibrium value of the exchange rate.

Self-Test

1. True or false: According to the theory of this section, the money supplies of two trading countries will have no effect at all upon their equilibrium terms of trade.

2. Multiple choice: At unchanged terms of trade, an increase in the German money supply will:
   2.1. Increase the French equilibrium exchange rate.
   2.2. Increase the German equilibrium exchange rate.
   2.3. Increase the French money supply.
   2.4. Lower the German equilibrium exchange rate.
   2.5. None of the above.

3. Multiple choice: If real outputs remain unchanged in France and Germany, a deterioration of the German terms of trade will:
   3.1. Increase the French equilibrium exchange rate.
   3.2. Increase the German equilibrium exchange rate.
   3.3. Increase the French money supply.
   3.4. Lower the French equilibrium exchange rate.
   3.5. None of the above.

Solutions to Problems from the Text

14.5 *Suppose that whiskey costs £120 per case, that wheat costs $90 per bushel, and that the relative price of whiskey in terms of wheat is two bushels per case. What is the U.S. exchange rate (the price of a pound in terms of dollars)? What is the dollar price of whiskey? The pound price of wheat?*

The U.S. exchange rate is $1.50/£, the price of whiskey is $180, and the price of wheat is £60.

14.6 *Suppose that America and Europe trade, America specializing in and exporting wheat and Europe specializing in and exporting cloth. American wheat production equals 1,000, and European cloth production 600. In equilibrium, 5 wheat exchange for 1 cloth. The American money supply consists of $2000, the European money supply consists of £3,000 and k = ½. Describe international monetary equilibrium and illustrate with a diagram analogous to Figure 14.1 on page 406 of the textbook. Suppose the American money supply increases to $4000; calculate the effect on your answer and illustrate the change in your diagram. Do the same if instead the terms of trade were to alter so that 5 wheat exchange for 3 cloth.*

The American exchange rate $R = \$2/£$. If $G^A = \$4,000$, then $R = \$4/£$. If $R(P_C/P_W) = 5/3$, then $R = \$.67/£$.

14.7   *In the discussion in the text, how will the equilibrium American exchange rate be affected by:*
   a.   An improvement in the American terms of trade
   b.   A growth of European income relative to American
   c.   An increase in the American rate of interest?

An improvement in the terms of trade (a fall in p) causes the dollar to appreciate (a fall in R); a relative growth of German income causes the dollar to depreciate; an increase in the interest rate (a rise in i_{US}) causes the dollar to depreciate.

14.8   *Suppose that the dollar becomes worth fewer marks (so R rises). What will be the direct impact of this on American and German firms if they pursue the following alternative pricing policies:*
   a.   Each firm holds the domestic currency price of its product fixed and adjusts the foreign currency price
   b.   Each firm holds constant in foreign currency the price of its product and adjusts the domestic currency price
   c.   Each firm holds constant both the domestic currency price at which it sells in domestic markets and also the foreign currency price at which it sells in foreign markets.
   What consequences would likely develop in each case for the respective firms? Can you think of any reason why firms might respond in one way rather than in others?

   a.   American firms lower the mark price of their exports and German firms raise the franc price of their exports, so that American goods become cheaper relative to German goods in both markets.

  b. American firms raise their domestic prices and German firms lower
      their domestic prices, so that American goods become more
      expensive relative to German in both markets.

  c. American firms receive a higher price for exports than for domestic
      sales, while German firms receive a lower price for exports than for
      domestic sales.

14.9 *Show the effects of an increase in the American money supply in Figure 14.1 in
the textbook. What happens to the equilibrium exchange rate if the Americans
increase their money supply by 25 percent each and every year? What happens
to the money prices of both goods?*

The *SS'* line shifts to the left, causing *R* to rise.

Additional Problems

1. Draw Figure 14.1 on page 406 of the textbook as it would appear if America
    were a very small country relative to Germany. (Imagine Germany to be the
    rest of the world.)

2. Suppose that Gormengast and Ditch trade, Gormengast specializing in and
    exporting zingoes and Ditch specializing in and exporting poobahs. Gor-
    mengast's zingo production equals 10,000 and Ditch's poobah production
    20. In equilibrium 100 zingoes exchange for 1 poobah. The Gormengastian
    money supply consists of 12,000 clams, Ditch's money supply is 12,000
    oysters, and $k = 2$. Describe international monetary equilibrium and
    illustrate with a diagram analogous to Figure 14.1 on page 406 of the
    textbook. Suppose the Gormengastian money supply increases to 18,000
    clams. Calculate the effect on your answer and illustrate the change in your
    diagram. Do the same if instead the terms of trade were to alter so that 150
    zingoes exchange for 3 poobahs.

3. The discussion in the textbook supposed that *k* had the same value in both
    countries. Show in detail how the argument would change if *k* were
    different in Germany and America. How would your answer to the first part
    of **Problem 14.6** above change if *k* were to fall to one-fourth in America but
    remain at one-half in Europe?

Answers to Self-Test

1. True

2. 2.2

3. 3.4

3.   EXCHANGE-RATE ADJUSTMENT

Basic Ideas

1.   If the actual exchange rate does not equal the equilibrium exchange rate, as described in the previous section, adjustment is necessary.

2.   This adjustment can take any of three alternative forms:
     a.   Through payments imbalances, which change the relative money supplies of the two countries
     b.   Through exchange-rate variations
     c.   Through a combination of payments imbalances and exchange-rate variations.

3.   If adjustment takes place through exchange-rate variations, there are two broad implications:
     a.   Individual countries can control their own money supplies.
     b.   Payments imbalances can be controlled or prevented by exchange-rate adjustment.

4.   Terms you should know: **appreciation; depreciation**.

Self-Test

1.   Suppose the dollar depreciates relative to all other currencies. For each of the following, write a "W" if, other things constant, the depreciation is likely to be welcomed by the person described, and a "D" if the depreciation is likely to be disliked.
     1.1.   Someone with wealth in dollars
     1.2.   Someone with wealth in British pounds
     1.3.   Someone selling goods priced in dollars
     1.4.   Someone selling goods priced in British pounds
     1.5.   Someone importing goods priced in dollars

2.   Multiple choice: Which of the following pairs represents two alternative methods of adjustment?
     2.1.   Appreciation or payments deficits
     2.2.   Depreciation or payments surpluses
     2.3.   Depreciation or revolution
     2.4.   All of the above
     2.5.   None of the above

Solutions to Problems from the Text

14.10   *As in **Problem 14.6**, America produces 1,000 wheat, Europe 600 cloth and in equilibrium 5 wheat exchange for 1 cloth. Initially, the American money supply consists of $2,000, the European money supply is £3,000 and k = ½. Now suppose that the American money supply increases to $4,000. Calculate the* *cumulative payments imbalance necessary to restore equilibrium if the exchange rate were held fixed. What exchange-rate adjustment would instead be required if the American money supply were maintained at $4,000? What would happen if, after the initial increase in the American money supply to $4,000, the authorities decided not to let it subsequently fall below $3,000?*

A cumulative U.S. deficit of $1,500, or a depreciation of the dollar to $4 per pound, or a cumulative U.S. deficit of $1,000 followed by a depreciation of the dollar to $2.57 per pound would each suffice to restore equilibrium.

14.11 *Suppose that German real income y^G grows by 10 percent each year, but that American real income y^{US} remains constant. What happens to international equilibrium if the American increase the supply of dollars by 5 percent a year and Germany increases the supply of marks by 10 percent per year?*

R rises (that is, the dollar depreciates) by 5 percent per year.

14.12 *In the last two columns of the table,* Selected Exchange Rates, *in the introduction to Part Four of the textbook, which currencies are shown to have appreciated and which to have depreciated relative to the U.S. dollar? Relative to the franc?*

The Canadian dollar, yen, franc, mark, and pound appreciated, and the peso depreciated relative to the U.S. dollar. The U.S. dollar, Canadian dollar, Argentine peso, U.K. pound, and the Liberian dollar depreciated, and the Japanese yen and the German mark appreciated relative to the franc

Additional Problem

1. In **Problem 14.10**, suppose that the American money supply remains equal to $2,000, but that economic growth in America raises wheat production to 2,000 units. Calculate the cumulative payments imbalance necessary to restore equilibrium. What exchange-rate adjustment would do so instead?

Answers to Self-Test

1. 1.1. D
   1.2. W
   1.3. W
   1.4. D
   1.5. W

2. 2.5

4.   EXCHANGE REGIMES IN PRACTICE

Basic Ideas

1.   This section examines present day exchange rate arrangements. The most notable characteristic of these arrangements is their diversity.

2.   The major industrial nations have managed floats with respect to each other. The notable exception is the adjustable peg arrangement among the nations participating in the European Monetary System.

3.   Most LDCs maintain an adjustable peg to the dollar or to a basket of currencies or, in some cases, to some single currency other than the dollar.

4.   Extensive exchange controls are also common among LDCs.

5.   Individual countries apply these regimes in quite different ways, and any single country is apt significantly to alter its practices over time.

6.   The basic advantage of fixed exchange rates is that they make a country's currency more useful as money.

7.   The basic advantage of flexible rates is that they allow a country to control its own money supply.

Self-Test

1.   What does EMS stand for?

2.   What is a dual exchange market?

3.   Multiple choice: Most LDCs
    3.1.   Have floating exchange rates because they cannot afford the reserves necessary to peg.
    3.2.   Cannot practice exchange control because of a lack of trained bureaucrats.
    3.3.   Encourage capital mobility.
    3.4.   Remain on the gold standard.
    3.5.   None of the above

Solutions to Problems from the Text

14.16   *This section of the textbook gave reasons why a country might wish to peg its currency rather than to float. But why might it want to peg to a currency basket rather than to some individual currency? What considerations might influence the decision of which currency basket to peg to?*

A country might hope to stabilize its terms of trade by pegging its exchange rate; if this is the motive, it is natural to peg to a basket reflecting the relative importance of the various currencies of denomination of that country's imports and exports. Alternatively, a country might peg in order to maximize the value of that country's currency as money, and thereby encourage people to hold that currency and also encourage the development of domestic financial facilities. In this case the most natural basket would be one reflecting peoples' patterns of purchases.

14.17 *With a pegged exchange rate the authorities usually establish a band around the peg within which the exchange rate is allowed to float, perhaps freely, perhaps not. Under the gold standard a similar band was common not because of policy, but because of the cost (shipping, insurance, and foregone interest) of transporting gold from one country to another. Suppose that in Paris the French authorities freely exchanged gold and francs at the rate of Fr100/ounce while in Berlin the German authorities bought and sold gold for DM50/ounce. Suppose it cost the equivalent of one-tenth of an ounce of gold to transport each ounce between Paris and Berlin. Calculate the band within which the franc price of a mark must fall.*

Between Fr1.8 and Fr2.22 per DM.

Additional Problems

1. Investigate which countries of the world peg their currencies and which float (see Appendix II of the textbook for data sources). Pick three examples of each and try to explain why they are doing what they are doing.

2. Do more countries peg than float, or is the reverse the case? Is more of world trade between countries whose currencies are pegged to each other, or between countries whose currencies float relative to each other?

Answers to Self-Test

1. European Monetary System

2. One in which current account transactions are segregated from capital account transactions, so that they are subject to different exchange rates. Often the current account rate is pegged while the capital account rate is not.

3. 3.5

5. INTERNATIONAL CAPITAL MOVEMENTS: INTERTEMPORAL TRADE

Basic Ideas

1. Two-commodity trade models can be used to study the current account (capital account) from the essential intertemporal perspective if the goods are thought of as "present goods" and "future goods."

2. The relative price of present goods in terms of future goods is one plus the rate of interest.

3. A net import of present goods in exchange for future goods constitutes a present current account deficit (or capital account surplus).

4. Since the demand for money in a country depends upon the quantity of goods currently being consumed in that country, the intertemporal view of the current account also offers an explanation for the behavior of the exchange rate over time.

Solutions to Problems from the Text

14.18   *Suppose that the U.S. and Germany move from autarky to the situation shown in Figures 14.5 and 14.6 on pages 420 and 421 of the text. Describe in detail the effects on firms and consumers in both countries, and the effects on money market equilibrium.*

Initially the interest rate in the U.S. is *OU* minus one, in Figure 14.5 in the text. When free international transactions are allowed, U.S. residents find themselves exposed to a lower interest rate. This induces U.S. consumers to save less (and spend more now) and U.S. firms to invest more. The opposite takes place in Germany. The increased present consumption of goods in the U.S. and the reduced present consumption in Germany raise the demand for dollars relative to the demand for marks, and the dollar appreciates.

14.19   *The discussion in the text assumed a single world rate of interest was established. Suppose instead that in the present everyone believes that the German government will in the future impose a tax on interest income received from abroad. How does this affect international equilibrium?*

The German excess supply curve shifts up by the amount of the tax. The intersection of the U.S. curve with the new German curve determines the interest rate in the U.S., and the interest rate in Germany is lower by the amount of the tax.

14.20* *The equilibrium depicted in Figures 14.5 and 14.6 on pages 420 and 421 of the text calls for the dollar to depreciate in the future. But if people realize that this is going to happen, they will want to take care that, when the future arrives, they are holding few dollars and many marks. How would this consideration affect the analysis in the text?*

People would be less willing now to hold dollars and more willing to hold marks. Thus today's *DD'* curve will shift up because of expectations about how the exchange rate will behave in the future. This shift causes the dollar to depreciate now.

Additional Problems

1. What happens to the equilibrium in Figures 14.5 and 14.6 on pages 420 and 421 of the text if the U.S. imposes a tariff on the import of German goods, and spends the proceeds on future goods?

2. What happens to the equilibrium in Figures 14.5 and 14.6 on pages 420 and 421 of the text if German lenders begin to fear that there is a chance that U.S. borrowers will default on their loans when the future arrives?

6.   INTERNATIONAL CAPITAL MOVEMENTS: EXPECTATIONS

Basic Ideas

1. International capital movements constitute *intertemporal* trade, and a key characteristic of the future is that it is uncertain. Thus *expectations* about the future are critical.

2. In particular, the expected change in the exchange rate matters because it is part of the expected yield of holding assets denominated in terms of foreign currency.

3. Home and foreign bonds give the same yield when *interest parity* holds: the expected depreciation of the exchange rate equals the excess of the domestic interest rate over the foreign interest rate.

Solutions to Problems from the Text

14.25   *If the U.S. rate of interest is 6 percent and the comparable U.K. interest rate is 9 percent, what must the consensus view be about the likely future course of the dollar-sterling exchange rate, if interest parity is to hold?*

That the pound is expected to depreciate by 3 percent relative to the dollar.

14.26   *The formula for interest parity given in the text applies instantaneously, for assets that are about to mature. The formula varies slightly for different maturities. Suppose, for example, that* r *denotes what a dollar invested in the U.S. will earn in interest over the next three months, that* r* *is the number of pounds sterling a pound invested in the U.K. would earn over the next three months, that* R *is the current U.S. exchange rate (the number of dollars required to buy one pound now), and that* E *denotes what this exchange rate is*

*expected to be in three months. Then interest parity will hold if (1+r) =
(1/R)(1+r*)E. Explain why. The formula can also be written:*

$$\frac{E - R}{R} = r - \frac{E}{R} r*.$$

*Derive this expression. The term on the left is the expected depreciation of the
dollar relative to the pound over the next three months. Newspapers will quote
three month interest rates on an annualized basis. To obtain r from such a
quote, divide the latter by 4 (to change it from an annual basis to a three-month
basis), and then divide it by 100 (to change it from a percentage to a decimal).
Thus a three-month interest rate of 12 percent corresponds to a value of r of
.03.* (The above formula converges to the one in the text as the time to
maturity becomes arbitrarily small.)

If a dollar is invested in the U.S. it will be worth $1 + r$ dollars in three
months. If it is instead invested in the U.K., the dollar will buy $(1/R)$ pounds
now, each pound invested in the U.K. will be worth $1 + r^*$ pounds in three
months, and it is expected that in three months each pound will be sold for
E dollars. Thus a dollar invested in the U.K. now is expected to be worth
$(1/R)(1 + r^*)E$ dollars in three months. Interest parity implies that a dollar
invested now in the U.S. is expected to be worth the same number of dollars
in three months as a dollar invested in the U.K.: $1 + r = (1/R)(1 + r^*)E$.
Subtract $1 - (E/R)r^*$ from both sides to obtain the other version of this
formula.

14.27 *Suppose that the present exchange rate is $1.50/£ and that in the U.S. the three-
month, six-month, and one-year interest rates are respectively 12 percent,
10 percent and 8 percent, on a yearly basis. The corresponding U.K. interest
rates are 6 percent, 10 percent and 10 percent. Describe what the market must
expect the future course of the exchange rate to be, if interest parity holds.*

The dollar is expected to depreciate to $1.5225/£ in three months, to then
appreciate back to $1.50/£ in six months, and to appreciate further to
$1.47/£ in one year.

7.   INTERNATIONAL CAPITAL MOVEMENTS: IMPERFECT CAPITAL MOBILITY

Basic Ideas

1. The degree of international capital mobility determines how closely linked
    together are interest rates of assets denominated in different currencies.

2. With perfect international capital mobility, interest parity will hold: the
    excess of domestic interest rates over foreign interest rates will exactly
    reflect the expected rate of depreciation of the domestic currency.

3. It is very difficult to tell how closely interest parity actually holds because we cannot observe expected rates of depreciation.

Self-Test

1. True or false: With imperfect capital mobility, an expected appreciation of the exchange rate will reduce interest rates at home, relative to those abroad, but not by as much as it would if there were no capital mobility at all.

Answer to Self-Test

1. True.

8. MONETARY POLICY AND EXCHANGE RATES

Basic Ideas

1. This section puts the model to work to analyze the effects of monetary policy.

2. An open-market purchase of bonds reduces interest rates at home absolutely and relative to interest rates abroad. The changes in interest rates cause shifts in the demands for home and foreign money, producing a depreciation.

9. REVIEW QUESTIONS

1. Discuss the implications of exchange-rate adjustment.

2. Discuss alternative methods of international adjustment.

3. What are the implications of the degree of international capital mobility for exchange-rate adjustment?

CHAPTER 15

The Automatic Adjustment Process

KEY IDEAS of Chapter Fifteen

1. If international monetary equilibrium cannot be attained through variations in exchange rates, *payments imbalances* will arise, redistributing money supplies across countries.

2. Payments imbalances are benign in the sense that they allow the world to maintain *fixed exchange rates*, but they deprive individual countries of permanent *control* over their own money supplies.

3. Countries routinely *sterilize* payments imbalances to try to control their money supplies, but sterilization vitiates the self-correcting nature of payments imbalances, and there is little evidence that sterilized intervention is effective in controlling exchange rates.

4. If a country supplies a *reserve currency*, then payments imbalances of that country may change the world stock of international reserves and may be automatically sterilized.

1.   INTERNATIONAL MONETARY EQUILIBRIUM

Basic Ideas

1.   This chapter examines the operation of an international monetary system characterized by fixed exchange rates. With fixed rates it is meaningful to add together the money supplies of different countries to obtain the size of the world money supply.

2.   Assuming the quantity theory of money, the equilibrium terms of trade determines the equilibrium relative sizes of various countries' money supplies.

3.   The size of the world money supply then determines the equilibrium absolute sizes of various countries' money supplies and absolute price levels.

Self-Test

1.   Multiple choice: The crude quantity theory of money implies that:
     1.1.   The price level is proportional to the money supply.
     1.2.   Real output is proportional to the money supply.
     1.3.   The price level is proportional to real output.
     1.4.   All of the above
     1.5.   None of the above

2.   True or false: According to the theory of this section, the money supplies of two trading countries will have no effect at all upon their equilibrium terms of trade.

Solutions to Problems from the Text

15.1   *Suppose that America and Europe trade, America specializing in and exporting wheat and Europe specializing in and exporting cloth. American wheat production equals 1,000 and European cloth production 600. In equilibrium, 5 wheat exchange for 1 cloth. The world money supply consists of 2,000 gold coins, and* $k = \frac{1}{2}$. *Describe international monetary equilibrium and illustrate with a diagram analogous to Figure 15.1 on page 439 of the textbook. Suppose the world money supply increases to 4,000 gold coins. Calculate the effect on your answer and illustrate the change in your diagram. Do the same if instead the terms of trade were to alter so that 5 wheat exchange for 3 cloth.*

Thus, $L^A = 500$, $L^E = 1500$, $P_W = 1$, $P_C = 5$.
If $L^A + L^E = 4000$, then $L^A = 1000$, $L^E = 3000$, $P_W = 2$ and $P_C = 10$.
If $P_W/P_C = 3/5$, $L^A = 1000 = L^E$.

15.2   *The discussion in the textbook supposed that k had the same value in both countries. Show in detail how the argument would change if k were different in Germany than in the U.S. How would your answer to the first part of the above problem change if k were to fall to one-fourth in America but remain at one-half in Europe?*

If k differed in the two countries, then equation (15.3) in the text would become: $L^G/L^{U.S.} = p(y^G/y^{US})(k^G/k^{US})$. If k were to fall to one-fourth in America, in **Problem 15.1**, then the American money supply would equal 285.7 and the European money supply would equal 1714.3 in equilibrium.

15.3   *Assume that in equilibrium the German supply of butane is 111 and supply of apples is 21, that America exports 70 apples to Germany for 30 units of butane, and that American production is 100 apples. Suppose that the world money supply consists of 1,520 gold coins and that k = 2. Find the equilibrium money supplies in the two countries and the equilibrium money prices of the two goods.*

The German money supply is 1,120, the American money supply is 400, the price of butane is 4.67, and the price of an apple is 2.

15.4*   *England has 100 labor units, of which 5 are required to produce either a cask of wine or a bolt of cloth. The English always consume equal quantities of the two goods. Portugal has 100 labor units with 1 required to produce a cask of wine and 4 to produce a bolt of cloth; the Portuguese always consume equal valued quantities of wine and cloth. The world money supply consists of 150 gold coins, and k = 1. Describe and illustrate international monetary equilibrium. Show what happens if England's labor force increases to 1,000.*

In equilibrium the English money supply is 66.67 gold coins and the Portuguese is 83.33; the price of cloth is 3.33 coins and the price of wine is .83. If the English labor force increases to 1,000, then in the new equilibrium the English money supply is 100 gold coins and the Portuguese is 50; the prices of wine and cloth each equal one-half of a gold coin.

15.5*   *Show how the discussion in this section of the textbook changes if, instead of remaining fixed,* G *constantly* increases *at the rate of 10 percent per year.*

The two money supplies and the two nominal prices all increase at 10 percent per year. All other magnitudes are unchanged.

Additional Problems

1.   Draw Figure 15.1 on page 439 of the textbook as it would appear if the U.S. were a very small country relative to Germany. (Imagine Germany to be the rest of the world.)

2.   Suppose that Gormengast and Ditch trade, Gormengast specializing in and exporting zingoes and Ditch specializing in and exporting poobahs. Gormengast's zingo production equals 10,000 and Ditch's poobah production 20. In equilibrium 100 zingoes exchange for 1 poobah. The world money supply consists of 12,000 clams, and $k = 2$. Describe international monetary equilibrium and illustrate with a diagram analogous to Figure 15.1 on page 439 of the textbook. Suppose the world money supply increases to 18,000 clams; calculate the effect on your answer and illustrate the change in your diagram. Do the same if instead the terms of trade were to alter so that 150 zingoes exchange for 3 poobahs.

Answers to Self-Test

1.   1.1

2.   True

2.   THE AUTOMATIC ADJUSTMENT PROCESS

Basic Ideas

1.   The automatic adjustment process is concerned with the way in which the equilibrium described in the previous section is attained.

2.   There are three constituents of the automatic adjustment process.

   a.   The quantity theory of money determines the equilibrium allocation of the world's money supply among countries, as discussed in the first section of this chapter.

      b.   Disequilibrium allocations generate payments imbalances, in ways to be examined subsequently.

      c.   The payments imbalances redistribute money supplies among countries so as to attain the equilibrium allocation.

3.   There are two implications of the automatic adjustment process.

      a.   Payments imbalances are caused by monetary misallocations among countries and serve to correct these misallocations; thus they are temporary.

      b.   Individual countries cannot pursue independent monetary policies, except transitorily.

4.   Be sure you understand: **The Rules of the Game; the sense in which countries cannot have independent monetary policies.**

Self-Test

1.   What are "The Rules of the Game?"

2.   True or false: The classical automatic adjustment process states that national monetary authorities have little scope for independent action because the classical writers thought the authorities would usually do something stupid if allowed to act independently

Solutions to Problems from the Text

15.6   *As in Problem 15.1, America produces 1,000 wheat, Europe 600 cloth and in equilibrium 5 wheat exchange for 1 cloth. Initially, the world money supply consists of 2,000 gold coins, and k = ½. Now suppose that the world money supply increases to 4,000 coins, with the increase taking place in America. Calculate the cumulative payments imbalances necessary to restore equilibrium.*

A cumulative American deficit (or cumulative European surplus) of 1,500.

15.7   *In Problem 15.6, suppose that the world money supply remains equal to 2,000 gold coins, but that economic growth in America raises wheat production to 2,000 units. Calculate the cumulative payments imbalance necessary to restore equilibrium.*

A cumulative American surplus (or cumulative European deficit) of 300.

15.8   *Suppose that, in Problem 15.4*, Portuguese tastes permanently change so that each Portuguese now spends one-fourth of her income on cloth and three-fourths on wine. Find the new monetary equilibrium and calculate the*

cumulative payments imbalances necessary in order to reach this new equilibrium from the old one.

No payments imbalances are necessary. The Portuguese shift their pattern of production to 91 cloth and 2.25 wine and the new equilibrium is attained, with the same money supplies and prices as the old.

15.9*   *Show how the discussion in this section of the textbook changes if the Americans, instead of doubling their money supply just once, double it every year forever.*

The Americans will experience a permanent balance of payments deficit.

Additional Problems

1.   In **Additional Problem 2** in Section 1 above, suppose that the increase in the world's money supply is brought about by money creation in Gormengast. Calculate the cumulative payments imbalances necessary to restore equilibrium.

2.   In **Problem 15.4***, calculate the cumulative payments imbalances necessary to restore equilibrium after England's labor force increases from 100 to 1,000.

Answers to Self-Test

1.   The monetary authorities in a country experiencing a balance of payments deficit should allow that country's money supply to fall by at least the amount of the deficit, and the monetary authorities in a country experiencing a balance of payments surplus should allow that country's money supply to rise by at least the amount of the surplus.

2.   False

3.   THE BALANCE OF PAYMENTS AND THE DOMESTIC BANKING SYSTEM

Basic Ideas

1.   This section concerns the mechanics of payments settlements and imbalances with modern banking systems.

2.   The basic agents in each country are the public, the commercial banks, and the central bank.

3.   Each agent has assets and liabilities, with the excess of the former over the latter equal to net worth.

4. The public's assets consist of deposits in the commercial banks and other assets, and their liabilities are loans from the commercial banks.

5. The assets of the commercial banks are the loans to the public and their reserves (on deposit with the central bank), and their liabilities are the deposits of the public.

6. The assets of the central bank are government bonds and international reserves; their liabilities are the reserves of the commercial banks.

7. The commercial banks are required to hold reserves equal to some fraction of deposits.

8. A balance-of-payments deficit (surplus) will be reflected by an equal reduction (increase) in the central bank's stock of international reserves, and the commercial banks' reserves with the central bank. This will require, for the reserve requirement to be met, a larger reduction (increase) in deposits at commercial banks, and in those banks' loans to the public.

Solutions to Problems from the Text

15.10   *Work through the example in the textbook if the French reserve requirement is one-tenth rather than one-fifth (keep the German equal to one-fifth).*

The demand deposits of the French public in the French commercial banks would have decreased from Fr5,000 to Fr4,000.

15.11   *Suppose that in Italy the money supply is 300,000 lire while the Spanish money supply equals 60,000 pesetas. In each country money is in the form of paper notes, but the central bank will exchange its money on demand for gold. In Spain the central bank will buy or sell pesetas for 2 ounces of gold each, and the Italian central bank will exchange a half ounce of gold for each lira. Each central bank has 50,000 ounces of gold in its international reserves. Suppose that Italy experiences a balance of payments deficit of 40,000 lire, and Spain accordingly has a surplus of 10,000 pesetas. Describe what happens, and calculate the money supplies and international reserve stocks in the two countries after the payments imbalance takes place.*

After the imbalance takes place, Italy has a money supply of 260,000 lire and international reserves equal to 30,000 ounces of gold, while Spain has a money supply of 70,000 pesetas and international reserves equal to 70,000 ounces of gold.

15.12   *In Problem 15.11, suppose that Italian law or custom guarantees that at all times the size of the Italian money supply equals exactly 6 lire for each ounce of gold contained in the international reserves of the Italian central bank. How does your answer to Problem 15.11 change?*

The Spanish surplus is 10,000 pesetas or 20,000 ounces. Thus the Spanish gold stock increases to 70,000 ounces and the Spanish money supply to

70,000 pesetas. Italian reserves fall to 30,000 ounces and the Italian money supply falls to 180,000 lire.

15.13   *Suppose, in Problems 15.11 and 15.12, that each central bank initially has a stock of reserves equal to 50,000 dollars, that the Italian central bank will exchange 2 lire for a dollar, and that the Spanish central bank will exchange a peseta for 2 dollars. How do your answers change?*

Replace "ounce of gold" with "dollar."

Additional Problems

1.   Using Federal Reserve data (see Appendix II of the textbook for data sources), try to compile a table for the United States, as close as possible to Table 15.1 on page 450 of the textbook, for the beginning of 1994.

2.   Answer the analog to the preceding problem for Canada.

4.   THE RULES OF THE GAME AND MONETARY POLICY

Basic Ideas

1.   This section discusses the third ingredient of the automatic adjustment process (the Rules of the Game): payments deficits should reduce a nation's money supply and surpluses should increase it.

2.   National monetary authorities often attempt to maintain independent monetary policies by *sterilizing* payments imbalances, that is, by creating new money to replace that lost through a payments deficit or by contracting the money supply to eliminate that acquired through a payments surplus. Thus sterilization means violating the Rules of the Game.

3.   Successful sterilization allows a country to control its own money supply, but it also prevents (or retards) payments imbalances from redistributing money between countries. Thus it prevents those imbalances from being self-correcting.

4.   There are two limitations to the ability of a country to sterilize payments imbalances:

   a.   *Central bank assets*: a deficit country, for example, will eventually run out of reserves if it does not first allow the payments imbalance to be corrected.

   b.   *Offsetting capital movements*: a deficit country which creates additional money, for example, will find that its residents increase their purchase of foreign assets, so that the sterilization enlarges the size of the deficit. The extent of this offset depends upon the degree of capital mobility. With perfect capital mobility sterilization will be entirely offset, so that it will only magnify payments imbalances and will not enable countries to control their money supplies.

5.   Sterilization, or attempted sterilization, has been quite common in practice.

Self-Test

1.   True or false: Countries with very large stocks of international reserves are likely to be able to force the burden of adjustment to payments imbalances onto those countries with small stocks of international reserves.

2.   Why should a rise in the degree of international capital mobility cause countries to abandon fixed exchange rates?

3.   Multiple choice: An increase in the degree of capital mobility can be expected to cause countries to:
   3.1.   Need fewer international reserves because private capital movements could substitute for official ones.
   3.2.   Want fewer reserves because they would be better able to borrow abroad should a crisis arise.
   3.3.   Want more reserves to be better able to counter increased offsetting capital flows.
   3.4.   All of the above
   3.5.   None of the above

Solutions to Problems from the Text

15.14   *In Problem 15.11, suppose that the Italian central bank sterilizes completely the Italian deficit, and that there is no offset. How do your answers change? What are the changes in the bond holdings of the Italian public? The Italian central bank? How do your answers change if the Spanish authorities also fully sterilize the Spanish surplus?*

The Italian money supply remains equal to 300,000 lire, the Italian public has fewer bonds—and the central bank more bonds—by an amount equal in value to 40,000 lire.

15.15   *Suppose, in Problem 15.14, that the Italian authorities completely sterilize and the Spanish do not sterilize at all. Suppose also that one-half of any Italian sterilization is offset by a purchase of foreign bonds: whenever the Italian central bank buys 2 lire worth of bonds from the Italian public, the public then buys 1 lira's worth of bonds from abroad. How do your answers to* **Problem 15.13** *change? How do they change if, instead, three-fourths of any sterilization is offset?*

The Italian money supply remains equal to 300,000 lire, the public has 40,000 lire's worth of fewer bonds, the central bank has 80,000 lire's worth of additional bonds, the total Italian payments deficit has been 80,000 lire, and central bank reserves have fallen by 40,000 dollars.

Additional Problems

1. Complete the analog for Germany of Table 15.5 on page 459 of the textbook, assuming alternatively that:
   a. The German central bank attempts to sterilize its surplus.
   b. The German central bank does not attempt to sterilize its surplus.

2. Sterilization is simply monetary control motivated by the balance of payments, so any method of monetary control can be used for sterilization. The text discussed open market operations; alternative methods are changes in reserve requirements and in discount rates. How would the latter two be used to sterilize the effects of a deficit? Rework the example of Tables 15.4 and 15.5 on pages 455 and 459 of the textbook if the French authorities try to sterilize by changing reserve requirements rather than by open market operations.

Answers to Self-Test

1. True

2. Maintaining control over their own money supplies after the increase in offsetting capital flows makes sterilization more difficult.

3. 3.3

5. RESERVE CURRENCIES

Basic Ideas

1. A reserve currency is one which other countries hold in their international reserves. The U.S. dollar is the most important example.

2. If other countries respond to surpluses or deficits by adding to or subtracting from their holdings of a reserve currency, then payments imbalances of the reserve currency country:

   a. Do not change that country's stock of international reserves, since the country need not use its reserves to purchase its currency,

   b. Change the total world stock of reserves, by an amount equal to its own payments imbalance,

   c. Are automatically sterilized, since foreign central banks will hold their reserves of that country's currency in the form of interest earning assets.

Solutions to Problems from the Text

15.17   *The textbook showed that imbalances of a reserve-currency country could be automatically sterilized. But sterilization will be offset, to some degree, if capital is internationally mobile. Suppose that foreign central banks hold reserves only in the form of U.S. dollars. What does this imply about a U.S. balance-of-payments deficit if there is partial mobility of capital between the U.S. and the rest of the world? If capital is perfectly mobile? How do your answers change if foreign central banks always hold half of their international reserves in the form of dollars and half in the form of gold?*

With capital mobility, the automatic sterilization of U.S. deficits magnifies the size of those deficits, to an extent depending on the degree of capital mobility. Perfect mobility would render automatic sterilization impossible and/or force down interest rates worldwide. If foreign central banks held half of their reserves in the form of gold, only one-half of any U.S. deficits would be automatically sterilized. If the U.S. does not attempt to sterilize the other half, and if capital mobility is perfect, U.S. deficits will be twice as large as they would be without the automatic sterilization.

15.18   *In Figure 15.4 on page 456 of the textbook, suppose that the U.S. supplies a reserve currency for the rest of the world. Show what happens if the U.S. increases its money supply and the rest of the world sterilizes its own imbalances; if the rest of the world does not sterilize. If the rest of the world tries to increase its money supply.*

Suppose that the U.S. is initially at point A in Figure 15.4 and increases its money supply by AH. If the rest of the world consciously sterilizes its own surpluses, and if the U.S. deficits are automatically sterilized, the world remains at D. If the rest of the world does not sterilize its surpluses, the world moves to point B, assuming again that the U.S. deficits are automatically sterilized.

Additional Problems

1.   How does your answer to **Problem 15.11** change if the Spanish authorities add to their reserves any lire acquired through payments surpluses, instead of holding all their reserves in the form of gold?

2.   How does your answer to **Problem 15.14** change if the Spanish authorities add to their reserves any lire acquired through payments surpluses, instead of holding all their reserves in the form of gold?

6. REVIEW QUESTIONS

1. Write an essay on sterilization. Be sure you discuss what it is, why it has been done, what limits it, and practical experience.

2. What are the basic constituents and implications of the automatic adjustment process?

3. Discuss the importance of the degree of international capital mobility for a fixed exchange rate system.

CHAPTER 16

The International Monetary System

KEY IDEAS of Chapter Sixteen

1. The *Bretton Woods system* is the international monetary arrangement, designed at the end of the Second World War, which lasted until the 1970s.

2. The Bretton Woods system featured *adjustable pegs* for the currencies of the major industrial countries.

3. Current international monetary arrangements are less formal and quite *diverse*, featuring managed floating, adjustable pegs, joint floating, and other practices.

4. Major industrial countries have undertaken intermittent *coordinated intervention* since the Plaza agreement of 1985, and secret target zones for the U.S. dollar-Japanese yen and U.S. dollar-German mark exchange rates have sometimes been used since 1987.

1.   THE BRETTON WOODS SYSTEM

Basic Ideas

1.   A new international monetary system was designed by the United Nations member states toward the close of the Second World War.

2.   The International Monetary Fund (IMF) and the World Bank (IBRD) were established as institutional components of the new system.

3.   The system was to feature an adjustable-peg exchange-rate arrangement and the free convertibility of national currencies for the purpose of current account transactions.

4.   Quota subscriptions of member states supply resources for the IMF, which uses them to make various loans, both conditional and unconditional, to members.

5.   The Bretton Woods system was an example of a gold exchange standard, with the United States obligated to exchange gold for dollars at a fixed price with foreign central banks, and the latter obligated to peg their currencies to the U.S. dollar. As a result the dollar is an intervention and reserve currency.

6.   The Special Drawing Right (SDR) is an international reserve asset created by the IMF.

7.   Be sure you understand: **the mechanics of IMF functions; the basic outline of the Bretton Woods System; the nature of and reasons for the special role of the dollar; what SDRs are and how they are used.**

Self-Test

1.   What does each of the following stand for: IMF, IBRD, SDR?

2.   True or false: The "reserve tranche" is a quantity of funds the IMF keeps as a reserve to lend to countries should a global crisis seem imminent.

3.   List the types of international reserve assets under the Bretton Woods system.

Solutions to Problems from the Text

16.1   *On April 11, 1994, the dollar exchange rate of the German mark was $.58, of the French franc was $.17, of the Japanese yen was $.01, of the pound sterling* was $1.47, and of the Italian lira was $.0006. What was the price of one SDR in terms of U.S. dollars? In terms of French francs? In terms of Italian lire?

SDR1 = $1.41. It was also worth 8.28 French francs or 2,347 Italian lire.

16.2   *Until the creation of SDRs, there were three international reserve assets under the Bretton Woods system. The rapid growth of the world economy and of the volume of international transactions during the years that this system existed certainly made for a substantial increase in the world's need for international reserves. How reasonable do you think it would have been to expect this increased need to actually have been met by increases in each of the three reserve assets?*

Increases in gold could have been expected to be modest at best, since they could come about only through new mining or by enticing some out of private hoards, both unlikely with a fixed gold price. Increases in aggregate reserve tranche positions could have been accomplished by IMF quota increase, but these would entail a corresponding reduction in other reserve assets. Increases in reserve currency holdings were the most likely.

16.3   *In view of the intervention obligations of the Bretton Woods system, what was the maximum percentage by which the market value of the dollar could fluctuate relative to any other currency? What was the maximum percentage by which any two (nondollar) currencies could fluctuate relative to each other?*

With all (nondollar) currencies restricted to be within 1 percent of their dollar pegs, the exchange rate of the dollar in terms of any other currency could vary within a 2 percent band, whereas the exchange rate of any two nondollar currencies could vary within a 4 percent band.

Additional Problems

1.   Answer **Problem 16.1** above with recent values of the relevant exchange rates. Compare your answers with the actual values of the SDR (see Appendix II of the textbook for data sources).

2.   What do you think is the role of the IMF in dealing with the recent debt problems of many LDCs?

Answers to Self-Test

1.   International Monetary Fund; International Bank for Reconstruction and Development; Special Drawing Right.

2.   False

3.   Gold, reserve currencies, unconditional borrowing rights at the IMF, SDRs

2. THE BRETTON WOODS SYSTEM IN OPERATION

Basic Ideas

1. The Bretton Woods system went into operation in the late 1940s, though it wasn't until 1959 that most industrial countries had accepted the convertibility obligation, and the majority of LDCs still have not.

2. The early years were characterized by "dollar scarcity," the 1960s by "dollar glut."

3. There was a series of steadily worsening balance-of-payments crises during the 1960s.

4. **Be sure you understand: the confidence problem; the nature of the debate surrounding the asymmetric position of the dollar; the problems involved in maintaining an adjustable peg in the face of national autonomy and a high degree of international capital mobility.**

Self-Test

1. Who are in the "Group of Ten?"

2. Multiple choice: Which of the following is the "confidence problem?"
   2.1. It is unrealistic to expect private markets to maintain confidence in currencies not linked to gold, but impossible for all currencies to be linked to just one metal.
   2.2. The U.S. must run deficits to satisfy the world need for dollar reserves, but those deficits undermine world confidence in the value of the dollar as a reserve asset.
   2.3. The Arabs could not have been expected, in the early 1970s, to have much confidence in the currencies of countries dependent upon them, but there was nowhere else they could have turned for a store of value for their new-found wealth.
   2.4. All of the above
   2.5. None of the above

3. True or false: The U.S. government thought that the reserve currency status of the dollar was an unmixed blessing.

Solutions to Problems from the Text

16.4 *Discuss how each of the following might be interpreted as evidence in the debate over whether U.S. payments deficits were supply-determined (due to a failure of the U.S. to adopt measures to eliminate its deficit) or demand-determined (due to the failure of foreign countries to eliminate their surpluses):*
   a.   The U.S. improved its current-account position in the early and mid 1960s, but the over-all payments deficits continued.

      b.   *Even as the IMF was allocating a new reserve asset, in the early seventies, the American deficit exploded.*

      a.   Demand-determined
      b.   Supply-determined

16.5   *The text discussed the role of speculative capital movements with an adjustable peg. How would this discussion change in the presence of each of the following alternative exchange regimes: free floating, managed floating, fixed exchange rates.*

The problems discussed in the text would be absent with free floating, since the authorities would not stake out a position to be defended at all costs (or at any costs, for that matter), and with fixed rates, where there would be no possibility of an exchange rate change in any case. With managed floating, it would depend on the way in which the authorities managed their float.

Answers to Self-Test

1.   The United States, Canada, Britain, Japan, Sweden, France, Germany, Italy, Belgium, the Netherlands, and (the eleventh member) Switzerland.

2.   2.2

3.   False

3. COLLAPSE OF THE BRETTON WOODS SYSTEM

Basic Ideas

1.   With huge U.S. deficits, the Bretton Woods system collapsed in the early 1970s. Industrial countries abandoned their obligations to peg to the dollar and the U.S. renounced its obligation to sell gold to foreign central banks for dollars.

2.   Attempts to design consciously a new international monetary system—or to redesign the old system—came to nought.

3.   As a result we now have a hybrid system. Most industrial countries have managed floats, with the notable exception of the EMS. Most LDCs peg their currencies, either to the dollar or some other major currency or else to a basket of currencies or to the SDR.

Solution to Problem from the Text

16.6   *The Smithsonian negotiations included considerable debate over whether the depreciation of the dollar should involve a dollar devaluation or just the revaluation of other currencies. Can you think of any reasons for this, since everyone knew that the United States would not restore official gold convertibility in any case?*

For reasons of national pride mainly. However, there were some outstanding contracts and international agreements and obligations expressed in terms of gold. The values of these in terms of national currencies were sensitive to the exact combination of dollar devaluation and revaluation of other currencies adopted.

Additional Problems

1.   Give a narrative of the major events in the three years leading up to the collapse of the Bretton Woods system in 1973.

2.   Describe the Committee of 20, the Rambouillet meeting, the Jamaica Agreement, and the Second Amendment to the IMF Articles of Agreement.

4.   INTERNATIONAL MONETARY REFORM ISSUES

Basic Ideas

1.   Debate over reform of the international monetary system has centered on reserve assets and the nature of the exchange-rate regime.

2.   Gold has become an inactive reserve asset, currencies can no longer be pegged to it, and the IMF is attempting to replace it with the SDR.

3.   It has been proposed that the IMF establish a substitution account to trade SDRs to central banks for their dollar holdings. But agreement has not been reached on this.

4.   It has also been proposed that there be intervention with a number of currencies, rather than with just dollars.

5.   There have been many proposals for regulating, mandating, or otherwise restricting national intervention in the exchange markets, but nothing has been done.

6.   There have been isolated instances of coordinated intervention by several central banks.

7. Be sure you know about: **the dollar overhang; the substitution account; multicurrency intervention; the IMF Guidelines and Decision on Surveillance.**

Solutions to Problems from the Text

16.7 *Under what circumstances could the existence of a substitution account lessen the asymmetric position of the United States?*

By itself, the establishment of a substitution account would not alter intervention practices. Also, if the IMF held its dollars in interest-earning form (a matter for negotiation during the establishment of such an account) and if the IMF were neither more nor less willing to accumulate dollars than central banks had been (or if the latter were neither more nor less willing to accumulate additional dollars than they had been before the account) the U.S. position would be no different.

16.9 *Suppose that the fluctuations of some exchange rates consist of random deviations from a constant equilibrium value. If a central bank then undertakes to lean against the wind, would its intervention on balance serve to move the exchange rate toward equilibrium or away from it? Answer the same question if the exchange rate fluctuations instead consist of random deviations from a moving equilibrium.*

Leaning against the wind could be expected, on balance, to move an exchange rate neither closer to nor further from a constant equilibrium, but further from a moving one.

Additional Problem

1. Discuss the likely consequences of a unilateral U.S. return to the gold standard, under the assumption that other major countries do not follow suit and that the IMF's rules and policies are not altered.

5. REVIEW QUESTIONS

1. Describe the basic features of the Bretton Woods system.

2. Analyze the Bretton Woods system in the light of section 1's discussion of policy dilemmas.

3. Describe the basic features of the present international monetary system.

4. Analyze the present international monetary system in light of the discussion of policy dilemmas in Section 1.

Part Six

Open-Economy Macroeconomics

CHAPTER 17

Incomes and Adjustment

KEY IDEAS of Chapter Seventeen

1. Income-expenditure theory attempts to describe how *aggregate demand* is determined if prices are rigid.

2. International trade affects the basic income-expenditure model in two ways: the multiplier is reduced because some spending "leaks" into imports, and the economy is subjected to disturbances originating from abroad.

3. The balance-of-trade surplus, or excess of exports over imports, can equivalently be described as the excess of national income over *absorption*.

1.   BASIC INCOME-EXPENDITURE THEORY

. Basic Ideas

1. This section is simply a review of basic multiplier theory. If you have any difficulty at all, you should consult the textbook used in your principles course.

2. Be sure you recall and understand: **multiplier; marginal propensity to save.**

Solutions to Problems from the Text

17.1   *Suppose in England consumption equals 100 units plus three-fourths of the English income. What is the English multiplier? What is English income if investment equals 200 units? How much does income increase if investment increases to 300? Answer this by the method of successive rounds, calculating the increase in income after 6 or 7 rounds.*

Multiplier = $1/MPS$ = $1/(1 - [3/4])$ = 4.
If investment is 200, income = 1,200; if investment is 300, income is 1,600.

17.2*   *We can investigate the* stability *of the equilibrium in Figure 17.1 on page 497 of the textbook. Suppose that investment is* OI_0 *but that income is* OI_1*, so that saving exceeds investment. Then some output is not being sold, so we would expect firms to cut back production. This suggests the disequilibrium hypothesis:* Y *is falling when* S *exceeds* I *and rising when* I *exceeds* S*. Is the equilibrium in Figure 17.1 stable? Draw an unstable equilibrium. What is the stability condition?*

The equilibrium in Figure 17.1 is stable, as the stability condition is simply that $MPS > 0$. Thus for an unstable equilibrium, the S line in the figure would have to be downward sloping.

Additional Problems

1. Spanish consumption always equals 500 plus one-half of any income above 500 plus one-fourth of any income above 1,000. What is the Spanish marginal propensity to save, and what is the Spanish multiplier, at all income levels?

2. In the above problem, suppose that investment I is not completely autonomous, as in the discussion in the textbook, but rather equals the sum of an autonomous component plus one-eighth of national income. What is the Spanish multiplier at each income level?

2.   THE DEMAND FOR IMPORTS

Basic Ideas

1.   In an open economy, the equilibrium level of national income is that for which $S + M = I + X$.

2. X is regarded as autonomous spending, like I, while M depends upon income, like S.

3.   The simple Keynesian theory introduced in this part of the chapter makes four basic assumptions:

   a.   The prices of goods are fixed by producers in terms of their own currency.

   b.   Fixed exchange rates

   c.   No international capital movements except for official intervention.

   d.   Payments imbalances are completely sterilized.

4.   Terms you should know: **marginal propensity to import; average propensity to import.**

Self-Test

1.   Multiple choice: In a certain country, *MPM* > *APM*. If the country experiences a rise in income, the *APM* will:
   1.1.   Rise.
   1.2.   Fall.
   1.3.   Remain unchanged.
   1.4.   Can't tell without more information

2.   How would an increase in the European demand for American wheat affect the U.S. import curve?

Solutions to Problems from the Text

17.3   *Suppose that English imports always equal 50 units plus one-fourth of English income. Draw the English import function, and calculate the marginal propensity to import, average propensity to import and the income elasticity of imports.*

$MPM = 1/4$; $APM = (1/4) + (50/Y)$; elasticity $= 1/[1 + 200/Y]$.

17.4   *Portugal always spends one-half of its income on imports. Draw the Portuguese import curve and calculate the marginal propensity to import, average propensity to import, and income elasticity of imports.*

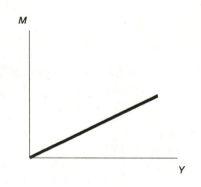

$MPM = \frac{1}{2}$; $APM = \frac{1}{2}$; elasticity $= 1$.

Additional Problem

1.   Spain exports goats and imports olives. The Spanish always consume 3 goats with each barrel of olives. If a goat costs 100 pesetas and a barrel of olives costs 150, what is the Spanish marginal propensity to import? How does your answer change if the price of olives increases to 200 pesetas?

Answers to Self-Test

1. 1.1

2. No effect

3. CASE STUDY: MEXICO, FRANCE, AND OTHER COUNTRIES

Basic Ideas

1. Import curves vary substantially from country to country, depending upon such things as country size, willingness to trade, income, etc.

2. Be sure you understand: **the difficulty in inferring the value of the MPM from trade and income data**.

Solutions to Problems from the Text

17.5 *Describe the effect of each of the following on a country's import curve.*
   a. *The country imposes a tax on imports.*
   b. *The country's residents decide to save less, thereby boosting income and imports.*
   c. *The country establishes an import quota, prohibiting imports above a certain amount, M_0.*
   d. *The rest of the world imposes a tax upon imports from this country.*

   a. The import curve becomes flatter and shifts down.
   b. The import curve shifts up.
   c. The import curve becomes flat when M equals the quota amount, but is unchanged before that.
   d. No effect on the import curve of this country

17.6 *Using the 1993 U.S. APM of 0.11 and the estimate of the U.S. income elasticity shown in Table 17.2 on page 503 of the textbook, calculate an estimate of the U.S. MPM. Calculate the actual increase in U.S. imports for 1993-94 as a fraction of the actual U.S. increase in GNP (see Appendix II of the textbook for data sources). Compare the two results. List all the reasons you can think of why they might differ from each other and from the true MPM. Do the same for Canada.*

   Estimate of U.S. $MPM = 1.7 \times 0.11 = 0.19$.

4.   THE SIMPLE FOREIGN TRADE MULTIPLIER

Basic Ideas

1.   The total of exports and investment determines equilibrium levels of income and of the balance of trade simultaneously. Thus policies which influence one of the latter influence the other as well.

2.   The multiplier, which measures the change in Y brought about by a change in X and/or I, is larger the smaller are MPM and MPS.

Self-Test

1.   Which of the following policies, if undertaken by the home government, would not affect the home foreign trade multiplier?
     1.1.   A tax on imports from abroad
     1.2.   A tax credit for domestic investment
     1.3.   A tax exemption for interest income
     1.4.   An export subsidy

2.   Would the multiplier for the state of California be greater or less than that for the U.S. as a whole?

Solutions to Problems from the Text

17.7   *Use the method of successive rounds to derive the foreign trade multiplier.*

$$Y_1 - Y_0 = [I_1 - I_0] + [1 - MPS - MPM][I_1 - I_0]$$

$$+ [1 - MPS - MPM]^2 [I_1 - I_0] + \cdots$$

$$= \frac{[I_1 - I_0]}{[MPS + MPM]}.$$

17.8   *Find the multiplier for England if consumption equals 100 units plus three-fourths of English income and if imports equal 50 units plus one-fourth of income. What is English income if investment equals 200 units and exports 100? If investment increases to 300? Suppose instead that investment remains at 200 but trade policy is used so that English imports now equal 40 plus one-fifth of English income; calculate the effect on income.*

$MPS = 1/4$; $MPM = 1/4$; multiplier $= 2$.
Income initially $= 700$; after the rise in investment, it $= 900$.
With trade policy the multiplier is $20/9$ and the new income is instead 800.

17.9   *Suppose that the Portuguese always save one quarter of their income and spend one half on imports. Calculate the multiplier. What is Portuguese income if investment equals 50 and exports 100?*

Multiplier = 4/3.
$Y = 200$.

17.10   *Calculate a formula for the term that must be multiplied by a change in I to obtain the effect on the trade balance X – M.*

-[MPM/(MPM + MPS)].

17.11   *The discussion in the textbook assumed that autonomous expenditure was all devoted to domestic goods. Suppose instead that the fraction MPM of an increase in I is spent on imports. Calculate the formula for the multiplier in this case. How would your answer to* **Problem 17.10** *above change?*

[(1 – MPM)/(MPM + MPS)];
– [MPM(1 + MPS)/(MPM + MPS)].

17.12   *The discussion of trade policy assumed that the reduction in M for any Y was all spent on domestic goods, that is, that trade policy switched expenditure from foreign goods to domestic ones. Suppose instead that the income no longer spent on foreign goods is simply saved. How would trade policy affect income and the trade balance in this case?*

Trade policy has no effect on income, and the trade balance is affected by an amount equal to the direct impact of the trade policy.

Additional Problems

1.   In the **Additional Problem** in Section 2 of this chapter, suppose that the Spanish always save one-tenth of their income. Calculate the Spanish multiplier both before and after the price rise.

2.   Suppose that the foreign country institutes a subsidy on exports to our country. Depict geometrically the effect on domestic income and the trade balance.

Answers to Self-Test

1.   1.2 and 1.4

2.   Less

5.* EXPLORING FURTHER: GENERAL EQUILIBRIUM

Basic Ideas

1. Domestic income depends upon exports, which depend upon foreign income, and foreign income depends upon foreign exports, which depend upon domestic income. Thus domestic and foreign income are jointly determined.

2. An increase in autonomous spending at home will increase imports, since income goes up, and this will increase foreign income. This causes foreign imports to rise, which in turn increases domestic income again, and so on. Exact expressions for the multipliers must take such "secondary repercussions" into account.

3. An increase in autonomous spending at home increases foreign income, and vice versa. Thus there are "cross multipliers" to consider.

Solutions to Problems from the Text

17.14 *Using the method of successive rounds, derive the multiplier that relates changes in* Y^F *to changes in* I^F *when all repercussions are accounted for.*

$$(Y_1^F - Y_0^F) = (I_1^F - I_0^F)$$

$$\times \left(1 + \left[(1 - MPM^F - MPS^F) + \frac{(MPM^F MPM^G)}{(MPM^G + MPS^G)} \right] \right.$$

$$\left. + \left[(1 - MPM^F - MPS^F) + \frac{(MPM^F MPM^G)}{(MPM^G + MPS^G)} \right]^2 + \cdots \right)$$

$$= (I_1^F - I_0^F)$$

$$\times \left[\frac{(MPM^G + MPS^G)}{(MPS^G MPS^F + MPM^G MPS^F + MPS^G MPM^F)} \right].$$

17.15 *Using the method of successive rounds, derive the multiplier that relates changes in* Y^F *to changes in* I^G *when all repercussions are accounted for.*

The "cross multiplier" is:

$$\frac{MPM^G}{(MPS^G MPS^F + MPM^G MPS^F + MPS^G MPM^F)}.$$

17.16   *In England consumption equals 100 units plus three-fourths of GNP and imports equal 50 units plus one-fourth of GNP. England trades with Portugal, where savings are one-fourth of GNP and imports are one-half of GNP. Calculate multipliers for each country. What is each country's GNP if English investment equals 200 units and Portuguese investment equals 50 units? Calculate the effects of each of the following:*

    a.   *An increase in English I to 300.*

    b.   *An increase in Portuguese I to 100.*

    c.   *A shift in the English import curve to 40 units plus one-fifth of GNP.*

   Show how your answers illustrate the use of the formulas you derived in Problems 17.15 and 17.16.

In England the direct multiplier is 3 and the cross multiplier is 2; in Portugal the direct multiplier is 2 and the cross multiplier is 1. Initially, English income is 950 and Portuguese income is 450. Thus a rise in English investment to 300 will increase English income to 1,250 and Portuguese income to 650. Alternatively, a rise in Portuguese investment to 100 would raise Portuguese income to 550 and English income to 1,050.

6.   INCOME ADJUSTMENT

Basic Ideas

1.   In a Keynesian context, an increase in the domestic money supply will reduce savings, S, and/or increase investment, I, so that $S - I$ falls.

2.   This causes an increase in domestic aggregate demand, in an amount determined by the foreign trade multiplier.

3.   The rise in aggregate demand causes a rise in imports, in an amount determined by the marginal propensity to consume, and thereby induces a payments deficit. Thus both aggregate demand and the balance-of-payments deficit increase.

4.   The rest of the world experiences an increase in aggregate demand also, but a reduction in its payments deficit.

5.   The balance of trade, or excess of exports over imports, can equivalently be defined as the excess of national income over absorption. This reflects a macroeconomic point of view.

6.   A depreciation of the exchange rate, by switching demand from foreign goods to domestic goods, increases aggregate demand.

7.   The increase in aggregate demand increases the demand for imports and thereby nullifies at least part of the increase in the trade balance brought about by the depreciation.

8. If the economy is initially operating at full capacity, it cannot produce the additional goods demanded as a result of the depreciation, and so there will instead be domestic inflation that will continue until the other effects of the depreciation are nullified.

Self-Test

1. True or false: "Absorption" refers to the money acquired by a country as a result of a balance of payments surplus.

2. In a Keynesian context, what will be the consequences of exchange depreciation by a country operating at full capacity?

3. In a Keynesian context, what will be the consequences of exchange depreciation by a country operating with excess capacity?

4. In a Keynesian context, what will be the consequences of exchange depreciation by a country operating with unemployment and an excessive balance of payments surplus?

Solutions to Problems from the Text

17.17   *How does the discussion in the text change if the home country is so small that the flow of money abroad brought about by the home balance of payments deficit has no significant effect on the rest of the world? Show the final equilibrium in Figure 17.11 on page 512 of the textbook.*

The $X - M$ line does not now shift up in response to the flow of money abroad, so that the new equilibrium is attained only when the $S - I$ line shifts all the way back to its initial position. Thus the initial domestic income level will eventually be restored.

17.18   *Suppose that domestic residents suddenly decide to save more than before at each level of income. Discuss the consequences. Do the same if instead domestic goods become more attractive to foreigners, so that exports rise.*

The $S - I$ line shifts up, producing consequences just the reverse of those described in the text. In the second case, the $X - M$ line shifts up instead.

17.19   *Suppose the French suddenly acquire an enhanced taste for German goods. Analyze how the exchange rate must adjust to maintain balance of payments equilibrium.*

The franc must depreciate.

17.20   *Suppose that a country is initially at full employment and levies a tariff. Discuss the effects on the balance of trade and on aggregate demand, at the initial exchange rate. How must the exchange rate be altered to keep the balance of trade unchanged?*

The tariff would induce a trade surplus and an increase in aggregate demand; they could be prevented by an appreciation of the currency.

17.21 *Does it matter whether the axes in Figure 17.12, on page 513 of the textbook, are measured in terms of domestic currency or of foreign currency? Why?*

No, as long as both axes are measured in terms of the same currency.

17.22* *Must the discussion of Figure 17.12 on page 513 of the textbook be altered if the demand for imports is price inelastic?*

Yes, the conclusions would be reversed.

Additional Problem

1. Suppose that domestic residents suddenly decide to save more than before at each level of income. Discuss the consequences for the exchange rate, if the balance of trade is to remain unchanged. Do the same if instead domestic goods become more attractive to foreigners, so that exports rise.

Answers to Self-Test

1. False

2. Inflation, and nothing else

3. A rise in national income and an improvement in the trade balance

4. A reduction of unemployment but a worsening of the surplus

7.* *EXPLORING FURTHER:* IS-LM ANALYSIS IN AN OPEN ECONOMY

Basic Ideas

1. The *IS* curve shows those combinations of the interest rate and national income for which the demand for a country's output just equals that level of income.

2. The *LM* curve shows those combinations of the interest rate and national income for which the demand for a country's money just equals its supply.

3. The *T* curve shows those combinations of the rate of interest and national income for which a country's balance of trade is in neither deficit nor surplus at the existing level of the exchange rate.

4. The intersection of the *IS* and *LM* curves determines a country's short-run equilibrium interest rate and income. The position of this intersection relative to the *T* curve determines the trade imbalance.

5. Long-run equilibrium is illustrated by a simultaneous intersection of all three curves.

6. A depreciation of the exchange rate shifts the *IS* curve to the right and up.

7. A depreciation of the exchange rate shifts the *T* curve to the right.

Solutions to Problems from the Text

17.23 *How does a rise in the domestic price level affect the* LM *curve? The* T *curve?*

The *LM* curve shifts up, the *IS* curve shifts down, and the *T* curve shifts left.

17.24 *How is each of the curves affected by a rise in the foreign price level?*

The *IS* curve shifts to the right, the *T* curve shifts right, and the *LM* curve stays put.

17.25 *Analyze the effects of a permanent improvement in the terms of trade (due, say, to a shift in tastes from foreign goods toward domestic goods).*

The *IS* curve shifts to the right, causing the interest rate and income to rise, and the *T* curve shifts right, indicating a balance of trade surplus. The domestic price level begins to rise, shifting these curves back toward where they were originally. The balance-of-trade deficit and the rise in domestic prices produce more or less offsetting effects upon the position of the *LM* curve.

17.26 *Analyze the effects of a more expansionary fiscal policy with a fixed exchange rate and also with a floating rate.*

The *IS* curve shifts to the right, increasing the rate of interest and national income, and producing a balance-of-trade deficit if the exchange rate is fixed. The latter causes the *LM* curve to begin shifting up, further raising the interest rate but gradually forcing income back down. This continues until the three curves again come into a common intersection, when the deficit ceases. The interest rate is higher than originally, reflecting the shift in spending from private investment to the government deficit.

With a floating exchange rate, the expansionary fiscal policy again shifts the *IS* curve to the right. To prevent a deficit, the exchange rate depreciates, shifting the *T* curve to the right and the *IS* curve up and to the right.

17.28 *Analyze in detail the effects of an increase in the domestic money supply if the authorities adjust the exchange rate to prevent a balance-of-payments deficit.*

The increase in the money supply shifts the *LM* curve down and to the right. To prevent a deficit, the exchange rate depreciates, shifting the *T* curve to the right and the *IS* curve up and to the right. In order to keep the balance of trade equal to zero, the curves must shift so that the intersection of the *IS* and *LM* curves moves along *T*.

17.29   *The discussion in the text on the long-run consequences of depreciation assumed that the money supply remained constant, that is, that all payments imbalances were completely sterilized. How must the discussion change if instead there is no sterilization at all?*

The discussion in the text indicated a payments surplus, so if this is not sterilized it will cause the *LM* curve to shift down and to the right.

Additional Problems

1.   use *IS-LM-BP* analysis to discuss the effects of an increase in the money supply with complete sterilization of all payments imbalances.

2.   use *IS-LM--BP* analysis to speculate about the influence of the degree of international capital mobility on the effectiveness of monetary and fiscal policy, with fixed exchange rates and also with floating rates.

8. REVIEW QUESTIONS

1.   What are the four basic assumptions of the simple Keynesian model of an open economy? Describe the consequences of relaxing each assumption.

2.   Describe the macroeconomic performance of the U.S. economy during the 1980s in terms of the theory developed in this chapter.

CHAPTER 18

Prices and Adjustment

KEY IDEAS of Chapter Eighteen

1. In an open economy, prices are subject to two distinct influences: *domestic* macroeconomic conditions, and *international* price linkages.

2. The strength and the immediacy of international price linkages vary across commodities; they are strongest and fastest for standardized, traded goods and weakest and slowest for nontraded goods.

3. Prices influence adjustment through *relative-price* changes, notably changes in the prices of domestic goods relative to foreign goods and in the prices of traded goods relative to nontraded goods. Relative-price effects are investigated by the *elasticities* approach.

4. Prices also influence adjustment through *price-level* effects, that is, changes in the value of all goods relative to money. This is investigated by the *monetary* approach.

1.   THE AGGREGATE DEMAND CURVE

Basic Ideas

1.   An aggregate demand curve records what the equilibrium level of aggregate demand will be in a country at each value of the country's price level.

2.   A reduction in the price level causes the national money supply to be worth more in real terms and also causes domestic goods to be cheaper relative to foreign goods. This causes aggregate demand to rise; thus the aggregate demand curve has a downward slope.

3.   An aggregate demand curve is drawn for fixed values of the money supply, the exchange rate and the foreign price level. Thus a change in any of these shifts the curve.

4.   If the equilibrium level of aggregate demand is unequal to aggregate supply, the price level will eventually begin to adjust. This causes the economy to move along its aggregate demand curve.

5.   Full macroeconomic equilibrium is given by the intersection of the aggregate demand and aggregate supply curves. At this price level there will be no pressure on prices for further adjustments.

Self-Test

1.   For each of the following disturbances, write an *M* if it will cause a movement along a country's aggregate demand curve, and/or an *S* if it will cause a shift of that curve.
     1.1.   Depreciation of the exchange rate
     1.2.   A growth of productive capacity
     1.3.   An increase in the foreign price level
     1.4.   An increase in the domestic price level

2.   True or false: An aggregate demand curve shows how much an economy will demand at each price level, but this quantity can not actually be produced unless the economy is also on its aggregate supply curve.

Solutions to Problems from the Text

18.1   *Use the aggregate demand curve to discuss the effects of a fall in the price of oil, assuming a fixed exchange rate. How does your analysis change with a floating rate? In each case discuss how monetary policy might be used to respond to the price fall.*

Oil is an imported good, so a reduction in its price reduces the foreign price level relative to the home price level and can therefore be expected to shift the home aggregate demand curve to the left. Also oil is an intermediate good, giving it added weight in the home price level, which therefore also falls. However, in the short run, demand for oil is relatively unresponsive to price changes. If the economy continues to import the same quantity, it will now cost less. Thus the short-run effect of the price decline will be like an increase in income, shifting the aggregate demand curve to the right.

18.2   *What happens to the balance-of-trade surplus as we move down and to the right along a country's aggregate demand curve? Explain your answer.*

The increase in aggregate demand causes imports to rise and therefore reduces the balance-of-trade surplus, but the reduction in the domestic price level makes home goods cheaper relative to foreign goods, and this tends to increase the trade surplus. Whether the surplus actually rises or falls depends on which effect is the stronger.

18.3   *The three lines in Figure 18.3 on page 529 of the textbook divide the plane into six regions. Describe how the economy will behave in each of these regions.*

Suppose, for example, that the world is in Zone I in the figure below. Then inflation will eventually arise in both France and Germany. Thus each economy will be moving upwards and to the left along its aggregate demand curve. Also German prices are rising more rapidly than French. Thus the German aggregate demand curve will be shifting to the left and the French curve will be shifting to the right. Behavior in the other zones can be described analogously.

GERMAN INCOME

FRENCH INCOME

Additional Problems

1.   Discuss the short-run and long-run effects of an increased propensity to invest, using aggregate demand and supply curves.

2. Discuss the effects on the domestic economy of a constant rate of foreign inflation.

Answers to Self-Test

1. 1.1. M, S
   1.2. M
   1.3. M, S
   1.4. M.

2. False

2. INTERNATIONAL PRICE LINKAGES

Basic Ideas

1. Prices in an open economy are influenced by international conditions as well as domestic conditions.

2. The prices of standardized traded goods have the strongest international linkages. Domestic conditions cannot force them to depart from foreign prices, and exchange rate changes are offset by price changes.

3. The prices of nontraded goods have the weakest international linkages. They are not influenced directly by foreign conditions or by exchange rate variations.

4. The prices of differentiated traded goods are in between in terms of their international linkages.

5. The time horizon also matters. Domestic prices are more likely to move in line with foreign prices when more time is allowed for adjustment.

6. The Law of One Price has two versions:

   a. Identical goods should sell for the same price in different countries (except for tariffs, transportation costs, etc.), once the exchange rate is used to compare prices expressed in different currencies.

   b. Relative prices are determined by real considerations independently of the exchange rate, so that any change in the latter should be accompanied by offsetting changes in the prices of goods, unless real considerations also change.

7. If the Law of One Price holds, purchasing power parity will be observed: the depreciation of a nation's currency will just equal the excess of inflation in that nation above inflation abroad.

8. Purchasing Power Parity is in fact often violated, but it does appear partly true.

9. Terms you should know: **Law of One Price; purchasing power parity; real exchange rate; effective exchange rate.**

Self-Test

1. Multiple choice: The price of which of the following goods is most tightly linked to foreign prices?
   1.1. Automobiles
   1.2. Iron ore
   1.3. Haircuts
   1.4. Construction
   1.5. Peanut butter

2. Multiple choice: The price of which of the following goods is most tightly linked to foreign prices?
   2.1. Consumer goods
   2.2. Services
   2.3. Producer goods
   2.4. All of the above
   2.5. None of the above

3. True or false: Purchasing power parity implies that exchange depreciation is caused by differences in inflation rates across countries.

4. True or false: Purchasing power parity implies that differences in inflation rates across countries are caused by exchange depreciation.

Solutions to Problems from the Text

18.4 *What will Table 18.1 on page 533 of the textbook look like if the initial disturbance is cost inflation in the U.S. rather than a depreciation of the dollar? That is, suppose that initially all prices are $100 and both exchange rates are $1.00, and that the price of foreign currency remains $1.00 throughout. Instead, an increase in the U.S. money supply, for example, causes a 50 percent rise in all wages and costs, but there is no similar change abroad. Indicate the responses, and explain your answer.*

Response in:		Short-run	Medium-run	Long-run
Price of foreign currency		$1.00	$1.00	$1.00
Standardized	U.S.	$100	$100	$100
traded goods	Foreign	$100	$100	$100
Differentiated	U.S.	$125	$111	$100
traded goods	Foreign	$100	$100	$100
Nontraded goods	U.S.	$150	$125	$100
U.S. price index		$125	$112	$100
Real exchange rate		.80	.89	1.00
Price of traded goods relative to nontraded		.71	.82	1.00

18.5 *In Table 18.3 on page 536 of the textbook, calculate the 1986 average values of four bilateral exchange rates for South Korea. Calculate the South Korean effective exchange rate using the following weights: Japanese yen, 50 percent; U.S. dollar, 30 percent; deutsche mark, 10 percent; Canadian dollar, 10 percent. Using data in Table 18.2 on page 535 of the textbook to approximate inflation differentials, calculate the South Korean real exchange rate.*

Canadian dollar	123
Japanese yen	208
Deutsche mark	123
U.S. dollar	146
Effective	172
Real	155

Additional Problem

1. This section discussed changes in three types of price indices: the overall price index; the price of home-produced traded goods relative to foreign goods; and the price of traded goods relative to nontraded goods. On the basis of Table 18.3 on page 536 of the textbook, speculate how each of these behaved in the U.S. during 1980-1986.

Answers to Self-Test

1. 1.2

2. 2.3

3. False

4. False

3. RELATIVE PRICE ADJUSTMENT: THE ELASTICITY APPROACH

Basic Ideas

1. This section looks at the relation of relative price changes and exchange rate changes and at the role of relative price changes in the adjustment process. The terms of trade is the relative price examined.

2. An appreciation of one country's currency raises the prices of that country's goods relative to foreign goods. In response imports rise and exports fall.

3. An increase in the money supply—or a decrease in the demand for money— in one country raises the prices of that country's goods relative to foreign goods. In response imports rise and exports fall.

4. The trade price elasticities determine the size of the response to the price changes.

5. The analysis of this section of the textbook is more relevant the less rigid is the link between foreign and domestic prices.

6. The response of importers and exporters to the relative price change produced by a depreciation is often delayed, but the depreciation immediately increases the domestic currency cost of imports priced in terms of foreign currency. Thus depreciation often causes the balance of trade to deteriorate before it improves.

7. Be sure you understand: **elasticity of import demand; Marshall-Lerner condition; J curve.**

Self-Test

1. True or false: According to the theory of this section, a spontaneous shift in consumer tastes from foreign goods to domestic goods, with a floating exchange rate, would cause an appreciation of the domestic currency that would continue until domestic relative prices became high enough to clear commodity markets.

2. True or false: According to the theory of this section, a spontaneous shift in consumer tastes from foreign goods to domestic goods, with a fixed exchange rate, would induce a balance-of-payments surplus that would continue until the domestic economy accumulated enough money to raise domestic prices high enough to clear commodity markets.

3. True or false: With floating exchange rates, high elasticities are to be welcomed because they imply that exchange-rate variations will be rare and of modest size.

4.   True or false: With a fixed exchange rate, high elasticities are to be welcomed because they imply that payments imbalances will be gradual and of modest size.

Solutions to Problems from the Text

18.7   *When the California gold rush began, the prices of ordinary consumer goods and services were driven to very high levels in the mining regions. After a while these prices fell to more normal levels. Discuss in terms of the automatic adjustment process.*

The supply of gold (and the shortage of commodities) pushed up prices in California, leading to a balance-of-payments deficit. This continued until the outflow of gold (and the inflow of commodities) allowed prices to approximate more nearly those in the rest of the world.

18.8   *Suppose that Italy's income is 10,000 olives, Spain's is 4,000 goats, the equilibrium terms of trade equal 2 olives per goat, and k = 2. Initially Spain's money supply is 80,000 gold coins and Italy's is 100,000 gold coins. Whenever the relative price of goats in terms of olives increases by 1 olive, the Spanish respond by increasing their imports from Italy by 1,800 olives and the Italians purchase 900 fewer goats from Spain. Suppose the Spanish money supply increases by 72,000 gold coins. Describe in detail the resulting adjustment.*

Initially the price of a goat is 10 gold coins and that of an olive is 5 coins. When Spain's money supply increases from 80,000 coins to 152,000 coins, the price of a goat rises to 19 coins, so that the relative price of goats in terms of olives rises from 2 to 3.8. The Spanish then increase imports by 3,240 (= 1.8 x 1800) olives and the Italians reduce their imports from Spain by 1,620 goats. These changes in trade volumes produce a Spanish balance-of-payments deficit (Italian surplus) of 46,980 gold coins [(19 x 1,620 + (5 x 3,240)]. (NOTE: The price changes will also change the values of the initial trade volumes. But the problem supplies no data on the latter, so assume they are in fact zero.) The payments imbalances reduce the Spanish money supply to 105,020 coins, lowering the price of a goat to 13.1 coins, and increase the Italian money supply to 146,980 coins, raising the price of an olive to 7.3 coins. Thus the new relative price of goats in terms of olives is 1.8. The price change causes Spanish imports to fall by 3600 olives and Italian imports to rise by 1800 goats; thus Italy now imports 180 goats and 360 olives for a balance-of-payments deficit (Spanish surplus) of 4,986 gold coins. Proceed in this way to calculate subsequent developments.

18.9   *Suppose again that Italy produces 10,000 olives, Spain 4,000 goats, 2 olives exchange for one goat in equilibrium, k = 2, and that Spain's money supply consists of 80,000 pesetas and Italy's of 100,000 lire. Suppose the peseta depreciates by one half of its equilibrium value, and that the lira price of olives and the peseta price of goats are unchanged. What happens?*

The peseta price of olives doubles and the lire price of goats falls by one-half, so that the price of goats in terms of olives falls by 50 percent. This

should increase Spanish exports and reduce Spanish imports, etc., as
discussed in the text.

18.10   *Chapter 15's discussion of the price-specie flow mechanism assumed that the
demand for money in each country is proportional to that country's production
of goods. Sometimes it is argued instead that money demand is proportional to
demand for a country's goods. Can you think of any reason for one to be the
case rather than the other? To see what difference it makes, suppose that each
country consumes only the other country's products, that is, the French
consume only butane and the Germans only apples. Then French demand for
money will be proportional to (py^G) rather than to y^F, and German money
demand will be proportional to (y^F/p) instead of to y^G. What difference does
this make to the automatic adjustment process?*

In this case an increase in L^F relative to L^G causes p to rise rather than fall,
so that the discussion is reversed.

18.11   *Use the aggregate demand curve to discuss the effects of an increase in the
money supply with a floating exchange rate.*

The aggregate demand curve shifts to the right, and the exchange rate
depreciates. As domestic inflation develops, the economy moves up along
the new curve, with further accompanying depreciation.

18.12*   *The text pointed out that a 1 percent depreciation increased export receipts by
e* percent and reduced import expenses by e - 1 percent. These were then
added to conclude that the total improvement in the trade balance would be
proportional to e + e* - 1. Actually this addition gives only an approximation
that becomes less accurate the larger is the initial trade imbalance. Why is this?
Derive the true expression.*

A one percent depreciation reduces import expenses by e - 1 percent, as
discussed in the text. Export receipts increase by e^* percent, but this should
be expressed as a percentage of import expenses—not exports—if we are to
add the two together. As a percentage of the latter, export receipts increase
by $e^*(X/pM)$ percent. Thus the improvement in the trade balance is
proportional to $e^*(X/pM) + e$ - 1. If trade is initially balanced, $X = pM$, so
this reduces to the expression in the textbook.

Additional Problems

1.   How is the analysis of this section of the textbook affected if France is a
small country and Germany is the rest of the world?

2.   Suppose that the terms of trade is determined entirely by real
considerations and that exchange rate changes cannot influence it, but that
each country also has a class of nontraded goods, as discussed in the
previous section of the textbook. How is the analysis of this section of the
text affected?

Answers to Self-Test

1. False

2. True

3. False

4. False

4.* EXPLORING FURTHER: NONTRADED GOODS

Basic Ideas

1. Depreciation increases the price of traded goods relative to nontraded goods.

2. This change in relative prices causes firms to switch production from nontraded goods to traded goods, and consumers switch their purchases from traded goods to nontraded goods.

3. This change in production and consumption reduces the excess demand for traded goods, that is, it reduces the balance-of-trade deficit.

4. The change also creates an excess demand for nontraded goods. This causes the economy to move up along its aggregate demand curve until the demand for nontraded goods comes into line with the supply.

Solutions to Problems from the Text

18.13 *How does the analysis of this section change if, instead of a depreciation, the exchange rate remains fixed but the domestic money supply is increased?*

The increase in the money supply will promote inflation at home. But with the prices of traded goods held down by world markets, the inflation affects only nontraded goods. Thus the price of nontraded goods rises relative to traded goods. This is just the reverse of the case discussed in the textbook, so it produces just the reverse effects.

18.14 *How does the analysis of this section change if the exchange rate is allowed to float and the domestic money supply is increased?*

In this case the domestic prices of traded goods can also rise if the exchange rate depreciates a like amount. Thus the increase in the money supply causes exchange depreciation rather than an increase in the price of nontraded goods relative to traded goods.

5. HOARDING AND DISHOARDING: THE MONETARY APPROACH

Basic Ideas

1. If residents of a country have larger money balances than they wish, they will begin to dishoard—or spend some of the excess. This induces a balance-of-payments deficit if the exchange rate is fixed.

2. If residents of a country have smaller money balances than they wish, they will begin to hoard—or spend less than their incomes. This induces a balance-of-payments surplus if the exchange rate is fixed.

3. Relative price changes play no role in this facet of the automatic adjustment process. But the absolute level of world prices adjusts so that what one country wishes to hoard just matches what the rest of the world wishes to dishoard.

4. If purchasing power parity holds, a depreciation of the domestic currency will require that inflation at home rise relative to inflation abroad. This will increase the demand for money at home and reduce it abroad.

5. Since domestic residents now have smaller money balances than they wish, they will begin to hoard. Similarly foreign residents will begin to dishoard. In this way the depreciation of the domestic currency increase the domestic balance-of-payments surplus and reduces the foreign balance-of-payments surplus.

6. Term you definitely should understand: **propensity to hoard.**

Self-Test

1. Multiple choice: According to the mechanism studied in this section, disturbances to equilibrium produce price changes
   1.1. So that the terms of trade can adjust.
   1.2. To bring reciprocal demand into play.
   1.3. To cause hoarding in one country to just match dishoarding abroad.
   1.4. All of the above
   1.5. None of the above

2. True or false: An increase in the money supply of a "small" country would have a big impact on inflation in that country, since it can't influence foreign prices and thereby "export" inflation.

Solutions to Problems from the Text

18.15 *Suppose that Italy's income is equal in value to 10,000 olives and that Spain's consists of 4,000 goats. In equilibrium 2 olives exchange for 1 goat. If the world money supply consists of 180,000 ounces of gold, and if k = 2, what are the equilibrium money supplies and money prices? If a Spanish peseta equals 2 ounces of gold and the Italian lira equals ½ ounce of gold, what are the money supplies and money prices in terms of pesetas? In terms of lire?*

$L^S = 80,000$, $L^I = 100,000$, $P_G = 10$ ounces $= 5$ pesetas $= 20$ lire. $P_O = 5$ ounces $= 10$ lire $= 2.5$ pesetas.

18.16 *Suppose, in the previous problem, that Spain obtained 72,000 ounces of additional gold from the New World. How must the money prices of goats and olives change if the Spanish excess supply of money is to just equal the Italian excess demand? Suppose that the propensity to hoard of each individual is such that everyone wants to take exactly ten years to adjust money supply to demand, performing one tenth of the adjustment each year. What are the Spanish and Italian imbalances in the first year after the Spanish obtain the new gold? What are the new money supplies after one year, and the payments imbalances in the second year? Continue to give answers for succeeding years until the new equilibrium is reached.*

$P_G = 14$ ounces and $P_O = 7$ ounces. The initial Spanish deficit (Italian surplus) is 4000 ounces, so that after one year $L^S = 148,000$ ounces and $L^I = 104,000$.

18.17 *In Problem 18.15, suppose Spain and Italy have paper currencies, 100,000 lire and 80,000 pesetas. What are the equilibrium prices and the exchange rate?*

$P_G = 10$ lire $= 10$ pesetas; $P_0 = 5$ lire $= 5$ pesetas; and $R =$ one lira per peseta.

18.18 *Suppose, in **Problem 18.17** above, that the peseta depreciates relative to the lira, by one half of its equilibrium value. If PPP holds, what must happen to the money prices of the two goods in the two currencies if the excess demand for lire is to equal in value the excess supply of pesetas?*

Now the Italian exchange rate is ½ a lira per peseta. $P_G = 140/9$ lire $= 280/9$ pesetas; $P_O = 35/9$ pesetas $= 35/18$ lire.

18.19 *The discussion in the textbook showed that exchange depreciation tends to increase domestic inflation relative to foreign inflation. Suppose that some exogenous event causes the domestic inflation rate to rise but does not influence foreign inflation. What will be the likely effect on the exchange rate, if the latter is free to adjust? What, in turn, will be the consequences of this adjustment? Compare with the effects of increased domestic inflation when exchange rates are fixed.*

The domestic currency would likely depreciate.

18.20 *Show how Figure 18.8 on page 551 of the textbook can be used to analyze a depreciation of the franc if both axes are measured in marks.*

In Figure 18.8, instead of the *GG* line shifting out, the *FF* line would shift to the left and become steeper.

18.21   *The text described the response to a monetary disturbance: an increase in the French money supply. Suppose instead that the disturbance is real, say economic growth in Germany in the form of an increase in* y^G. *Analyze the response using diagrams such as Figure 18.7 on page 549 of the textbook.*

An increase in y^G increases the German demand for money and therefore shifts the *GG* schedule *downward*. This lowers the world price level and produces a German balance-of-payments surplus and a corresponding French deficit. These imbalances cause both schedules to rise until their intersection point reaches the P axis, when the new equilibrium is attained and the payments imbalances cease.

18.22*   *How do your answers to Problems 18.15 and 18.16 change if the Spanish obtain an additional 72,000 ounces of gold not just once, but each and every year?*

In **Problem 18.15** the equilibrium money supplies and money prices continue to increase in tandem (though at a decreasing rate). Spain develops a permanent balance-of-payments deficit.

Additional Problems

1.   In **Additional Problem 2** in Section 1 of Chapter 15, suppose that the increase in the world's money supply is brought about by money creation in Gormengast, and that the residents of each country always wish to eliminate one half of any discrepancy between money demand and supply in one year. Calculate the consequent payments imbalances for the first three years after the Gormengastian money creation.

2.   In **Problem 8.4***, calculate the payments imbalances in the three years following the increase in England's labor force from 100 to 1,000, if the English always wish to eliminate one-half of any discrepancy between money demand and supply in one year, and the Portuguese always wish to eliminate one fourth.

3.   Suppose that France discovers credit cards, so that *k* falls in France, but not Germany. Analyze the response using a diagram such as Figure 18.7 on page 549 of the textbook.

4.   In **Additional Problem 2** in Section 2 of Chapter 14, suppose that the residents of each country always wish to eliminate one-half of any discrepancy between money demand and supply in one year. Calculate the consequent exchange-rate changes during the first three years after the Gormengastian money creation, assuming that adjustment takes place entirely through exchange-rate alterations.

Answers to Self-Test

1.   1.3

2.   False

6.   REVIEW QUESTIONS

1.   Price changes can influence international adjustment either through changes in *relative commodity* prices or through changes in *relative national price levels*. Compare and contrast these two possibilities. Which do you think is more important?

2.   Suppose that the elasticity approach captures most of what is important in international adjustment. What does this imply about the adjustment problems of DC-DC economic relations relative to the adjustment problems of DC-LDC relations?

3.   Discuss the macroeconomic performance of the United States economy during the 1980s in terms of the theory developed in this chapter.

CHAPTER 19

Capital and Adjustment

KEY IDEAS of Chapter Nineteen

1. This chapter addresses the role of *international capital mobility* in international adjustment. Capital mobility was also examined in detail in Part Five; the present discussion has much less to say about the crucial intertemporal aspect, but instead uses a richer macroeconomic context.

2. In the short run, monetary and fiscal policies can be used to attain both *internal* and *external* balance even with a fixed exchange rate, because international capital mobility causes the two policies to have differential effects on the two targets.

3. The degree of international capital mobility influences how *temporary* the effects of monetary and fiscal policies will be, and how strongly they will have *foreign repercussions*.

4. Both expenditure policies and trade policies have international repercussions. Whether these bring governments into conflict or cause them to reinforce each other's efforts depends upon whether their economies are in phase or not.

1.   INTERNAL AND EXTERNAL BALANCE UNDER FIXED EXCHANGE RATES

Basic Ideas

1.   This section addresses the dilemma faced by national authorities who wish to use expenditure policy to attain simultaneously internal balance (the desired level of aggregate demand) and external balance (the desired size of the balance-of-payments deficit).

2.   If there is international capital mobility, a combination of monetary policy and fiscal policy—the two types of expenditure policy—can be found that will just attain both types of balance at once.

3.   The reason is that the two types of policy have differential effects on the two types of balance. Fiscal policy directly influences aggregate demand and, through the multiplier, the balance of trade. Monetary policy does the same but, in addition, it exerts a second effect on the balance of payments by changing interest rates and thereby influencing the capital account.

4.   However this argument is true only in the short run. Once individuals have responded to the change in interest rates and undertaken their desired capital transactions the effect on the capital account will cease.

Self-Test

1.   Multiple choice: Under which of the following circumstances would this section's conclusion about how to attain both internal balance and external balance no longer hold?
     1.1.   The absence of international capital mobility
     1.2.   Perfect capital mobility
     1.3.   The long run
     1.4.   All of the above
     1.5.   None of the above

2.   True or false: The presence of international capital mobility causes fiscal policy to exert a greater influence on the balance of payments relative to aggregate demand, compared to monetary policy.

Solutions to Problems from the Text

19.1   *The* IB *and* EB *lines in Figure 19.1 on page 557 of the textbook divide the plane into four zones. What is the interpretation of each of these zones in terms of policy goals?*

In the zone NE of point *A* aggregate demand is excessive and the balance-of-payments surplus is too high; SW of point *A* just the reverse is the case.

In the zone NW of point *A* aggregate demand is deficient and the balance-of-payments surplus is too high; SE of *A* just the reverse is the case.

19.2 *Suppose that savings are small so that the increase in the capital account surplus caused by a rise in the domestic interest rate almost entirely disappears after the short run. Show what the relative positions of the IB and EB schedules in Figure 19.1, on page 557 of the text, look like in both the short run and the long run. What do you conclude about policy?*

The diagram would look qualitatively the same, but in the long run points above the *EB* line would correspond to payments deficits because of international interest payments.

19.3 *Suppose that the economy is initially in external balance at point* D *in Figure 19.1, on page 557 of the text, and, in order also to attain internal balance the interest rate is reduced by* BD *and the budget deficit by* AB. *Show in the diagram what happens after the short-run change in the capital account disappears, assuming that both the continuing effect on the capital account and the long-run effect on net interest income are small enough to be ignored. Show what additional policy measures the authorities must take in order to preserve internal and external balance.*

The country will develop a larger balance-of-payments surplus than it wants. To prevent this the authorities must either find an additional policy with which to reconcile internal and external goals, or they must be prepared repeatedly to change monetary and fiscal policies in order to attain the desired short run effects over and over.

19.4* *The intersection of the* IB *and* EB *lines in Figure 19.1, in the text, gives a specific policy prescription (point A). But in actual situations we will have at best only a very hazy idea of the shape and position of these curves, and so will not know where A is. It is therefore useful to have simple rules for adjusting the targets so as to "grope" toward* A. *One simple rule would be to assign each instrument to one target. For example, if the interest rate were assigned to internal balance and the budget deficit to external balance, one would reduce the interest rate whenever the economy was in a recession and reduce the budget deficit whenever there was a balance-of-payments deficit. An alternative assignment would be monetary policy to external balance and fiscal policy to internal balance. Discuss the relative merits of these two assignments as means to attain point* A.

Suppose that the economy is initially at point *E* in each panel of the following figure. This economy is in a recession and is experiencing a larger balance-of-payments deficit than the authorities wish. If the authorities assign monetary policy to internal balance and fiscal policy to external balance, they will lower interest rates in response to the recession and reduce the government budget deficit in response to the payments deficit. This is illustrated in panel (a). The result is that the economy moves to the southwest and both problems worsen! The influence of each policy tool on the target it is assigned to is overwhelmed by the influence of the other policy tool. If the authorities instead assign monetary policy to external

balance and fiscal policy to internal balance, they will act in the reverse
manner to that just described. This is illustrated in panel **(b)**. In this case
the policy actions improve matters. The point of this is that if policy tools
are to be assigned to particular targets, it is important that each tool be
assigned to the target on which it has relatively the most influence,
compared to the other tool. Note the analogy with the principle of
comparative advantage. In the above figure, the *IB* and *EB* lines divide each
panel into four zones. You should verify that if point *E* were instead in the
northeast zone it would still be crucial to properly match tools and targets,
but that this is less important in the northwest and southeast zones, where
each tool would used in a particular direction regardless of which target it is
aiming at. But even in these cases it is likely that the economy would sooner
or later move into one of the zones where the proper assignment becomes
vital.

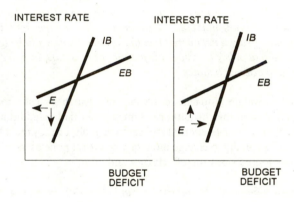

Answers to Self-Test

1.   1.4

2.   False

2.   AGGREGATE DEMAND MANAGEMENT WITH FLOATING EXCHANGE RATES

Basic Ideas

1.   With floating exchange rates, an expansion of the money supply will
     depreciate the currency and stimulate aggregate demand.

2.   The greater the degree of international capital mobility, the more transitory
     will be the influence of a monetary expansion on domestic aggregate

demand, and the greater will be its depressing influence on foreign aggregate demand.

3. With floating exchange rates, fiscal policy will be effective in influencing aggregate demand if capital is not very mobile, but will be ineffective with a high degree of capital mobility.

Solutions to Problems from the Text

19.5 *Suppose that France and Germany have a floating exchange rate, and suppose that there is an exogenous increase in the German desire to consume French goods. What will be the results? How does your answer depend upon the degree of capital mobility? Contrast your answer with what would happen under fixed rates.*

The immediate effect will be to generate a French trade surplus, to stimulate aggregate demand in France and to depress it in Germany. The changes in aggregate demand will limit the trade surplus, but they will also put upward pressure on French interest rates and downward pressure on German interest rates, thereby inducing a French capital account surplus. The franc will appreciate enough to cancel these effects.

19.6 *Suppose that France and Germany have a floating exchange rate, and suppose that there is an exogenous increase in the German desire to own French bonds. What will happen? How does your answer depend upon the degree of capital mobility? Contrast your answer with what would happen under fixed rates.*

The immediate effect will be a French capital account surplus, with downward pressure on French interest rates and the reverse in Germany. This will stimulate French aggregate demand and induce a trade deficit to partially cancel the capital surplus. Exchange rate changes will complete the cancellation.

19.7 *The textbook showed that, with floating exchange rates and perfect capital mobility, monetary policy could influence domestic aggregate demand, but the influence would be temporary. Fiscal policy would have no influence. Is this lack of influence of fiscal policy also temporary? Explain.*

No, because as long as the budget deficit continues new bonds will continually be sold to foreigners.

19.8* *How are our conclusions about the temporary effect of monetary policy in the presence of capital mobility altered when account is taken of: (a) the fact that there will be continuing capital flows in a growing world with positive net saving, and (b) international payments of interest income?*

a. In this case there will be permanent capital account deficit and therefore also a permanent trade surplus, which will require a depreciated exchange rate and consequent rise in aggregate demand.

b.   In this case there will eventually develop a permanent surplus due to interest income from abroad and therefore also a permanent trade deficit, which will require an appreciated exchange rate and consequent reduction in aggregate demand.

Additional Problems

1.   The main advantage of floating exchange rates is that they allow countries independent control over their own money supplies. Distinguish this from independent control over their own economic performances.

2.   Discuss why countries might want to limit, or to encourage, international capital mobility.

3.   CASE STUDY: U.S. EXPERIENCE IN THE 1980s

Basic Ideas

1.   This section uses the theory presented in the preceding section as a framework to discuss us experience in the 1980s.

2.   The us federal government ran a large budget deficit in the early 1980s. The current account developed a large deficit position and the dollar appreciated dramatically. This was followed by a large depreciation in the middle of the decade.

3.   The current account deficit and dollar appreciation can be explained in terms of a downward shift of $S - I$ and $X - M$. Explaining the subsequent depreciation requires us to augment the simple theoretical model.

Solutions to Problems from the Text

19.9   *When large federal budget deficits began to develop in the early 1980s, many commentators expected them to ignite a burst of inflation. But this did not happen. In fact, the inflation rate fell. Explain in terms of our theory.*

Commentators expected that the deficits would add to the demand for us goods and thus push prices up. Instead much of the added demand was satisfied by imports, as reflected in the large current account deficit.

19.10   *How is the discussion of intervention in this chapter sensitive to whether that intervention is sterilized or not?*

The chapter discussed the possibility that intervention to force the dollar down could help finance the us budget deficit. That is, that the deficit would be partly paid for with new dollars. This presumes that the intervention is not sterilized.

Additional Problem

1. Chapter 14 gave an alternative, intertemporal, explanation of the experience discussed in this section. How consistent are the two explanations? Do you prefer one to the other?

4.* *EXPLORING FURTHER:* IS-LM-BP ANALYSIS

Basic Ideas

1. The *IS* curve shows those combinations of the interest rate and national income for which the demand for a country's output just equals that level of income.

2. The *LM* curve shows those combinations of the interest rate and national income for which the demand for a country's money just equals its supply.

3. The *BP* curve shows those combinations of the rate of interest and national income for which a country's balance of payments is in neither deficit nor surplus at the existing level of the exchange rate.

4. The intersection of the *IS* and *LM* curves determines a country's short-run equilibrium interest rate and income. The position of this intersection relative to the *BP* curve determines the payments imbalance.

5. Long run equilibrium is illustrated by a simultaneous intersection of all three curves.

6. A depreciation of the exchange rate shifts the *IS* curve to the right and up.

7. A depreciation of the exchange rate shifts the *BP* curve to the right and down.

Solutions to Problems from the Text

19.12 *How does a rise in the domestic price level affect the* BP *curve?*

The *BP* curve shifts up

19.13 *How is the* BP *curve affected by a rise in the foreign price level?*

The *BP* curve shifts up.

19.15 *Analyze the effects of a more expansionary fiscal policy with a fixed exchange rate and also with a floating rate.*

The *IS* curve shifts to the right, increasing the rate of interest and national income, and producing a balance-of-payments deficit if the exchange rate is fixed. The latter causes the *LM* curve to begin shifting up, further raising the interest rate but gradually forcing income back down. This continues until the three curves again come into a common intersection, when the deficit ceases. The interest rate is higher than originally, reflecting the shift in spending from private investment to the government deficit.

With a floating exchange rate, the expansionary fiscal policy again shifts the *IS* curve to the right. To prevent a deficit, the exchange rate depreciates, shifting the *BP* curve down and to the right and the *IS* curve up and to the right.

19.17   *Analyze in detail the effects of an increase in the domestic money supply if the authorities adjust the exchange rate to prevent a balance-of-payments deficit.*

The increase in the money supply shifts the *LM* curve down and to the right. To prevent a deficit, the exchange rate depreciates, shifting the *BP* curve down and to the right and the *IS* curve up and to the right. In order to keep the balance of payments equal to zero, the curves must shift so that the intersection of the *IS* and *LM* curves moves along *BP*.

Additional Problems

1. Use *IS-LM-BP* analysis to restate the discussion, in Section 12 of the textbook, of internal and external balance.

2. Use *IS-LM-BP* analysis to discuss the effects of an increase in the money supply with complete sterilization of all payments imbalances.

3. Use *IS-LM-BP* analysis to discuss the influence of the degree of international capital mobility on the effectiveness of monetary and fiscal policy, with fixed exchange rates and also with floating rates.

4. Use *IS-LM-BP* analysis to discuss the effects of an increase in the money supply with complete sterilization of all payments imbalances.

5. Use *IS-LM-BP* analysis to derive the aggregate demand curve.

5.   FLOATING EXCHANGE RATES

Basic Ideas

1. This section examines the operation of floating exchange rates in a world with capital mobility.

2. Purchasing power parity requires a positive relation (the *PPP* line) between the exchange rate and the ratio of domestic prices to foreign prices.

3.   Equilibrium in the asset markets (money and bonds, the latter exchanged
     between countries) implies a negative relation (the *AME* line) between the
     exchange rate and the ratio of domestic prices to foreign prices.

4.   Because asset markets attain equilibrium quickly, the economy must be on
     the *AME* line even in the short run. In the long run purchasing power parity
     must also hold, so long run equilibrium is given by the intersection of the
     AME and *PPP* lines.

5.   Monetary disturbances can be depicted as shifts of the *AME* line, so that
     long run equilibrium moves along the *PPP* line. But if the exchange rate
     adjusts more rapidly than commodity prices, the former will "overshoot" its
     new equilibrium value and then have to backtrack. Thus monetary
     disturbances would make exchange rates volatile.

6.   Real disturbances can be viewed as shifts of the *PPP* line and movements
     along *AME*. Thus real disturbances would make exchange rates neither
     more volatile nor less volatile than commodity prices. Purchasing power
     parity would appear to be violated, but only because the equilibrium
     relation between prices was itself changing.

7.   Things oyou should understand: **the *AME* line and its slope;
     "overshooting;" the role and implications of relative speeds of adjustment.**

Self-Test

1.   Multiple choice: To maintain equilibrium in the asset markets, a
     depreciation of the exchange rate would have to be accompanied by which
     of the following?
     1.1.   An equal excess of domestic inflation over foreign inflation
     1.2.   A mass resignation of central bankers
     1.3.   An increase in foreign interest rates
     1.4.   An excess of foreign inflation over domestic inflation
     1.5.   None of the above

2.   Multiple choice: To maintain equilibrium in the commodity markets, a
     depreciation of the exchange rate would have to be accompanied by which
     of the following?
     2.1.   An equal excess of domestic inflation over foreign inflation
     2.2.   A mass resignation of central bankers
     2.3.   An increase in foreign interest rates
     2.4.   An excess of foreign inflation over domestic inflation
     2.5.   None of the above

3.   True or false: *Overshooting* of the exchange rate refers to the short-term
     overreaction, relative to the long-term effect, of the exchange rate to a
     monetary disturbance that is made necessary by the fact that commodity
     prices don't adjust for a while, so that in the meantime the exchange rate
     must overadjust to compensate.

Solutions to Problems from the Text

19.19   *Can the different responses of the exchange rate to monetary and real distur-*
         bances help explain why in Table 19.3 on page 563 of the textbook exchange
         rates were more volatile than commodity prices but less so than asset prices?

         The theory suggests that exchange rates were as volatile as asset prices
         (interest rates) in response to monetary shocks, but no more volatile than
         commodity prices in response to real shocks. Since actual experience
         presumably includes a mixture of both types of disturbances, this is not
         inconsistent with the observation that exchange rate volatility has actually
         been somewhere between that of asset prices and that of commodity prices.

19.20   *The monetary shock analyzed in this section was an unanticipated increase in*
         the home money supply. Suppose instead that the home authorities announce
         that in one year they will increase the money supply by a certain amount and
         that everyone believes them, and that they then do so. Discuss the likely conse-
         quences.

         With the money supply expected to increase in a year, people would be-
         come less willing to hold domestic currency now and the exchange rate
         would begin now to depreciate gradually in response. This would give
         commodity prices time to gradually adjust also, so as to preserve commodity
         market equilibrium. The *AME* curve would gradually shift outward and
         equilibrium would move along the *PPP* line, reaching the new equilibrium
         at point *C'* in one year, just as the money supply is actually increased to
         what everyone had correctly expected it to be.

19.21*   *The discussion in the textbook of the slope of the* AME *line assumed that*
         people expected the exchange rate to move toward its long-run equilibrium
         value. Suppose instead that they expect any departure from that value to be
         accentuated, at least for a while. How might this affect the slope of the AME
         line and the subsequent analysis?

         In this case the explanation of the slope of the *AME* line given in the
         textbook is just reversed, and so that line has a positive slope. The following
         figure shows the effect of an increase in the money supply when the *AME*
         line is flatter than *PPP* and when it is steeper.

         In both panels, the monetary expansion shifts the *AME* line outward to
         AME', and short term equilibrium shifts from point *C* to *D*. In panel **(a)** this
         does not involve overshooting, the equilibrium subsequently moves along
         AME' from *D* to the new long run at equilibrium at *C'*. In this case however,
         peoples' expectations are systematically incorrect: since the exchange rate *R*
         is lower at *D* than at its equilibrium at *C'*, people by assumption expect it to
         deviate even more, but it does just the opposite.

(a)   (b)

In panel (b), the short run adjustment of R from C to D is in the opposite
direction to its new equilibrium. From D, the exchange rate appreciates
even more and moves southwest along AME' ever further from C'. Equilibrium is unstable, with monetary disturbances causing explosive deviations.
However this behavior is consistent with peoples' expectations: at D they
expect the exchange rate to move even further from its value at C', and it
does.

Additional Problems

1. The discussion in the textbook assumed that the exchange rate adjusted
    much more rapidly than did commodity prices. Suppose that the opposite
    were in fact the case. How would responses to monetary and real shocks
    change?

2. The discussion in the textbook assumed that the asset markets adjusted
    much more rapidly than did commodity markets. Suppose that the opposite
    were in fact the case. How would responses to monetary and real shocks
    change?

Answers to Self-Test

1. 1.4

2. 2.1

3. True

6. POLICY DILEMMAS

Basic Ideas

1. The authorities cannot independently control the level of income and the trade balance if expenditure policy is the only available tool.

2. A second tool, such as the exchange rate, allows both targets to be attained, in principle. A combination of the exchange rate and expenditure policy can be found that will just attain both types of balance at once.

3. With a fixed exchange rate, expenditure policy influences foreign aggregate demand in the same direction as domestic aggregate demand. Thus if countries use expenditure policy for internal balance, their individual efforts will reinforce each other when the economies are in phase, but will breed international conflict when they are out of phase.

4. If expenditure policies are used for internal balance, and the exchange rate is allowed to adjust to achieve external balance, countries will not find themselves in conflict if the degree of international capital mobility is low.

5. If fiscal policy is used for internal balance and capital is highly mobile, countries will likely find themselves in conflict.

6. Exchange rate variations influence foreign aggregate demand in the opposite direction as domestic aggregate demand. Thus if countries try to use the exchange rate for internal balance, their individual efforts will reinforce each other when the economies are out of phase, but will breed international conflict when they are in phase.

7. If the exchange rate is regarded as a policy target, rather than an instrument, we are again in the situation of trying to attain internal and external balance with fiscal and monetary policies.

Self-Test

1. Multiple choice: Under which of the following circumstances would expenditure policy aimed at internal balance cause more international conflict with floating rates than with fixed rates?
    1.1. No international capital mobility
    1.2. When monetary policy is the instrument and capital mobility is high
    1.3. When fiscal policy is the instrument and capital mobility is low
    1.4. When fiscal policy is the instrument and capital mobility is high
    1.5. None of the above

2. Suppose that Italy has a *MPS* of one-sixth and a *MPM* of one-third. What increase in Italian autonomous spending would produce the same effect on foreign aggregate demand as would an increase of 100 in foreign autonomous spending?

Additional Problems

1. Discuss possible policy conflicts between countries if the authorities in each country are concerned about external balance.

2. What are "beggar-my-neighbor" policies?

Answers to Self-Test

1. 1.4

2. 150

7. REVIEW QUESTIONS

1. Describe the macroeconomic performance of the us economy during the 1980s in terms of the theory developed in this chapter.

2. Describe two distinct views of the role of the exchange rate in a floating rate system. Why does it matter whether one view or the other is correct? Is there any empirical evidence?

Part Seven

The Modern International Economy

CHAPTER 20

Economic Integration

KEY IDEAS of Chapter Twenty

1. Economic integration refers to the elimination of barriers to economic transactions between countries.

2. This chapter discusses *biased* integration: some countries reduce their mutual barriers but not the barriers between themselves and other countries.

3. Biased integration *creates* trade between the partners, *diverts* trade from nonpartners to partners, and *modifies* the structure of trade with partners and nonpartners.

4. We usually expect trade creation to be beneficial and trade diversion to be harmful. Trade modification may be either.

5. The most important example of biased integration is the EU. NAFTA is another, more recent, important example.

1.   BIASED INTEGRATION IN THEORY

Basic Ideas

1.   This section discusses reductions in barriers to trade or to factor mobility, or a unification of economic policies, between a group of countries.

2.   A reduction in trade barriers between a group of countries causes *trade creation* between them.

3.   The fact that each of these countries now discriminates in favor of its partners, relative to those countries that are not parties to the agreement, produces *trade diversion.*

4.   *Trade modification* results when a group of countries reduce their tariffs in a nondiscriminatory fashion, but the reductions take place on goods that are largely traded within the group.

5.   Mutual tariff reductions can alter the terms of trade between the partners, and also the terms of trade of the partners with the rest of the world.

6.   Integration can allow the partners to enjoy the benefits of international scale economies and increased product differentiation.

7.   Attempts of countries to integrate macroeconomic policies often focus on first maintaining fixed exchange rates relative to each other.

8.   Terms you should understand: **trade creation; trade diversion; trade modification; optimum currency area.**

Self-Test

1.   Multiple choice: Britain joins the Common Market and imports wheat from France rather than from Canada and the U.S. This is an example of which of the following?
     1.1.   Trade creation
     2.2.   Trade diversion
     2.3.   Trade modification
     2.4.   All of the above
     2.5.   None of the above

2.   Multiple choice: Britain joins the Common Market and begins importing wine from France in exchange for beer. This is an example of which of the following?
     2.1.   Trade creation
     2.2.   Trade diversion
     2.3.   Trade modification
     2.4.   All of the above
     2.5.   None of the above

3. Multiple choice: Britain joins the Common Market and reduces imports of tea from India because the British are now drinking wine from France instead of tea. This is an example of which of the following?
   3.1. Trade creation
   3.2. Trade diversion
   3.3. Trade modification
   3.4. All of the above
   3.5. None of the above

4. True or false: The formation of the EU was followed not by an increase in interindustry trade and specialization, but rather by an increase in intraindustry trade and a consequent reduction in specialization.

Solutions to Problems from the Text

20.2 *Should the existence of the quest-worker system discussed in Chapter 10 of the textbook prove a help or a hindrance in the effort of the EU to achieve monetary integration?*

If the guest worker systems of the various EU countries are in fact stabilizing aggregate demand in those countries, as they are intended in part to do, this should help the cause of monetary integration, because it would reduce the tendency for the individual EU countries to pursue divergent macroeconomic policies.

20.3 *Suppose the world is as described in the Heckscher-Ohlin-Samuelson model of Chapter 5 of the textbook, except that there are several countries instead of just two. Is integration more likely to be beneficial to two countries if their relative endowments are similar or if they are different?*

Greater differences in relative endowments could be expected to accentuate both trade creation and trade diversion.

20.4 *Are those gains from integration that are due to international scale economies and product differentiation more likely to be large if the partners are similar or if they are different?*

If they are similar.

20.5* *Suppose that F and G mutually eliminate tariffs on each other's products and then jointly levy an optimum common tariff on goods from R. Can you say anything about the significance of trade diversion?*

There would be no problem with trade diversion because F and G would be exploiting their position relative to R to the full. Any trade diversion that did occur would serve the purpose of helping to improve the partners' terms of trade with R.

Additional Problem

1.   In terms of the concepts discussed in this section of the textbook, speculate about the consequences for the United States of the formation of the EEC.

Answers to Self-Test

1.   1.2

2.   2.1

3.   3.3

4.   True

2.   BIASED INTEGRATION IN PRACTICE

Basic Ideas

1.   There have been many attempts at economic integration since the Second World War. Two of these are of major historical significance.

2.   The first of these is the large reduction on barriers to the trade of manufactures enacted by the DCs under GATT auspices.

3.   The second is the economic integration that has taken place in western Europe: the EU and also its free trade arrangements with other western European countries.

4.   There have been many attempts at integration between LDCs, but they have had quite limited success so far.

5.   There has been a resurgence of regional integration in recent years, most notably with the North American Free Trade Agreement and the expansion of the EU. There are also many new attempts at integration involving LDCs.

6.   Be sure you understand: **the distinctions between the major types of economic integration; the various attempts at integration.**

Self-Test

1.   What do the following stand for: CAP, EFTA, LAFTA, ASEAN?

2. Multiple choice: A common market differs from a customs union in which way?

    2.1. The countries in a common market agree to sell on equal terms to the rest of the world, but not necessarily to *buy* on equal terms, as is the case with a customs union.

    2.2. The countries in a common market agree to buy on equal terms from the rest of the world, but not necessarily to *sell* on equal terms, as is the case with a customs union.

    2.3. The customs union allows free factor mobility, as does a common market, but also free trade in goods.

    2.4. The common market allows free trade in goods, as does a customs union, but also free factor mobility.

    2.5. None of the above

Solutions to Problems from the Text

20.6 *Why is it necessary for a customs union to negotiate some way of distributing the joint tariff revenues, rather than simply letting each country keep what it collects (hint: consider the geographical position of Luxembourg)?*

Formation of a customs union itself alters the distribution of tariff collections among countries.

20.8 *The United States strongly supported formation of the EEC. Why?*

Basically for non-economic reasons.

20.9 *Discuss the implications of the GATT multilateral tariff reductions for the significance of the EU.*

The abolition of internal EEC tariffs became much less significant.

Additional Problem

1. Can you think of any reasons why the European attempts at integration were notably more successful than LDC attempts in the 1960s and 1970s?

Answers to Self-Test

1. Common Agricultural Policy, European Free Trade Association, Latin American Free Trade Association, Association of Southeast Asian Nations

2. 2.4

3. REVIEW QUESTIONS

1. What are the advantages and disadvantages of economic integration, such as the EU, for the participants and for the rest of the world?

2. Compare integration among DCs with integration among LDCs.

CHAPTER 21

The South and the East in Transition

KEY IDEAS of Chapter Twenty-One

1. This chapter investigates a different type of economic integration than that of the previous chapter. Here we look at countries undertaking *basic reform* of their economies that involve trading more with the outside world in general.

2. The two most important contemporary examples—both of major historical significance—are LDCs replacing inward-oriented policies with outward-oriented ones, and the former communist countries replacing soviet-style economic systems with market economies.

3. In the process of *transition*, the LDCs find themselves constrained by a serious debt problems, and the former communist countries are confronted with painful choices necessary for reform.

1. THE LDC DEBT PROBLEM

Basic Ideas

1. LDCs can be expected to be net borrowers from the DCs in normal circumstances.

2. After the oil price shocks, LDCs borrowed large sums from Western banks. Many of these funds had been deposited by oil exporters.

3. Since 1982, many LDCs have experienced difficulties in servicing their debts. There have been many crises and new lending has been sharply curtailed.

4. The large outstanding loans to LDCs with difficulties have left many banks in an exposed position.

Self-Test

1. Multiple choice: Which is the country with the largest foreign debt?
    1.1   Brazil
    1.2. Russia
    1.3. Argentina
    1.4. The U.S.
    1.5. Mexico

2. Multiple choice: Which of the following was *not* a major reason why the LDCs have found it difficult to service their debts?
    2.1. Recession in the DCs
    2.2. The appreciation of the dollar in the early 1980s
    2.3. High real interest rates
    2.4. All of the above
    2.5. None of the above

Additional Problems

1. Why don't the LDCs simply refuse to pay back their debts?

2. Discuss the consequences for the us of large scale LDC defaults on international debt.

Answers to Self-Test

1. 1.4

2. 2.5

2. THE INTERNATIONAL TRADE OF CENTRALLY PLANNED ECONOMIES

Basic Ideas

1. Since prices did not reflect opportunity costs in centrally-planned economies, those economies could not allow foreign residents freely to buy and sell there, or allow domestic residents to buy and sell freely abroad. That is, their currencies had to be inconvertible.

2. The international trade of these countries was instead handled by foreign trade organizations.

3. Trade among communist countries was basically bilateral and used prices derived from Western market prices.

4. Despite the political barriers, East-West trade grew relative to East-East trade. The former was in some ways easier, since it could use Western market prices directly.

Self-Test

1. What did COMECON stand for?

2. Multiple choice: Economic integration in Eastern Europe:
    2.1. Was a matter of course, since the Soviet Union called all the shots anyway.
    2.2. Was complete, because those countries had no tariffs.
    2.3. Became a reality when, after the formation of COMECON, those countries integrated their planning procedures.
    2.4. All of the above
    2.5. None of the above

3. True or false: East-West trade was usually conducted with Western currencies, not Eastern currencies.

Additional Problems

1. Suppose that COMECON had made the transferable ruble convertible into Western currency and pegged the ruble to a currency composite, such as the SDR. Discuss the implications. Could COMECON have survived that way?

2. Chapter 11 of the textbook discussed a theory of multinational enterprises. How does this theory seem to apply to the activities of large Western firms in centrally planned economies?

Answers to Self-Test

1. Council for Mutual Economic Assistance

2. 2.5

3. True

3. REVIEW QUESTIONS

1. Discuss international trade between centrally planned economies. Compare with trade between market economies.

2. What special problems arose in trade between market economies and centrally planned economies?

3. If the soviet-type economic systems were so inefficient, why are the former communist countries doing so badly now that they have abandoned their old systems and adopted market economies?

Appendices

Appendices

A Survey of the Pure Theory of International Trade

A.1.   THE NATIONAL INCOME OF A TRADING ECONOMY (CHAPTER 1)

Solutions to Problems from the Text

A.1.1   *Figure A.2 in the textbook was drawn by holding P_C constant and allowing P_W to vary. Derive an income curve by instead holding P_W constant and allowing P_C to vary.*

If you derive the curve properly it should resemble Figure A.2 qualitatively, with the roles of the two goods reversed. The upper and lower specialization values of P_C are P_W/c_o and P_W/w_o respectively.

A.1.2   *Equation (4) in the textbook holds for small (that is, differential) movements along the transformation curve, when both goods are being produced. What can you say about large movements? If only one good is initially produced?*

If the change in production is not infinitesimal, the left-hand side of equation (3) in the textbook could be strictly negative. Then the term in brackets in equation (4) would be negative, so that the left-hand side of that equation would be strictly less than S_C. If the economy is specialized a change in prices does not change production, so that the term in brackets in equation (4) would still be zero.

A.2.   THE NATIONAL EXPENDITURE OF A TRADING ECONOMY (CHAPTER 1)

Solutions to Problems from the Text

A.2.1   *Suppose a country has the utility function*

$$u(D_C, D_W) = D_C^{\alpha} D_W^{1-\alpha}$$

for some number a between zero and one. Derive a formula for $E(P_C, P_W; u)$. Verify the properties discussed in the text.

$$E(P_C, P_W; u) = \left(\frac{1}{\alpha^{\alpha}(1-\alpha)^{1-\alpha}} \right) u\, P_C^{\alpha} P_W^{1-\alpha}$$

A.2.2   *Derive $E(P_C, P_W; u)$ if consumers always demand wheat and cloth in equal amounts. If $u(D_C, D_W) = D_C + D_W$.*

$$E(P_C P_W; u) = (P_C + P_W)u. \qquad E(P_C P_W; u) = \min\{P_C, P_W\}u.$$

A.3.   INTERNATIONAL EQUILIBRIUM (CHAPTER 4)

Solutions to Problems from the Text

A.3.1   *Why is it that both cloth and wheat cannot be inferior?*

Income must always equal expenditure, but if both goods were inferior an increase in income would reduce spending on both goods, and therefore total expenditure as well.

A.3.2   For any variables x and y, show:

$$\left(\frac{1}{x}\right)^{\wedge} = -\hat{x}, \quad \widehat{(x \cdot y)} = \hat{x} + \hat{y}, \quad \left(\frac{x}{y}\right)^{\wedge} = \hat{x} - \hat{y}.$$

$$\left(\frac{1}{x}\right)^{\wedge} = \frac{d(1/x)}{(1/x)} = (-1/x)^2 \frac{dx}{(1/x)} = -\frac{dx}{x} = -\hat{x}$$

$$\widehat{(x \cdot y)} = \frac{d(x \cdot y)}{x \cdot y} = \frac{[y(dx) + x(dy)]}{x \cdot y} = \frac{dx}{x} + \frac{dy}{y} = \hat{x} + \hat{y}$$

A.3.3   *Find an explicit solution to the differential equation (DH) and use this to derive the stability condition (SC).*

Set $f(P) = M(P) - X^*(1/P)$ so that **(DH)** can be written:

$$\dot{P} = f(P).$$

Near equilibrium, this has the linear approximation:

$$\dot{P} = f'(P_0)[P(t) - P_0].$$

The solution to this linear differential equation is:

$$\dot{P} = ae^{f't} + P_0$$

where a is a parameter. It follows from this equation that $P(t)$ will converge to P_o as t goes to infinity if and only if $f' < 0$, which is the same as (SC) in the textbook.

A.3.4   *Derive the elasticity formulas for an economy with the tastes of* **Problem A.2.1** *above and a Ricardian technology. Derive the elasticiy formulas if* S_c *and* S_w *cannot be varied at all.*

If cloth is the imported good, $c = 1 - a$, $m = a$. If the economy is specialized to wheat production, $s = 0$. If both goods are being produced (that is, if the relative price is at its autarky value), s is infinite. Therefore e is infinite when P equals its autarky value and equals 1 for all other values of P.

A.4.   FACTOR ENDOWMENTS (CHAPTER 5)

Solutions to Problems from the Text

A.4.1   *Geometrically demonstrate exactly how an isocost curve can be derived from a given isoquant. Show how an isoquant can be derived from a given isocost curve.*

In the figure below, the curves in quadrants II and IV respectively graph $rK = 1$ and $wL = 1$. Quadrant I contains the isoquant for producing one dollar's worth of output.

To find the isocost curve corresponding to this isoquant proceed as follows. For any point on the curve, such as A in the figure, draw a tangent. Then points B and D measure the corresponding values of $1/r$ and $1/w$ respectively. Thus D and E measure r and w, so that point F must be on the corresponding isocost curve. Repeat this procedure for each point on the isoquant to trace out the entire isocost curve. To find the isoquant corresponding to a given isocost curve, simply reverse the procedure. That is, for point F draw a tangent. Then points D' and E' measure $1/K$ and $1/L$ respectively. Thus B' and C' measure K and L, so that A is the corresponding point on the isoquant.

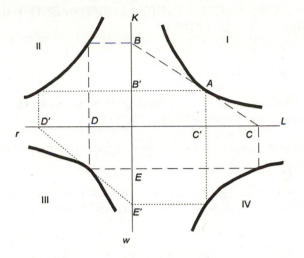

A.4.2   *Show how Figure A.11 in the textbook may alter in the presence of a factor intensity reversal. Trace out the values of S_C and S_W as K varies from zero toward infinity.*

A factor intensity reversal would raise the possibility that, in Figure A.11, there could be a second pair of intersecting K and L lines. Neither of these lines would intersect either of the first pair of lines, the second K line would intersect the second L line from above (or just the opposite of the first pair shown in the figure), and the second pair of lines would correspond to different factor prices from the first pair (but the same commodity prices).

A.4.3   *Derive the Rybczynski theorem if capital is immobile between sectors. What can you say about the factor-price equalization and Heckscher-Ohlin theorems?*

Suppose that commodity prices are held constant and that the stock of capital in the cloth sector rises. If factor prices did not change, cloth output would rise in the same proportion and wheat output would fall, as the cloth industry would attract labor from the wheat industry. This is very close to the standard Rybczynski result. But this would require that some wheat capital remain unemployed: the wheat sector has less labor but, at unchanged factor prices, uses the same capital labor ratio as before. Thus factor prices will change if factor markets continue to clear. With the wage rising and both rentals falling, cloth output will rise in a smaller proportion than the increase in cloth capital.

A.5.   HIGHER-DIMENSIONAL FACTOR-ENDOWMENTS THEORY*
         (SECTION 9* OF CHAPTER 6)

Solutions to Problems from the Text

A.5.1   *Show how the presence of factor intensity reversals can alter Figure A.13 in the
         textbook. Discuss the implications.*

         With factor intensity reversals, two isocost curves can intersect more than
         once.

A.5.2   *Suppose there are 3 goods and 2 factors, that all 3 goods are being produced in
         equilibrium, and that the techniques used in the 3 sectors relate to each other as
         follows:*

$$\frac{K_C}{L_C} > \frac{K_D}{L_D} > \frac{K_W}{L_W}. \tag{59}$$

         Now consider the price change:

$$\hat{P}_D > 0, \ \hat{P}_C = \hat{P}_W = 0.$$

         *What can you say about the consequences for factor rewards and the pattern of
         production?*

         The economy will cease producing either cloth or wheat. If it ends wheat
         production, the wage rises in terms of all three goods and the rent falls in
         terms of all three goods. If it ends cloth production, the wage falls in terms
         of all three goods and the rent rises in terms of all three goods.

A.5.3   *Suppose that there are 3 goods and 2 factors with relative intensities as in (59)
         above for all wage-rental ratios. If there are two countries, is it possible for one
         to specialize in deckles in equilibrium? Explain.*

         If prices were such as to cause one country to specialize in deckles (the
         three isocost curves would not have a common intersection), the other
         country could not produce both cloth and wheat. Thus such a case is
         impossible.

A.5.4   *How does our general version of the Stolper-Samuelson theorem change if we
         drop the assumption that the good whose price increases uses a nonspecific
         assortment of factors?*

         It would then be possible that an increase in the price of some commodity
         could cause some factor reward to rise in the same proportion, but no

factor reward to rise in strictly greater proportion. In this case the favored factor's reward would still rise in terms of all goods except that whose price itself rose. Thus recipients of income from that factor would find those incomes greater in real terms, unless they just happened to spend them entirely on the good with the increased price, in which case the real incomes would be unchanged. This very minor modification is the only consequence.

A.5.5 *What can you say about the general version of the Rybczynski theorem in the case of more goods than factors if, instead of holding factor prices constant, we fix commodity prices and suppose that all factors remain fully employed?*

The Rybczynski theorem derived in the textbook ceases to apply. But, on the other hand, the duality relations **(54)** now apply.

A.6.   TARIFFS (CHAPTER 7)

Solutions to Problems from the Text

A.6.1   *Explicitly derive (62) in the textbook.*

$$
\begin{aligned}
E(q, u_t) &= D_C + qD_W = [S_C + P(S_W - D_W)] + qD_W \\
&= [S_C + q(S_W - D_W) - tP(S_W - D_W)] + qD_W \\
&= (S_C + qS_W) + tP(D_W - S_W) \\
&= y(q,\dots) + tPM.
\end{aligned}
$$

A.6.2   *What will equation (65) in the textbook look like if we do not assume that* $t = 0$ *initially?*

$$
\hat{M} = -\frac{(c + s + m(1 - t))}{(1 - t)}\hat{P} \\
-\frac{(c + s)}{(1 - mt)}\frac{dt}{(1 + t)}.
$$

A.6.3   *What does the assumption of internationally identical tastes imply about the relative sizes of* $\hat{P}$ *and* $\hat{q}$?

They are both positive, with the latter exceeding the former (as always) by $dt/(1+t)$.

Sample Examinations

1.   ONE-HOUR EXAMINATIONS COVERING INTERNATIONAL TRADE

Examination I.

1. What does it mean for an import curve to be inelastic? Why does it matter? Discuss some theoretical issues where elasticity is crucial, and discuss some current policy issues as well. What can you say about actual values of these elasticities?

2. SHORT ANSWER. Give only the requested answer, with no explanation or derivation.
   - **2.1.**   State the factor price equalization theorem.
   - **2.2.**   Describe the us antidumping law.
   - **2.3.**   What is the Most-Favored-Nation clause?
   - **2.4.**   What do the following stand for: GATT, UNCTAD, OPEC, ITO?
   - **2.5.**   What is the Leontief Paradox?
   - **2.6.**   Write the optimum tariff formula.

3. In Pottstown, 2 units of labor are required to produce 1 beer and 10 units of labor are required to produce 1 mushroom. There are 1,000 laborers in Pottstown. As all the world knows, residents of Pottstown always eat 1 mushroom with each 5 beers that they drink. Describe autarky equilibrium. What happens if Pottstown can trade with Philadelphia at the relative price of 5 beers for 3 mushrooms?

Examination II.

1. In Grafton each pumpkin requires 2 units of labor in its production and each witch requires 4 units of labor. Grafton has 400 units of labor available. In Camden 10 units of labor are required to produce each pumpkin and 5 units to produce each witch. There are 1,000 units of labor in Camden.
   - **1.1.**   Who has a comparative advantage in what? Make two equivalent statements.
   - **1.2.**   Draw production possibility frontiers for Grafton, Camden and the world.
   - **1.3.**   How do your answers to **1.2** illustrate comparative advantage? What can you predict will happen if Grafton and Camden commence free trade in pumpkins and witches?

2. Write an essay on the "New Protectionism." Be sure you discuss what it is, how it differs from the old protectionism, and what its main instruments are.

3. SHORT ANSWER. Give only the requested answer, with no explanation or derivation.
   - **3.1.**   State precisely the Rybczynski theorem.
   - **3.2.**   Draw a diagram illustrating how a tariff could reduce the domestic relative price of importables.

3.3.   Define: demand reversal; factor intensity reversal.

3.4.   Define: elasticity of import demand; elasticity of export supply; What is the algebraic relation between the two?

3.5.   Define: specific tariff; ad-valorem tariff. How does it matter which type of tariff we have?

Examination III

1. Show geometrically that a tariff will increase the relative domestic price of importables in the tariff-levying country. Can this ever fail to happen? If so, demonstrate geometrically and explain why in words.

2. In a certain economy, an apple requires 2 units of land and 3 units of labor to produce, and a banana requires 3 land and 2 labor.

    2.1.   If an apple and a banana each cost $10 in long-run competitive equilibrium, what is land's rent and labor's wage?

    2.2.   using specific numbers, illustrate the Stolper-Samuelson theorem, and explain your illustration.

    2.3.   If, in the short run, factors are specific to industry, show how income distribution would instead be affected by a price change, and compare with your answer in **2.2**.

3. SHORT ANSWER. Give only the requested answer, with no justification or explanation.

    3.1.   State the Marshall-Lerner condition.

    3.2.   State Walras's Law.

    3.3.   What is a "beggar-my-neighbor" policy?

    3.4.   Define: MRT, MRS, MRTS.

Examination IV.

1. Briefly describe the salient features of international trade between and among the developed countries of the world, as a group, and the less developed countries. Show how the theoretical principles developed in this course can be used to explain various characteristics of this trade. Are there any respects in which the theory is deficient for this purpose?

2. "Nearly all valid arguments for a tariff are second-best arguments." Discuss.

3. Discuss international capital movements. Be sure your discussion thoroughly addresses intertemporal aspects.

2. ONE-HOUR EXAMINATIONS COVERING INTERNATIONAL MONETARY ECONOMICS

Examination V.

1. Describe the process of international adjustment under a gold exchange standard. Include in your discussion an evaluation of the advantages and disadvantages of the system and reference to historical performance.

2. What is meant by purchasing-power-parity? Exactly what roles does it play in international adjustment? Describe any relevant empirical evidence.

3. SHORT ANSWER. Give only the requested answer, with no justification or explanation.
   3.1. Define: perfect international capital mobility.
   3.2. What are the "Rules of the Game"?
   3.3. Suppose that the spot price of a U.K. pound in New York is $2.00/£, the three month forward rate is $1.96/£, the interest rate on us Treasury bills is 10 percent per annum and the interest rate on U.K. Treasury bills is 14 percent per annum. Describe the interest arbitrage that would likely result.
   3.4. What are Eurodollars? About how many are there?
   3.5. What does it mean for the foreign-exchange market to be efficient?
   3.6. Draw import curves for two countries and illustrate a case where the country with the higher APM has the lower MPM.
   3.7. What is sterilization and what is its purpose?
   3.8. Describe present exchange-rate arrangements.

Examination VI.

1. Suppose that France is specialized in wine production and Germany in machine production, and that the equilibrium terms of trade are two units of wine per machine. The following data apply:

	France	*Germany*
Constant Output	100 *W*	50 *Ma*
Velocity of Circulation	1	1
Price Elasticity of Imports	½	1
Marginal Propensity to Import	¼	½
Monetary Unit (gold)	Fr1 = 1 oz.	DM1 = 2 oz.

   1.1. If the world stock of gold is 1,000 ounces, what are the equilibrium price levels and money stocks?
   1.2. If France finds an additional 500 ounces of gold, what is the new equilibrium? Qualitatively describe the process of adjustment.

    1.3. How would your answer to 1.2 change if the French marginal propensity to import were instead three-fourths?

2. "In many ways the Bretton Woods international monetary system was designed in response to real or imagined lessons of experience before and after the First World War." Discuss this statement.

3. Write an essay on the covered interest parity theory of the forward exchange rate.

Examination VII.

1. Discuss the relative efficacy of monetary and fiscal policy for domestic stabilization purposes in an open economy.

2. Describe the mechanics of multiple deposit creation in the Eurodollar market.

3. Write a short essay on the intertemporal nature of the current account.

4. Discuss the forces that would tend to correct automatically an imbalance of payments of a country which maintained a fixed exchange rate and which was too small appreciably to influence world prices.

Examination VIII

1. What is sterilization and what is its purpose? What limits it? Is it common? Does it work?

2. In America, the money supply is $400, $k = 1$, and real GNP consists of 400 bushels of wheat. In Europe, the money supply = Fr800, the velocity of money is ½, and real GNP consists of 100 barrels of wine. The terms of trade are one barrel of wine per bushel of wheat, and the American exchange rate $R = \$1/\text{Fr}$.
    a. If America and Europe maintain a fixed exchange rate, what cumulative payments imbalance is necessary to establish equilibrium? What are the equilibrium price levels?
    b. Suppose that instead America and Europe maintain their initial money supplies and allow their exchange rate to float. How must it change in order to establish equilibrium?

3. SHORT ANSWER. Write only the requested answer, with no explanation or justification.
    3.1. Write the formula for purchasing power parity.
    3.2. What special role did the dollar play in the Bretton Woods system?
    3.3. What were the Smithsonian Agreement, the Second Amendment to the IMF Articles of Agreement, and the Plaza Accord?
    3.4. EMS stands for:
        a. Export Mobilization System

        b.   Eastern Magical Snake
        c.   European Monetary Scale
        d.   European Monetary System
        e.   None of the above

3.5.   The balance-of-trade deficit can be thought of as:
        a.   Insoluble
        b.   The excess of exports over imports
        c.   The excess of income over absorption
        d.   The excess of absorption over exorption
        e.   None of the above

3. TWO-HOUR EXAMINATIONS COVERING INTERNATIONAL ECONOMICS

Examination IX.

1. The rapid growth of the international economy since the Second World War has been a recurring theme of this course. Briefly describe the nature of this growth. Discuss its implications, using the theory developed in the course.

2. Sharp fluctuations of exchange rates have taken place with some frequency since the adoption of managed floating by major industrial nations. Discuss in terms of the theory developed in this course.

3. Write an essay on the optimum tariff. Make sure that your discussion includes: an analysis of the optimum tariff, the relation between the optimum tariff and the revenue-maximizing tariff, welfare implications, and the relevance of this to actual experience.

4. SHORT ANSWER. Give only the requested answer, without explanation or derivation.
   4.1.   What does OECD stand for?
   4.2.   What are the "Rules of the Game?"
   4.3.   Show in a diagram the effects on the forward exchange rate of a fall in the foreign interest rate.
   4.4.   What is the effective rate of protection? Give a formula.
   4.5.   Define: gold exchange standard, adjustable peg, managed floating.

Examination X

1. The degree of international capital mobility has played an important role in the analysis of international economic phenomena at several points in this course. What is meant by the degree of international capital mobility; is there more than one meaning? Mention and briefly discuss several issues where it is important. What can you say about the degree of capital mobility in the world economy since the Second World War?

2. In Europe cloth production requires 10 labor per unit and food production requires 5 labor per unit, whereas in Asia cloth requires 30 labor and food 20 labor. The European labor force equals 300 and the Asian 3,000. Europe always spends two-thirds of its income on cloth and Asia always spends one-half of its income on cloth. The world money supply consists of 4,200 identical gold coins. In each country $k = 1$. Find the complete world equilibrium. Draw all relevant diagrams (*PPFs*, import curves, etc.) and find the magnitudes of all economic variables (prices, quantities traded, money supplies, etc.).

3. SHORT ANSWER. Give a short, direct answer to each question, without justification or derivation.
   3.1. Define a gold exchange standard.
   3.2. Define ad-valorem and specific tariffs.
   3.3. Has it ever mattered whether tariffs were ad-valorem or specific? When?
   3.4. What are the short-run consequences of a tariff for domestic income distribution?
   3.5. What are the long-run consequences of a tariff for domestic income distribution?
   3.6. Describe current exchange-rate arrangements in the world.
   3.7. Write the formula for an optimum tariff in terms of export supply elasticities.
   3.8. Define "purchasing power parity" and "interest parity."

Examination XI.

1. Write an essay on the principle of comparative advantage. Be sure to include a precise statement of the principle in its most general form.

2. What are multinational enterprises, why do they exist, and where are they located?

3. Discuss the relative merits of fixed and floating exchange rates.

4. SHORT ANSWER. Give only the requested answer, without explanation or derivation.
   4.1. What are Eurodollars?
   4.2. What does it mean for foreign exchange markets to be efficient?
   4.3. Why is it difficult to determine whether the foreign exchange markets are efficient or not?
   4.4. Define: income elasticity of import demand.
   4.5. What is the Leontief Paradox?
   4.6. Describe covered interest arbitrage.
   4.7. What is sterilization? Offset?
   4.8. Define: countervailing duties. Describe the pertinent U.S. law.
   4.9. Briefly describe the role of the LDCs in the present international monetary system.

Examination XII

1. Write an essay on U.S. trade policy since the Second World War. Be sure to include a discussion of the Uruguay Round, NAFTA and the New Protectionism.

2. State and prove the Rybczynski theorem.

3. Write an essay on international migration.

4. There are two distinct theories which purport to explain the forward premium. Briefly describe each of these theories. Which of the two seems to offer a better explanation? Can the two be made consistent with each other?

Examination XIII.

1. Discuss the principle of *comparative advantage*. Be sure you define the principle, explain what it implies, and discuss its relevance to the world in which we live. How general is it?

2. In America, the money supply is $800, $k = 1$, and real GNP consists of 400 bushels of wheat. In Europe, the money supply = Fr800, $k = 2$, and real GNP consists of 100 barrels of wine. The terms of trade are 1 barrel of wine per bushel of wheat, and the American exchange rate $R = \$2/\text{Fr}$.
   a. If America and Europe maintain a fixed exchange rate, what cumulative payments imbalance is necessary to establish equilibrium? What are the equilibrium price levels?
   b. Suppose that instead America and Europe maintain their initial money supplies and allow their exchange rate to float. How must it change in order to establish equilibrium?

3. SHORT ANSWER. Give only the requested answer, with no explanation or justification.
   3.1. Define: intraindustry trade.
   3.2. Distinguish between national and international returns to scale.
   3.3. Briefly describe recent changes to us immigration law.
   3.4. Write the formula for covered interest parity.
   3.5. Write the formula for purchasing power parity.
   3.6. Describe the U. S. countervailing duty law.
   3.7. State the Rybczynski theorem in precise form.
   3.8. What is a dual exchange market? Cite an actual example.
   3.9. Describe the present international monetary system.
   3.10. What is forward exchange?

4. When does a tariff on imports raise the relative domestic price of imports? Prove that your answer is correct.

Examination XIV

1. In our study of the real theory of international trade we considered three different approaches summarized respectively by comparative advantage, economies of scale and imperfect competition. What are the basic questions that any pure theory of trade must attempt to answer? To which of these questions do each of the above theories principally address themselves? Contrast the theories with respect to basic assumptions and conclusions. To what extent does each of these theories provide answers to these basic questions?

2. Show geometrically how a tariff affects domestic and international prices. Enumerate alternatives and show when they happen.

3. In America, the money supply is $400, $k = 1$, and real GNP consists of 400 bushels of wheat. In Europe, the money supply = Fr800, the velocity of money is 1/2, and real GNP consists of 100 barrels of wine. The terms of trade are 1 barrel of wine per bushel of wheat, and the American exchange rate $R = \$1/\text{Fr}$.
    a. If America and Europe maintain a fixed exchange rate, what cumulative payments imbalance is necessary to establish equilibrium? What are the equilibrium price levels?
    b. Suppose that instead America and Europe maintain their initial money supplies and allow their exchange rate to float. How must it change in order to establish equilibrium?

4. SHORT ANSWER. Supply *only* the requested answer, with no explanation, justification, or derivation.
    4.1. Describe the present international monetary system.
    4.2. Write the formula for purchasing power parity.
    4.3. Write the formula for covered interest parity.
    4.4. What is forward exchange?
    4.5. What are guest-worker systems?
    4.6. A Japanese firm uses dollars, deposited in a New York bank, to buy rubber from Indonesians. Which of the following entries appears on the us accounts?
        a. A credit in merchandise trade
        b. A debit in merchandise trade
        c. A debit in short-term capital
        d. A debit in long-term capital
        e. None of the above
    4.7. With flexible exchange rates, a high degree of capital mobility means that:
        a. Monetary policy has little effect on the domestic or foreign economies.
        b. Fiscal policy has little effect on the foreign economy.
        c. Fiscal policy has little effect on the domestic economy.
        d. Fiscal policy has great effect on the domestic economy.
        e. None of the above.
    4.8. Which of the following generally characterizes firms that go multinational?

    a.   They have unique attributes that can be exploited in different countries.

    b.   Locational characteristics make it cheap to produce goods in a number of countries.

    c.   It is cheaper to internalize the transfer of these attributes than to transfer them through markets.

    d.   All of the above

    e.   None of the above

4.9. France and Germany abolish all tariffs on each other's goods and establish a common tariff on goods from the rest of the world. This is an example of:

    a.   Discriminatory tariff preferences

    b.   A free-trade area

    c.   A customs union

    d.   A common market

    e.   None of the above

4.10. Which of the following is *not*, by itself, an international capital movement?

    a.   South Korea buys advanced capital goods from the U.S.

    b.   A French firm sells bonds in New York to finance a new plant in Paris.

    c.   A U.S. firm borrows from New York banks and uses the money to buy out a British competitor.

    d.   Hans Schmid borrows $2,000 from a New York bank, goes to Munich, and spends it all on beer at the Oktoberfest.

    e.   None of the above